THE MENTORING ROADMAP

First published by Catherine Hodgson in 2023

© Catherine Hodgson, 2023

ISBN 978-1-991220-37-0   Print
ISBN 978-1-991220-38-7   d-PDF
ISBN 978-1-991220-39-4   ePUB
ISBN 978-1-991220-40-0   mobi file

Produced by Staging Post, a division of Jacana Media (Pty) Ltd
Cover design by Joan Baker
Layout by Sam van Straaten
Editing by Margot Bertelsmann
Proofreading by Lara Jacob
Set in Avenir 10/14.5pt
Job no. 004016

THE MENTORING ROADMAP

The ultimate guide for mentors and mentees

Catherine Hodgson

Praise for *The Mentoring Roadmap* and Catherine Hodgson

"Catherine brings an energy and focus to the topic of mentoring that parallels the best of mentoring relationships."
David Clutterbuck, the international pioneer of developmental mentoring, author and co-author of over 75 books on HR, coaching, and mentoring

"I've never seen anyone take mentoring as far, as fast, and as deep as Catherine has in her unique protocol and insightful methodology. This inspiring and profound book is perfect for anyone who wants to mentor or be mentored."
Marcia Weider, CEO of Dream University and best-selling author

"Catherine's book on mentoring is a masterpiece on the subject. She pours her heartfelt knowledge, processes, and personal experience into a comprehensive guide to becoming a better mentor. Her book covers both the science and art of mentorship with a great deal of supporting worksheets. Highly recommended for mentors and mentees across all industry types."
Rob Katz, DPhil, PhD, CEO of Spiritpower and YPO (Young Presidents' Organization) member

"Catherine has created a world-class mentoring product that has positively impacted the lives of so many."
Alan Hepburn, managing partner, Asia ABA, and YPO (Young Presidents' Organization) member

"Catherine, virtually single-handedly, created, designed, and launched the YPO Mentorship program and not only delivered the initial trainings,

but ensured that execution and improvements were established and followed through on. She has a warm yet professional manner and is highly organized and diligent in everything she does. Her evolved self-awareness and high EQ stand out for me as the key behaviors behind her success."
Sean Magennis, past president, COO and YPO (Young Presidents' Organization) member

"Catherine is a strategic leader who is never afraid of taking on a huge challenge. She has the gifts of empathy and compassion, combined with the ability of building broad coalitions around big ideas. We served together on an international board where I witnessed her resolve to create a mentoring culture and transform the organization forever."
Paul Lamontagne, non-executive director, Sustainable Development Goals advisor and YPO (Young Presidents' Organization) member

"Catherine is insightful, extraordinarily emotionally intelligent, authentic, and a gifted teacher. I have done almost 50 events for YPO, and Catherine and I have led workshops at the same events across the globe. I am grateful to have had the opportunity to watch many gifted speakers. That said, Catherine is my favourite. I prioritize attending her workshops not only because I learn so much from her, but simply because witnessing her teach makes my heart sing.

"Catherine is a true servant leader who lives her purpose every day. Each time I've interacted with her, I've come away with new knowledge and perspective that have been immediately relevant to my work and life. Her workshops are practical, thought-provoking, and emotional. It doesn't get much better than that."
Annie Sarnblad, global expert in microexpressions, author of *Annie Unfiltered: Facial Expressions in Love, Lust and Lies*

"I was fortunate to experience one of the biggest innovations in Young Presidents' Organization: mentoring, created and led by Catherine Hodgson. More importantly, I got to work very closely with Catherine as part of the mentoring sub-committee to launch YPO Mentoring. Catherine is a pioneer, creating and promoting the mentoring concept in the African region before using technology to take it pan-YPO. Catherine is a born leader with an infectious smile and positive attitude.

With a very high emotional quotient, she understands the power of mentoring. I have seen her design and develop material for mentoring based on her vast experience. She has trained numerous people across the world with the unique Mentoring Masterclass. This was successful because of her ability to connect and engage, which has helped her become a YPO mentoring facilitator."
Jayant Mammen Mathew, CEO of The Malayala Manorama Co Ltd and YPO (Young Presidents' Organization) member

"In 2020 I worked with Catherine on Empowr, a female mentor project. Catherine facilitated various workshops for both mentors and mentees as well as consulting us on our program. Not only does she have an extended skill set in mentorship and coaching, her presentation and workshop skills are impeccable. She made a fundamental impact on the lives and careers of our participants."
Anouk Moll, innovation manager at ABN AMRO, founder of Empowr & Binfluence

"I was lucky enough to have worked with Catherine, who was leading the YPO mentoring program over the period of time when I became involved both as a mentor and a mentee. Because this program is powered by the YPO network, the quality of mentors that you are paired with for starters is of an exceptionally high quality. Her incredible attention to detail throughout the entire process meant there was always full support and consideration at every step of the way. Her teaching and knowledge come from her own deep experience, which she is always happy to share.

"Not only is Catherine an incredibly committed and highly capable leader, she was also at the forefront of developing new mentoring material and many innovative concepts in this particular area of learning. She has campaigned tirelessly for mentorship around the globe, fully believing both in the power of this incredible process and, in addition, what a difference mentoring can make in a person's life. This is the real passion that drives her. I have no doubt that this book will be the essential go-to resource in mentoring for many years to come."
Julia Raphaely, CEO of Paradigm Connect and YPO (Young Presidents' Organization) member

"Catherine established the mentoring training program for Young Presidents' Organization and developed 'The Catherine Wheel', which essentially outlines the elements of a successful mentoring partnership. This model has been taught to thousands of YPO members and spouses/partners across the globe and has provided them with a tangible model and process to follow while conducting a mentoring partnership. There are many aspects of this model that can be applied to organizations, particularly the importance of listening skills and effective communication."

Julie Davis (YPO Oceana Integrated), YPO spouse partner community network chair (2017–2020)

"Catherine is known affectionately within Young Presidents' Organization as 'the mother of mentoring'. A true inspiration and visionary, she created the Catherine Wheel Mentoring Model and all the other supporting mentoring tools. This is a crucial part of members' lifelong learning journey."

Roy Moëd, co-founder of LifeBook Memoirs Limited and YPO (Young Presidents' Organization) member

"In Catherine's service on the YPO global learning committee, and in her pioneering work around developing mentoring within YPO, I have seen Catherine demonstrate an ability to connect with people from different parts of the world and from very different backgrounds."

Justin Taylor, CEO of Kaer Pte Ltd and YPO (Young Presidents' Organization) member

"Catherine has, in my opinion, been the most outstanding facilitator that we have had the privilege of contracting. She has always been extremely well versed, prepared, passionate, professional, articulate, and knowledgeable. She is also exceptional at receiving, understanding, and responding to questions with empathy, so that our staff feel psychologically safe to make themselves vulnerable and ask questions or express views freely. Catherine has the unique ability and capacity to facilitate conversations at any level in the organization."

Terry Bantock, CEO of Unitrans Supply Chain Solutions (Pty) Ltd

"I had the honour of serving with Catherine on the international learning committee of Young Presidents' Organization between 2016 and 2018, where she was overseeing and strategically guiding the roll-out of mentoring across the organization. Her passion and drive for mentoring are still examples that I share with incoming members about servant leadership delivering rewards to both our community as well as those who take on leadership roles.

"I always found Catherine to be present, authentic, and willing to share her experiences for the whole group to benefit. Her great success in business, raising two wonderful young ladies who have followed in their mothers' entrepreneurial shoes and her ability to find a life balance where she and her husband spend months at sea indulging their passion for sailing speak volumes of the credibility, diversity, and gifts of wisdom."
Kavit Handa, co-founder and partner at Africa Capital and YPO (Young Presidents' Organization) member

The Mentoring Roadmap *is dedicated to my husband, best friend, and life partner, Nicholas, who has lovingly supported and encouraged me along this journey as well as being my greatest mentor. To my two daughters, Sarah-Jane and Emily, who have taught me how important it is to have open and honest conversations, to be non-judgmental and to love unconditionally.*

CONTENTS

PREFACE

Mentoring is not a sprint, where you finish the race shortly after you have begun. Nor is it a marathon, which can be difficult and tiring, something that you must endure. Mentoring is more like a road trip, a journey that needs to be planned and prepared for, a trip you are excited to undertake.

Along the way are unexpected "(in)sights", lots of learning, detours, maybe some easy long roads and some twisty hairpin bends. This book is your roadmap, your compass, your GPS. It will help you be better prepared and feel more confident for your trip. It will give you directions on where to start, where to go along the way and what to do once you are on your journey. This roadmap will make your experience a whole lot more successful and enjoyable.

A road trip is often shared with another person. Think of the mentee as the driver. They are taking responsibility for the journey and looking in front at the road ahead. In the passenger seat is the mentor. They have travelled these roads before and are there to support and guide the driver, but not to interfere with the driving. They will be looking in the side and back mirrors, pointing out any blind spots that the driver may not have seen. Along the way the mentor will share their experiences of their previous trips, but will also learn from this new journey they are taking with their mentee.

Are you ready to find out more? What are you waiting for? Climb in. Join me as I take you on a mentoring learning journey – and show you how to use this roadmap.

INTRODUCTION

What's in it for you?

Life is not plain sailing. You probably know this already. I know because I spend part of each year sailing, and it certainly is never calm seas all the way. In fact, there is a saying: "Smooth seas don't make skilled sailors." It's the rough seas and storms, the difficult experiences and events, the failures, the transitions in your life, those tough times, when we learn the most. However, it's more difficult to get through it when you have to do it on your own, without another person to help you learn the ropes or just be by your side. We all know that having a person to guide and share our journey with us gives us the confidence and ability to learn better and faster. And what a gift to be that mentor who walks alongside another person on their journey.

Whether you are a mentor or wanting to be mentored, by the end of this book you will have the confidence to embark on your mentoring journey with a structure, knowledge of your mentoring role, and key skills for the conversation. My hope is that this book will be a compass for you on your journey and enrich your mentoring experience.

I am certain that you have experienced a mentor in your life at some point, or been a mentor yourself, whether it's been a formal or informal mentoring relationship, a mentoring encounter with a parent, a spouse, a friend, a child, or a boss. I want you to think about how those mentors helped you at that point in your life, or how you may have been that to someone when they needed it most. Most importantly, I want you to think of how they made you feel, or how you may have made someone else feel.

You are going to have mentoring relationships for the rest of your life. Some are going to have a great impact, and in return you may perhaps have an impact on other people's lives. Mentoring can be a powerful experience – so powerful that it can change your life. You can have that effect on another person too if you remain open to being a mentor.

I have been amazed at the impact mentoring has had not only on my own life but also on the lives of others. I have learnt so much during my journey in the field of mentoring that I want to share my learnings with you.

One of the biggest learnings for me is that having a structure around your mentoring journey will help you and your mentor or mentee get more out of your mentoring relationship. In this book, you will learn about **The Catherine Wheel Mentoring Model**, which will provide a **roadmap for your mentoring journey**. This is a comprehensive model that will give you all the tools you need to effectively be a mentor or a mentee.

This book is divided into five parts:

Part 1: About Mentoring
Part 2: The Catherine Wheel Mentoring Model – A Roadmap for Your Mentoring Journey
Part 3: Key Mentoring Skills
Part 4: It's a Wrap – Ending Your Mentoring Journey
Part 5: Resources, Worksheets and Meeting Agendas

Part One includes why mentoring is so important now and the benefits of mentoring to organizations. It covers understanding where mentoring started, what mentoring is, the difference between sponsorship and developmental mentoring, between coaching and mentoring, and the various formats of mentoring available. We will look at why training for both mentors and mentees is vital for the success of a mentoring relationship. Finally, we will look at the benefits of being a mentor as well as a mentee on this journey.

Part Two introduces you to a roadmap for your mentoring journey – **The Catherine Wheel Mentoring Model**. This roadmap is a comprehensive model that I created after seven years of developing a global mentoring program and facilitating mentoring workshops and masterclasses. Many mentors came to me saying that they were struggling with how to conduct their mentoring conversations and how to ensure the mentee gets the most value from them. I developed the Catherine Wheel Mentoring Model, which consists of three wheels. The outer wheel is the mentoring **journey** you embark on; the middle wheel is the **relationship** that you will build; and the inner wheel is the flow of your mentoring **conversations**. The heart of the wheel is the trust, honesty, and confidentiality that are core to any mentoring relationship.

I will introduce you to the **Seven Strengths of Highly Effective Mentors and Mentees** models, which I created to have a visual view of what good mentors and mentees do well. It's important at the beginning of your mentoring relationship to really understand your role as a mentor and what your mentee expects from you, and vice versa. This lays the ground rules so that you ensure the relationship is based on a firm understanding and there are no unfulfilled expectations. We will look at how mentors and mentees are matched in a mentoring program as well as how to find your best mentor or mentee. Since many people are now experiencing mentoring virtually, we will also look at the benefits and pitfalls of virtual mentoring and how to get the most out of your virtual sessions.

Building a connection is key in your first mentoring meeting, which I call the chemistry meeting. We will cover how to prepare for it and how to get the most out of the session.

Building rapport and trust is important for creating the foundation of your relationship, so we will look at the middle wheel of the Catherine Wheel, **the relationship**, and cover how to build that trust and what to do if it is broken.

We will also talk about goal-setting, including the Seven Steps to Goal-Setting, a crucial step in your mentoring journey so that you both have something to work towards.

Part Two also covers your **mentoring conversation**, the inner wheel of the Catherine Wheel, and how to make the best use of your time together. We will go into detail of how you should prepare for your mentoring meeting. I will introduce you to the **Conversation Flow**, how to generate insights, ask the right questions and ensure that the meeting ends with a sense of achievement for both of you.

Part Three looks at **key mentoring skills** needed for your conversation. These skills include listening skills, which are most important for your mentoring conversation, as well as ways to improve your listening, which can also help you in all aspects of your life. We will look at reflecting, a skill we do not use very often, as well as summarizing, and when to do so. Questioning is a key skill to master, and we will look into the types of questions asked, such as open and closed questions, narrow and broad questions, as well as leading questions. We will explore questioning techniques such as probing questions, challenging questions, powerful questions, unlocking questions, pause questions, and tone. We will cover how to give, receive, and ask for feedback, which is important for both mentors and mentees to do frequently. We will also look at feedforward and how useful this can be, not only in your mentoring relationships but in your personal and business relationships too. Finally, advice will be discussed, being a trusted advisor, and how to build storytelling into your mentoring conversation.

Part Four is about reviewing your journey and relationship, what can go wrong along the way, and how to wrap up and end your journey. Finally, we will end with mentoring best practices that I have come across during my years in this field, my reflections, and my "ask" of you.

Part Five is filled with resources, worksheets, and meeting agendas. I will also cover the most frequently asked questions that I hope will help you with any possible questions that you may have.

This is an interactive book – you will get more out of it if you pause along the way, reflect, make notes, and complete the worksheets. Throughout the book, there will be exercises that you can do to practise your mentoring skills, practising what you have learnt to make it more sticky, as well as questions to reflect on to prepare you for your mentoring journey.

I will intersperse mentoring stories that I have come across over my years of being involved in this field. I have changed names for confidentiality purposes. I will also share some of my own personal mentoring experiences with you.

This book can be read from chapter 1 through to the end, or you can dip into the chapters that are most useful to you.

I'm sure you're as excited as I am to get started. But wait... do you want to hear a little bit about what got me here? My personal story follows.

What got me here?

I fell into mentoring by chance, got hooked, and found my passion and purpose. But it didn't happen overnight... it was a 12-year journey of hope, frustration, elation, disappointment, long hours, celebrations, and hard work, as well as dealing with a lot of egos. I'll tell you my story by starting at the beginning of my journey.

After graduating from university with a business degree in marketing, I worked in the corporate world for seven years, earning my stripes by working long hours, travelling, and dealing with a lot of corporate stress. I was fortunate to get married to an entrepreneur, who ignited my own entrepreneurial spirit, and we started a business together when I fell pregnant with our first child. I realized that a corporate life was not, at that stage, conducive to having a family and flexible working hours. Raising a family and starting a business, as you may know, are not to be entered into lightly. But we somehow managed, juggling family life and careers at the same time. I was fortunate that my husband supported my need to have a career and also be a mother, and he wanted to be an involved father, so we played a relay game of caring for our children and running our businesses, covering for each other along the way.

My father-in-law was a great mentor to me as we started our business, teaching me how to manage the finances of the business and to write out the cash book by hand! He was probably one of my greatest fans and believed in me right from the start.

However, it was my husband who was to become my mentor in my pursuit of being my own boss. He was there at every turn, encouraging me along the way, being an ear to talk to and a sounding board, believing in me and supporting me. He was there to rejoice in every success as well as to pick me up when something went wrong. I could not have had a better mentor to walk beside me along my journey. Over those years I had staff joining our company as we continued to grow it. I believed in supporting and growing them, being a role model for them, and believing in them. I, too, was becoming a mentor to them and it brought me so much joy to see them grow and develop. When I meet some of these former employees now it gives me great pride to see how they have succeeded.

In 2009 I decided to expand my learning, while still running our business, and joined a business organization called Young Presidents' Organization (YPO), a global leadership community of more than 35 000 CEOs from more than 142 countries. I had hit a brick wall in my career; I was a bit bored and looking for some contemporaries in the business world. When I joined, they asked if I could please ensure I was an active member, as they only had one other female member in the chapter and had not seen her since she joined. Being the enthusiastic person that I am, I told them that I'm a "boots-and-all kinda girl". Little did they know how full of mud those boots would get!

Six months into my membership, I was wanting to get involved in some aspect of the organization, but I was also looking for something that felt meaningful to me. My whole career until then had been a whirlwind of growing businesses, leading people, driving sales, and making a profit. It was exhilarating, creative, and entrepreneurial, but I felt that I needed to find my heart. When I saw an email about a mentoring pilot program, I immediately accepted the invitation.

The first year of our mentoring pilot in Cape Town saw us with only three pairings. We were finding our way and seeing what worked and what needed to be improved. However, I was convinced that this was something that could grow and make a significant impact in people's lives. The following story really convinced me that we were onto something significant and meaningful.

> In our first round of interviews when we were looking for mentees, one of our candidates, Jonathan, was a young man who had a business training firefighting in businesses. He was enthusiastic, he employed five people, but he was really struggling with the financial side of his business. He was looking for a mentor who could help him understand finances, of which he knew very little, and help him grow his business. One of my fellow mentoring committee members, Roy, took an interest in him and said he would step in as his mentor. I was a little surprised. Here was Roy, a CA and the CEO of a listed logistics company employing over 5 000 people, willing to mentor Jonathan, an entrepreneur who employed just five people. I had some doubts that this was going to work. I checked in regularly with Roy to see if the mentoring relationship was working, and it seemed to be, but I had not seen Jonathan, the mentee, since that initial interview until 18 months later when he arrived at one of our mentoring

8

workshops. During one of the breaks, I had the chance to speak to him and asked him to tell me about his mentoring experience and whether it had impacted his business at all. His face lit up as he told me his story…

At the first meeting with his mentor, he arrived at Roy's head office and had to walk up a big staircase after entering the front door. Jonathan felt intimidated, nervous, and unsure of what to expect. Roy's PA asked him to sit on a chair outside Roy's office, and as he looked around he felt many pairs of eyes on him, wondering what his business was with the CEO. He eventually went into Roy's office, where they sat in easy chairs with coffee and tea brought to them. Jonathan spent more than an hour with Roy. He was made to feel relaxed, and they started to get to know each other and Roy to understand his business. Each month, Jonathan arrived at Roy's offices and had a one- to two-hour meeting with him. His confidence grew and everyone would greet him when he arrived, wondering who this person was who commanded a monthly meeting with their busy CEO.

Jonathan then looked at me and beamed with pride as he told me the impact mentoring had on his business and him personally. Over the last 18 months he had been able to employ more people and now had 20 people working for him. He was able to buy a speedboat, his lifelong dream, and felt as though he was a respected person in his community. This was a very different man from the one I had met 18 months ago. I wiped a tear from my eye as I realized what an incredible impact mentoring had had on this one man's life. Imagine: if this could be rolled out globally, how many lives could we then impact?

After that first year, I chaired the mentoring committee and we increased the pairings, first to nine, and then to 21 a year later.

I took on a mentee in that first year and soon realized how difficult it was to be a mentor without any training… I could easily mentor people in my own business, but was I doing it right when I was mentoring other people? Was I making a difference? I had no idea. It felt as though we were just having chats and becoming friends, but I didn't feel that we were moving forward towards any goals. And so began my mission to introduce training workshops into the program.

The next five years I spent trying to perfect the workshops, running them in Cape Town, Johannesburg, and London, changing the material continually based on the feedback we received. I consumed every book I could on coaching, mentoring, and training. I sought out mentoring and coaching experts around the world. I attended my first Nancy Kline workshop, where I learnt about creating a thinking environment and the impact listening can have on another person's thinking. I was on a mission to change the world through mentoring!

After two years of running the mentoring program in Cape Town, I took over the position of chairing the mentoring program for Africa, rolling out mentoring programs in six countries in the continent. And then the second turning point happened.

I was asked to attend the YPO Global Leadership Conference in Istanbul to meet other members who were also running mentoring pilots around the world. Once there, I was asked if I would be interested in applying for a position on an international committee to take on the role of global mentoring chair for YPO and to expand the program globally.

So began my five years as global mentoring chair rolling out the mentoring program. We developed a marketing campaign and launched an online mentoring platform. We collaborated with David Clutterbuck, the international pioneer of developmental mentoring, to help us develop mentoring material, and we launched the Mentoring Masterclasses, training 30 mentoring facilitators to run them. We launched an online platform with MentorCloud, which allowed our members to find mentoring matches globally. I also developed a mentoring model, which I called the Catherine Wheel, incorporating all my work into a model so there was a structure to the program.

So how did the Catherine Wheel Mentoring Model come about?

I had been looking for a model that we could use for the structure of the program, but couldn't find anything that inspired me. I had so many members on the program coming to ask me for more specific structures on how to do mentoring. What should they be discussing? How long is a mentoring relationship? What should the agenda look like? I wanted everything to be included in a single model so that it would be easy for both mentors and mentees to see at a glance. I started to use The Catherine Wheel in our mentoring material, and it soon was incorporated into the Mentoring Masterclass.

I now use the model in all my training, and it really has been wonderful to see the positive response to it by participants as well as organizations.

By the end of five years of leading mentoring globally, I had to step off the committee to allow others to lead.

In my last year as global mentoring lead, I asked a fellow member in Cape Town, Rob Katz, who also happens to be an executive coach, if he would be available to mentor me for a year. Until then, I had not had the chance to be a mentee in the program and felt like a bit of a fraud, having not experienced both sides first-hand. Plus, I thought I may need a mentor to help me transition out of my mentoring role and back to my business. I put a theme to my mentoring journey: Transition.

I don't think that I would have been able to transition out of my role so easily without having had Rob as a mentor by my side. Even then, it was painful. I felt I had given birth to a baby, this program called mentoring. I had nurtured it, lived with it every day and now I had to leave it to strangers to do with it what they wanted. I was sad and lost for a few months, not knowing if I would find anything that fulfilled me as much as running this global mentoring program.

But, as we all know, time truly does heal. Being a mentoring facilitator and running workshops kept me connected to mentoring. I decided to do my certification in Conversational Intelligence with the late Judith Glaser, an intense 18-month course that kept me stimulated and inspired. I then went on to do my Coaching certification with the NeuroLeadership Institute, all the while continuing to run my business, which my husband by now had mostly stepped out of. I was also facilitating a lot of mentoring workshops, and in 2020 decided to launch my mentoring business, SHIFT Mentoring (www.shiftmentoring.com). I started consulting work for companies running mentoring platforms, including MentorCloud, as well as facilitating mentoring workshops for companies outside of YPO. In 2022 I was certified as a forum facilitator for YPO, continuing my training and facilitation work within the organization.

It's funny how one can stumble across something, and it can change the course of one's life forever.

For me, finding mentoring was finding my purpose. I've always been an ambitious businesswoman, but something was always missing in my work life. What was missing was "making a difference in other people's lives" and "giving back". Through mentoring I have found my meaning and purpose. I finally connected with my heart. I found my ikigai.

(**Ikigai** is a Japanese concept that means **your reason for being**. Iki in Japanese means life, and gai describes value or worth. Ikigai is the convergence of four areas of life: **what you love, what you're good at, what the world needs, and what you can be paid for**. Your ikigai is your life purpose or your bliss. It's what brings you joy and inspires you to get out of bed every day.)

PART 1: ABOUT MENTORING

1

MENTORING IS AGE-OLD

Mentoring is how we learned and grew as humans. It can be linked to words such as:

- Giving back
- Sharing
- Gifting wisdom
- Becoming an elder
- Sage
- Being a good ancestor
- Leaving a legacy
- Trust
- Support and encouragement
- Storytelling
- Advising

Close your eyes for a few minutes and think back to who your mentors have been in your life and who you have been a mentor to. Do it now.

You can probably name a number of people. We are all mentors and mentees throughout our lives, although we don't think of ourselves as such. Often, we just fall into a mentoring role and only realize it afterwards.

Let me ask you a few questions to reflect on:

- What do you want to be known for?
- What legacy do you want to leave?
- What impact do you want to have?
- What would people say about you when you are gone?
- Who have you encouraged and inspired on this journey of life, growth, and business? If no one, why not?
- Who have you reached out to in order to grow and expand your learning? If no one, what would you like to learn and who could you learn from?
- How many people do you mentor or have you mentored?

I believe that everyone should move from a phase of only receiving learning to a phase of giving back as well. It is the responsibility of all of us to start looking outwards, to nurture talent, youth, and excellence. We all have so much to offer – we need to be generous and offer it. It is only by giving that we also receive, and as a mentor you receive so much in return.

Now, more than ever in our lifetime, is the time to take action and make an impact in another person's life.

Mentoring is incredibly powerful and important in career and personal success, as well as in progression and transitions in our lives. You will see from the following list that mentoring is not all about business mentoring.

Mentoring Relationships

Here are 15 famous mentoring partnerships to show that mentoring can be applied in all aspects of our lives.

1. Socrates mentored Plato and Plato mentored Aristotle.
These relationships date as far back as 400BCE – to put mentoring into perspective and show how long it has been around! This trio show how the student can become the master – that is, the mentee can become the mentor.

2. Steve Jobs from Apple mentored Mark Zuckerberg from Facebook.
Whether you like them or not, these are two men who have had a significant impact on the world. It is said that the two of them used to walk around Palo Alto discussing entrepreneurship and how Zuckerberg

might manage and develop Facebook. When Steve Jobs died, Mark Zuckerberg posted on Facebook, thanking Steve for being a mentor and a friend to him.

3. Warren Buffet mentored Bill Gates from Microsoft.

These two successful businessmen have met for years. Gates admits that, over the years, he turned to Warren Buffet for advice and referred to Buffet as one of a kind. Buffet has repeatedly mentioned the importance that mentorship can have in someone's career development. Buffet challenged Gates, asking questions that made him think differently about his businesses, both IBM and Microsoft. Bill Gates said that he learnt to manage his time and prioritize people as a result of his meetings with Buffet. When Gates turned to philanthropy, Buffet ignited in him the desire to be more impactful in other ways, not just business.

4. Maya Angelou mentored Oprah Winfrey.

Oprah turned to Maya Angelou as a mentor, saying that she was always there for her, guiding her through some of the most important years of her life. Oprah Winfrey was looking for ways to grow her business and personal relationships, and looked to Maya Angelou for advice on how to build relationships and trust. She said that one of the best pieces of wisdom that Angelou gave her was that actions speak louder than words. Oprah believes that mentors are important, and that it is difficult for anybody to make it in the world without some form of mentorship.

5. Mahatma Gandhi mentored Nelson Mandela.

Mandela, who ensured a peaceful transition of power in South Africa, referred to Mahatma Gandhi as his mentor, a man who greatly influenced him through his books and writings. Mandela credits Gandhi with influencing his leadership, even though the two of them never met. Mentors can influence people they have never met.

6. Michelle Robinson mentored Barack Obama.

You may be wondering who Michelle Robinson is… She is better known as Michelle Obama! Michelle was designated as Barack Obama's mentor at the law firm where they both worked while he was an associate for the summer. Barack credits Michelle for being the support and success behind his great achievements.

7. Professor Dumbledore mentored Harry Potter.

A fictional relationship, but a mentoring relationship all the same! Harry respected Dumbledore and his development was attributed to Dumbledore's teaching.

8. Christian Dior mentored Yves Saint-Laurent.

Did you know that Saint-Laurent became Christian's personal assistant, learning the secrets of haute couture and how to run a company?

9. Sir Freddie Laker mentored Richard Branson.

When Branson was struggling with Virgin Atlantic, he went to Laker, to get advice and support. Branson believes that every successful businessperson will have had a great mentor at some point along the road. Branson credits Laker with helping him get rid of his ego and learn from failure.

10. Father Michael van der Peet mentored Mother Theresa.

Mother Theresa met Father Michael in Rome while waiting for a bus. They soon became close friends and confided in each other over the years.

11. Simon Sinek and Ron Bruder mentored each other.

Simon Sinek, author and inspirational speaker, reached out to Ron Bruder, an American entrepreneur, founder and chair of Education for Employment (EFE), when he had a question, and their mentoring relationship started from there. However, it was not a one-way relationship, as Bruder looked to Simon as his mentor too. They realized that mentoring is mutually beneficial for both parties and that both can be mentors and mentees to each other.

12 Jane Fonda mentored Meryl Streep, who paid it forward.

Both extremely famous actresses, Meryl Streep met Jane Fonda in the 1970s on set and learnt a lot from her in the time they spent together. Streep in turn has been able to do the same, being a mentor for others who have wanted to learn from her. Meryl learnt to "pay it forward", helping younger actresses, including Viola Davis, with guidance and wisdom, especially in how to be more confident.

13. Ray Charles mentored Quincy Jones, who paid it forward.

Ray Charles, singer, songwriter, and pianist, mentored Quincy Jones, who was then a young energetic "kid" who loved music and was eager to learn. Charles was able to show him things, giving him much joy in return at seeing this young man grow into a talented musician. Jones, in turn, mentored many young musicians and has been a long-time spokesperson for National Mentoring Month.

14. Luther Powell mentored his son, Colin Powell.

Former US Secretary of State, Colin Powell, considered his father as his most influential mentor. Powell Jr has said that everyone should make a commitment to mentoring, in order to help the next generation take their country to a higher level and a better place.

15. Elton John mentored Lady Gaga.

Elton John, singer, composer, and pianist, continues to play a crucial role in Lady Gaga's life. Having struggled with self-acceptance following trauma from her past, Gaga turned to Elton John for invaluable emotional support and he challenged her to really take care of herself.

As you can see in these relationships, mentoring does not always need to be about suits, ties, and business plans! Mentoring has no boundaries and can be applied to all aspects of life – personal, professional, political, and religious. We see successful mentoring programs in schools, colleges, prisons, and hospitals. Mentoring crosses time frames, ages, and cultures, making a significant impact on people's success, helping them find their purpose and a sense of well-being.

If these people all needed mentors, then why are we not ensuring that everyone has a mentor in their life, as well as being a mentor to someone else?

2

MENTORING IS GOOD FOR BUSINESS

Benefits of mentoring to the organization

Mentoring is not just a fad or a "nice to have"; it is a "must-have" for any organization that wants to survive. If an organization does not offer a mentoring program in the future, it may find it more difficult to grow, attract the right talent, create and maintain a positive company culture, improve minority representation at management and board level, retain key employees and keep them engaged, fill its leadership pipeline, and develop its employees to fulfil their learning needs.

Do you have a mentoring program in your organization? If not, why not? What can **you** do to make it happen?

It is my belief, now more than ever, that younger generations are attracted to organizations that are interested in their development and wellbeing. It is not only about the pay; it is about how much the organization is perceived to care about their employees in every way.

In its 2022 L&D Social Sentiment Survey, Donald H. Taylor discovered that mentoring is now #4 on a list of learning and development strategies L&D teams are looking at. That's an increase from #6 in the 2021 survey and the largest rank increase of any other strategy on the list.

A win-for-all

According to Forbes 2019, one of the most impressive things about an effective mentoring program is how far the positive ripple effects reach. Mentoring benefits an organization by improving job satisfaction and retention, and aids in the personal and professional development of the mentee. Moreover, mentors themselves seem to gain just as much.

An in-depth case study at Sun Microsystems is a good illustration:
- Employees who participated in the program were five times more likely to advance in pay grade, and mentors made even more progress.
- Mentees were promoted five times more than those not in the program, and mentors six times more.
- Retention rates were significantly higher for mentees (72%) and for mentors (69%) than for employees who did not participate (49%).

Mentoring has been shown to attract the best talent into an organization, integrate new people faster, help retain existing talent, accelerate talent and leadership development, fill leadership pipelines, increase diversity and integration, integrate mothers returning from maternity leave, and increase overall staff satisfaction in an organization. Let's look at each one in a bit more depth.

Leadership development

One of the biggest complaints that I have encountered when speaking to CEOs is the lack of a pipeline of leaders in their organization. This is another avenue that a mentoring program addresses. Mentors gain more leadership skills and confidence the more engaged they are with mentoring. Mentoring facilitates a ready pipeline of leaders.
- According to Accountemps, 96% of executives say mentoring is an important development tool.
- 75% of executives say mentoring played a key role in their careers, according to a survey by the American Society for Training and Development (ASTD).

Diversity and inclusion

I have seen over the last few years how organizations are using mentoring programs to improve minority representation at management and executive level; to improve inclusion of minority groups throughout the organization; as well as to improve promotion and retention rates of minorities and women. More can be done in this field, but it is positive to see organizations making headway in this area.

This is also where reverse mentoring can be so powerful, with minority employees mentoring senior and executive staff on minority needs. I have found in my years of experience, especially in South Africa, where we have such diversity of culture, race, and wealth, that senior management and board members understand diversity, equity, and inclusion (DEI) from an intellectual level, but it is only when they **experience or connect with it emotionally** that they are moved to make changes that are authentic, positive, and long lasting.

Here are some interesting stats:

- 44% of CEOs list mentoring programs as one of the three most effective strategies to enhance women's advancement into senior management, says the ASTD.
- Cornell University's School of Industrial and Labour Relations found that mentoring programs boosted minority representation at the management level by 9% to 24% (compared to -2% to 18% with other diversity initiatives).
- The same study found that mentoring programs also dramatically improved promotion and retention rates for minorities and women, an increase from 15% to 38% as compared to non-mentored employees.
- Companies that have racially diverse leadership teams are 33% more profitable, research by McKinsey found.
- 67% of women rate having a mentor as extremely important to their career advancement, according to DDI.
- Firms with a larger number of women serving in executive-level positions enjoyed a 6% increase in net profitability, research by the Peterson Institute for International Economics (PIIE) found.

Positive company culture

I strongly believe that mentoring creates a sense of caring and wellbeing for employees. In all my years of running my own business and being involved in connecting with other business leaders, I have seen that employees stay in an organization because of the people and the culture. Mentoring can strengthen employees' sense of belonging and connection, thus creating a positive company culture. Mentoring helps employees understand the organization's values, stories, culture, and organizational knowledge.

Imagine you join a tech company and you are told on your first day that you have a "big sister" or "big brother" who will be there for you. You can ask them anything and they will show you the ropes, inform you of the company history and culture, sit with you at lunch and introduce you to new people, teach you the "tech lingo" so you understand what they are talking about in meetings and generally be your friend. How would that make you feel? Does that sound comforting? This is what organizations can do to ensure that employees are enfolded in the company and supported along the way – this is mentoring!

Terri A. Scandura, a management professor at the University of Miami, says it is positive to see that 71% of Fortune 500 companies have mentoring programs and clearly think mentoring is an important business development tool.

Recruitment

Now more than ever, organizations need to attract the best talent and become the desired organization to work for. Having a mentoring program in your organization is an attractive reward for recruiting millennials who value learning as much as high salaries.

More than 60% of college and graduate students listed mentoring as a criterion for selecting an employer after graduation, MMHA found.

Integration

New employee onboarding

In my experience with talking to learning and HR directors in organizations, incorporating mentoring into an onboarding program is often the easiest way to start implementing mentoring into an organization. Most organizations have an onboarding program for new employees. Combining this with a mentoring program will help onboard new employees more quickly and with greater success.

An onboarding mentoring program gives employees an opportunity to develop and become more competent in their roles faster. It also gives them a great support system.

A listed logistics company I have worked with has a strong graduate onboarding program in which each new graduate is assigned a mentor from their division. This mentor ensures that the graduate settles into their job quickly and easily, while being there to support them. Feedback has shown that the graduates settle into their jobs more quickly and have a great sense of belonging.

According to togetherplatform.com, there are three key benefits to incorporating mentoring programs into onboarding programs:

1. Getting a new hire up to speed quickly: many organizations have buddy programs in place. This is where peer mentoring fits in. A peer mentor, at the same level as the new hire rather than a more senior person, is great because it's more casual for the new hire.
2. Allowing a new hire to meet the team and adjust to the company culture: the mentor helps the new person learn about the company, meet the team, and adjust to the company culture.
3. Setting them up for success so they don't turnover.

Employees returning from maternity leave

I've been encouraged to see new mentoring programs starting up over the past few years focusing on integrating employees returning from maternity leave. Many organizations are losing top employees when they go on maternity leave and then decide not to return to work.

A mentoring program offered to employees who are already on maternity leave, and who may now be apprehensive about leaving their baby and returning to work, can help alleviate the stress of returning and help them feel integrated more quickly back into the organization. An employee would be paired with a mentor while still on maternity leave. The mentor would meet with the mentee to listen to any concerns they may have about returning, while also bringing them up to speed with what has happened in the organization since they went on maternity leave.

I firmly believe that this is a solution that prevents the attrition of employees once they have had a child.

Employee development

Over my 27 years of running my own company, I have learnt that employees need to know they are growing and developing in an organization. That is why learning and development have become such an integral part of an organization. Imagine you have been working for a company for three years, and you know how to do the job and have learnt most of what can be learnt in your area. You are now asked if you would like to learn more and develop more hard and soft skills by being involved in the company's mentoring program. How would you react to that and, more importantly, how would that make you feel? I'm sure you would feel that the company cares for you, is genuinely interested in your development, and that your superiors want you to progress within the organization.

The human resources department at Sun Microsystems compared the career progress of approximately 1 000 employees over a five-year period. This is what they found:

- Both mentors and mentees were approximately 20% more likely to get a raise than people who did not participate in the mentoring program.
- 25% of mentees and 28% of mentors received a raise – versus only 5% of managers who were not mentors.
- Employees who received mentoring were promoted **five** times more often than people who didn't have mentors.
- Mentors were **six** times more likely to have been promoted to a bigger job.
- 89% of those mentored went on to become mentors themselves, contributing to a culture of learning and mentoring.

Employee engagement

Employee engagement is the emotional commitment an employee has to an organization. When an employee is engaged, they care about the company and work hard to help achieve their company's goals. Engaged employees are more proficient and productive.

Organizations have a distinct interest in ensuring their employees remain engaged. According to haiilo.com, employee engagement has become one of the top priorities for most businesses, and here's why:

- Employee engagement **increases productivity in the workplace**. Engaged employees outperform their peers who are not engaged.

Overall, companies with high employee engagement are 21% more profitable.
- Employee engagement **improves morale in the workplace.**
- Employee engagement **reduces absenteeism.** In fact, a Gallup study shows that highly engaged workplaces saw 41% lower absenteeism.
- CNBC found in a survey that 90% of workers who have a mentor report being happy in their job.
- Mentoring can help increase employee engagement.

Employee retention

The pandemic saw a rise in employees seeking new jobs, what was called "The Great Resignation" or the "Turnover Tsunami". What we saw were employees demanding more remote work, better work-life balance, a better quality of living, more money, and more upskilling and re-skilling, as well as more meaningful connections and interaction. This has continued after the pandemic.

We know the cost of hiring a new employee – it costs 33% of an employee's annual salary to replace them. It is my belief that an organization needs to do everything possible to retain their key employees.

1. 49% of millennials are looking at quitting their jobs within the next two years. (Deloitte)
2. Millennials are more likely to quit because of a lack of career advancement opportunities (35%) and a lack of learning and development opportunities (28%). (Deloitte)
3. Gen Z strongly believes in learning, as 76% see learning as critical to their career advancement. (Forbes)
4. 4% of workers would stay longer if their employer offered more learning and career development opportunities. (LinkedIn)

Mentoring programs help with employee retention.
- Employees who are involved in mentoring programs have a 50% higher retention rate than those not involved in mentoring and 93% of mentees believe their mentoring relationship was useful. (MentorcliQ)
- Millennial and Gen Z workers who have a mentor are 21% to 23% more likely to report being satisfied with their current job than those without a mentor. (CNBC/Survey Monkey)

Employee apprehension

Following the Ukraine-Russia war, we are seeing a global recession looming, with inflation at record highs and listed companies leading the way in stalling new employee hires. As a result, employees are now apprehensive about losing their jobs as companies face potential retrenchments. Mentoring can alleviate the apprehension and provide psychological safety for employees so that they can continue to perform at their best. In my experience with mentoring since 2009, I have seen that sometimes a mentee just needs a sounding board, someone to listen to them and bounce their ideas off. Having a mentor can alleviate stress and tension felt in the workplace due to these uncertain times and what may lie ahead for the individual.

The rapid acceleration of the number of online mentoring platforms is testament to how many large organizations are seeing mentoring as a way to attract, develop, and retain talent.

When I was first looking at online mentoring platforms to accelerate the mentoring program I was managing globally, I came across a handful of platforms, some of which were expensive and not very flexible. Nowadays, there are hundreds of mentoring platforms to choose from – they are an easy technology. Really, it's just like a dating platform. A mentor or mentee signs up, gets matched on certain criteria, and then is matched with someone who fits what they are looking for.

Mentoring platforms will be set apart in future by the extras that they can offer. What expertise can they offer their clients and what experts do they have on board to help guide their clients? How efficient are they in helping the organization set up a mentoring program? How is their onboarding and pilot program? What training can they offer their program manager as well as the mentors and mentees on the program? What support do they offer the program manager? What learning materials can they offer their clients? How easy is it for mentors and mentees to reach out to each other and how integrative is the platform with other systems and platforms, such as LinkedIn, Salesforce, Freshsales, etc. Does it integrate well with a smartphone? Is there an app? Is it affordable for any size of company or organization?

It is my belief that these factors will set the good mentoring platforms apart and be most attractive for organizations to adopt.

WHY YOU SHOULD BE SERIOUS ABOUT MENTORING

Positive Company Culture

Strengthens employees' sense of belonging and connection, while maximizing organizational knowledge. 71% of Fortune 500 companies have a mentoring program.

Leadership Development

Mentors gain more leadership skills and confidence the more engaged they are with mentoring. Mentoring facilitates a ready pipeline of leaders.

Diversity & Inclusion

Improves minority representation at management level. Increases inclusion by 20%. Improves promotion and retention rates for minorities and women by 15–38%.

Recruitment

79% of the millennial workforce see mentoring as critical to their workplace success.

New Employee Onboarding

Mentoring programs help to onboard new employees quicker and more successfully.

Employee Development

Mentees are five times more likely to be promoted and mentors six times more likely to be promoted compared to their peers.

Employee Engagement

90% of employees who have a mentor are more satisfied with their jobs. Employee performance can increase by up to 20%.

Employee Retention

Retention rate for mentees: 72%
Retention rate for mentors: 69%
Retention rate for employees not participating in mentoring: 49%

Key takeaways:

✓ Mentoring is a "must-have" for any organization that wants to survive.

✓ Mentoring benefits an organization by improving job satisfaction and retention, and aids in the personal and professional development of the mentee.

✓ Mentoring has been shown to attract the best talent into an organization, integrate new people faster, retain existing talent, accelerate talent and leadership development, fill leadership pipelines, and increase diversity.

3

WHAT IS MENTORING?

What mentoring is and is not

I've realized over the years that people have their own ideas of what mentoring is, which may be very different from someone else's ideas. People understand mentoring based on their own experience as well as their culture. Some people are very familiar with it, while others may only understand it as something that is done in internships or at college. So, let's start at the beginning and go through what mentoring actually is as well as the different types of mentoring.

We all have some kind of idea of what mentoring is. However, we usually know what mentoring **IS NOT.**

- Mentoring is not a silver bullet to success.
- It is not an advice session in which the mentor does all the talking, dispensing their advice.
- It is not a one-way learning experience. The mentor learns as much as the mentee.
- It is not counselling or a visit to a psychologist.

There should be no expectation that the mentor will accelerate their mentee's career or open up their network to them.

What mentoring IS is a mutually beneficial experience, where the mentor helps the mentee explore their own thinking so that they can gain greater insight, knowledge, and the confidence to reach their goals.

A mentee will learn from their mentor, someone who has experience in the area that the mentee may be seeking. A mentor is a sounding board and someone who challenges their mentee's thinking. This is an opportunity for both to grow, reflect, and learn – it's a mutually beneficial experience and journey. It is also a safe place where a mentee can do deep thinking, explore their ideas, be open to new ideas, and ask advice.

A mentor is a guide and a thinking partner who helps their mentee think clearly and expansively about challenges, opportunities, and issues that need addressing. The objective of mentoring is to enable the mentee to identify personal and/or business goals, develop strategies and action plans intended to achieve these goals, and monitor progress towards implementing them. The mentor will be open to sharing their experience with their mentee as well as acting as an advisor, if required. A mentor will also hold their mentee accountable and ensure they are moving forward towards their goals.

Where did mentoring start?

The word has its roots in Greek mythology. Odysseus left his son with Mentor while he went to war. The story goes as follows:

> During the ten-year Trojan War (yes, remember the one with the wooden horse?), Odysseus, the king of Ithaca, left his wife, Penelope, and his son, Telemachus, in order to lead his army. He placed Telemachus under the care of a guardian called Mentor, whose job it was to protect and guide him.
>
> In the *Odyssey*, Homer describes how Odysseus faces a series of obstacles and challenges that stop him from returning home for another 10 years. While this is happening, young noblemen put pressure on Penelope in the hope that she'll marry one of them, denying Telemachus his birthright.
>
> Luckily for Odysseus, the gods liked to interfere in the lives of mere mortals, and the goddess Athena, in particular, was following closely. Athena wanted Odysseus back on the throne and so appeared to young Telemachus to offer him guidance.
>
> With Athena's guidance and the help of his dad, Telemachus killed all his mother's suitors and established

both his claim and his authority.

It's this godly intervention from Athena that ultimately lends the meaning to our modern word "mentor", and not the personality of the person himself.

It wasn't Mentor who provided Telemachus with the guidance – it was the Greek goddess of wisdom, Athena.

Mentoring is **the way we learnt**, a wiser person giving support and encouragement to a younger person. Mentoring was **an act of service**; it was what was expected of you. In indigenous societies, as you became an elder, it was often a rite of passage that you moved into the role of being a mentor. Being an elder was not defined by age, but rather elders were recognized because they had earned the respect of their community through wisdom, harmony, and balance.

According to the website *Art of Manliness*, in an article titled "Lessons from the Sioux in How to Turn a Boy into a Man", when a Sioux boy became a young man, his education was turned over to his father or an elder in the community, who became his mentor. A boy was taught how to be a warrior and a hunter, to understand the tribe's code of honour. His mentor would teach him about natural phenomena such as how to identify certain plants, animal tracks, and weather patterns. Sioux knowledge and traditions were passed down through stories, which boys had to listen to and then be prepared to recite. Part of their tribe's code of honour was understanding achievement to be about becoming their best selves, recognizing that failures and successes bring public consequences, and that manly honour must be earned by having skin in the game.

With colonization and modernization, the population of many tribes was decimated, and many stories were lost and forgotten.

In an article by the National Mentoring Resource Centre titled "Mentoring for American Indian and Alaska Native Youth", it was noted that in 2017, there were 370 million indigenous people worldwide, equalling less than 5% of the world's population. In 2015, there were 5,4 million people in the United States who identified as American Indian and Alaska Native (AI/AN), composing 2% of the total population. Many indigenous people suffered historical traumas that were exacerbated by assimilation programs practised just a generation or two ago, including residential, military-style boarding schools and foster care/adoption programs in which Native children were placed in the homes of non-Native families. In these programs, many Native children experienced verbal, emotional, spiritual, physical, and sexual abuse, and were often removed from their culture, including their people, language, religion, and customs. Mentoring programs have been established to help youths of these indigenous tribes to learn about their history and retain their culture. Providing access to trained mentors via a mentoring program can help reduce challenges such as drug and alcohol abuse, risk of suicide, teen pregnancy, geographic isolation, limited health care, and high school dropout rates. Mentoring is connecting them with their culture again.

Mentoring is thus age-old, but it is also crucial for learning today.

Sponsorship mentoring versus developmental mentoring

Sponsorship mentoring

Now, I want you to think of how you traditionally understand mentoring – think of that apprentice who is taken under the wing of a master and taught the trade to eventually be moulded into the image of the master himself. That's really how mentoring formally started and still exists in a different form today, called **sponsorship mentoring.** This type of mentoring exists in many organizations today, being very popular in the United States, where a younger person learns from an older person who ensures and promotes their professional development. They take the younger person under their wing, teaching them, advising them, introducing them to their network as well as opening doors for them to promote them upwards.

What do mentors do for their mentees in a sponsorship relationship?

Sponsorship mentoring requires a mentor to make a bigger investment in their mentee by using their clout and influence to advocate for them, seeing their mentee as having high potential. A mentor shares their protégé's accomplishments with others in order to help create a positive impression of them. They help boost them, connecting them to their network and the right people to accelerate their career, giving them access to people they would not otherwise be able to meet. For example, a mentor might invite their mentee to an exclusive event in order to increase their visibility to more important people. Annie Young-Scrivner, a Chinese-American business executive who previously held senior positions at Godiva Chocolatier, PepsiCo, and Starbucks, benefitted from the sponsorship she received from Indra Nooyi, while at PepsiCo. Annie was invited by Indra to attend meetings in China, which proved to be valuable learning and exposure for her career development.

While I was facilitating virtual mentoring masterclasses for a hotel group, the focus for them was on developmental mentoring. However, they found that many of the mentees were expecting their mentors to advocate for them and help them with their promotion within the organization. I had to ensure that during the Mentoring Masterclasses I explained the differences between sponsorship and developmental mentoring as well as the expectations of each.

Many mentees may be expecting sponsorship mentoring, so guidelines need to be put in place about what type of mentoring is being offered in the organization so that expectations are met for both mentors and mentees.

Developmental mentoring

Another type of mentoring has developed over the past few decades called **developmental mentoring**. This is non-directive, mutually beneficial, and more of a peer-to-peer relationship.

While I was running a mentoring program in Cape Town, I had a mentee who was looking for someone to help him expand his fruit business in South Africa. Until then he had only been exporting his fruit overseas. At that time, I was still manually matching mentors to mentees, often approaching other members at cocktail parties, where after a drink or two they would agree to be a mentor for someone. After meeting Ian, I thought of the perfect mentor for him, someone I knew very well. I did a good job convincing Carlos to mentor Ian. Why did I think Carlos would make a good mentor for Ian? Well, Carlos was a farmer himself, running a large, profitable farm, not fruit, but a commercial farm. Carlos was also working for a large retailer in South Africa, not in the fresh foods area, but he had been in retail long enough to know what it was like to deal with South African retailers. The relationship took off and after it was finished, I had a conversation with Carlos to find out how it went. He said the following, which I will never forget:

"I feel quite embarrassed to say this, but I think I learnt more from my mentee than he did from me."

That was when I realized that the relationship really is **mutually beneficial** – the mentor learns as much as the mentee, if not more.

Yes, as a mentor you may be wiser, or have more knowledge on the subject, or more experience, but you are not going to tell your mentee what to do. Your job is to get them to do their thinking first, explore all the options, and **then** share your thinking and stories with them.

It is not just an advice session (even though it may feel good to do so and you may feel as though you are helping by dishing out instructions). But it's not helpful for your mentee unless you have explored all their own thinking first. Advice and sharing your experience are part of mentoring, but need to be done at the correct time and in the correct manner.

In developmental mentoring, the mentor is **your equal**; there is no hierarchy.

They are your **thinking partner** with your best interests at heart.

The following diagram shows the differences between developmental and sponsorship mentoring.

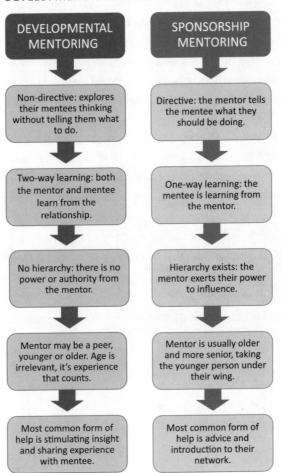

DEVELOPMENTAL VS SPONSORSHIP MENTORING

DEVELOPMENTAL MENTORING	SPONSORSHIP MENTORING
Non-directive: explores their mentees thinking without telling them what to do.	Directive: the mentor tells the mentee what they should be doing.
Two-way learning: both the mentor and mentee learn from the relationship.	One-way learning: the mentee is learning from the mentor.
No hierarchy: there is no power or authority from the mentor.	Hierarchy exists: the mentor exerts their power to influence.
Mentor may be a peer, younger or older. Age is irrelevant, it's experience that counts.	Mentor is usually older and more senior, taking the younger person under their wing.
Most common form of help is stimulating insight and sharing experience with mentee.	Most common form of help is advice and introduction to their network.

Mentoring versus coaching

In every Mentoring Masterclass I run, I have at least one participant eager to know what the difference is between mentoring and coaching. For me, these are the main differences:

- Coaching is **performance-focused** while mentoring is **development-focused** – focused on the mentee's development as a whole.

- A mentor usually has **experience** in the issue or area in which a mentee is seeking mentoring. They share their experience and knowledge with their mentee. A coach does not need to have any experience with the issue or area in which the client is seeking coaching. A coach follows a **process** in which they have been trained. They believe that the client has the best answers within themselves. The coach is trained to listen and ask questions to get the client to think about their own solutions and work towards goals.

- A mentor can give **advice** as a last resort and preferably only when asked. They are often sought by the mentee for the advice they can give them. However, caution needs to be taken when giving advice. A coach generally does not give advice. (Read more about advice in chapter 25).

A mentor is **not usually paid,** while an outside coach usually is, although there are professional mentors who are now being paid.

The fact that mentoring is usually not paid is powerful and potentially disruptive and exciting in the Western paradigm in which business operates.

In an organization, your line manager can coach you on the job and the method used is usually more directive. Mentoring in an organization is often **at least two levels apart** and the method is usually non-directive (if it is developmental mentoring), while it is directive if its sponsorship mentoring.

The next diagram explains the differences:

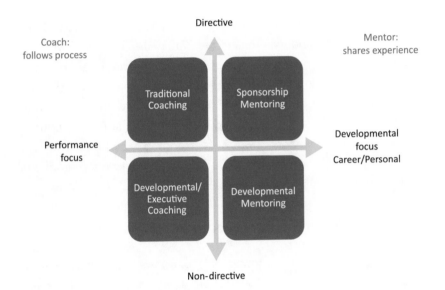

Reverse mentoring

We traditionally think of mentoring as an older person mentoring a younger person. Today the word "reverse mentoring" is used to describe a younger person mentoring a more senior person. A definition of reverse mentoring is when a more junior individual or employee is paired with a senior employee to share skills or knowledge on various topics such as diversity, technology, cultural relevance, Generation Z, etc.

I don't really like the term reverse mentoring. I think it's still just mentoring. Who cares how old or senior the person is? If one person needs to learn and the other person can help them, then there can be a mentoring relationship. However, many organizations are now implementing so-called reverse mentoring programs to allow older or more senior employees to learn from the younger generation. The pace of change is increasing in this information age and organizations are realizing that everyone needs to keep abreast of change in order to stay relevant. Creating an environment of lifelong learning is what most organizations are embracing, and this includes ensuring that **everyone** is learning. Organizations do not want to lose critical knowledge and skills, hence reverse mentoring allows senior employees to share their corporate cultural knowledge and technical experience, while younger talent can share their new skills and cultural perspective. Understood like that, reverse mentoring is crucial.

One organization that implemented a successful reverse mentoring program is the UK NHS Foundation Trust. The focus was on supporting BME (Black and minority ethnic) staff within the Trust. A BME staff member, who was the mentor, was paired with a senior board member, the mentee. The learning was profound and has changed the way the organization supports its BME staff. For board member Sandra Mellors, deputy chief executive and COO, and Diana Belfon, equality and engagement manager, it was a life-changing experience. They said that reverse mentoring developed a safe culture and deep emotional understanding for BME staff.

Types of mentoring or mentoring formats

Mentoring does not need to be only one-to-one, which is how we traditionally understand mentoring. I am seeing a plethora of different mentoring interactions. Today there are mentoring groups, team mentoring, mentoring circles, mentoring forums, reverse mentoring, and flash mentoring. Let me explain a little about each so you have a clearer idea of what they are and if any of these formats may interest you.

One-to-one mentoring: A mentor and a mentee meet regularly for a set period of time and have a definite beginning and ending. This is a one-to-one relationship where the mentor usually has experience in what the mentee is seeking mentoring about. This can be sponsorship mentoring (where the mentor is more senior and directive) or developmental mentoring. This has been the most common form of mentoring to date and one with which we are most familiar.

Peer-to-peer mentoring: This is also one-to-one mentoring, but both are mentors and mentees to each other. One of them does not need to have more experience than the other. They both learn from each other and mentor each other.

Group mentoring: The group consists of a mentor and a group of mentees. The mentor provides mentoring to the group as they usually have experience in the area in which the mentees are seeking mentoring. For example, an organization may want to set up group mentoring for new interns with one senior member in the organization. They may meet once a month to go through the culture of the organization and check if they are fitting in and so on. It's a very common form of mentoring for onboarding and is also useful if you do not have a large pool of mentors.

Mentoring circles and mentoring forums: This is peer mentoring where all participants in the circle or forum are mentors and mentees to each other. They do not need to be from the same team, division, or department. It is a trusted group sharing information and learning from one another. In organizations, it's often around a topic or field of interest. For example, if an organization wants to explore the topic of diversity a bit more, and this is a topic that is of interest to the participants, then they can explore the topic in several sessions. Mentoring circles and forums provide great support for employees.

Team mentoring: This is peer mentoring among a team in an organization. Each team member can be both a mentor and a mentee to one another. They have team mentoring sessions where they mentor one another around a subject or topic that is brought to the table by the manager, the team, or an individual.

Reverse mentoring: A younger person mentors an older or more senior person, or the mentee offers mentoring to the mentor, such as asking your mentor, "What would you like to learn from me?" Lately, we have found that this is happening when a more senior staff member may need mentoring in the areas of technology or social media, for instance.

Flash mentoring: This is a once-off mentoring conversation, usually around a certain issue that the mentee is dealing with. It is not mentoring in the traditional sense, but often a flash mentoring session can lead to a longer relationship. It may also be that you are looking for some expertise or input on one issue that you are dealing with, and it can be resolved in one session.

Whatever type of mentoring you choose, you will benefit from it, whether you are a mentor or mentee.

MENTORING FORMATS

ONE-TO-ONE

PEER-TO-PEER

REVERSE

GROUP: ONE-TO-MANY

CIRCLE OR TEAM

Key takeaways:

✓ Reverse mentoring flips the conventional mentoring relationship. The more senior employee is the mentee, and the more junior employee is the mentor.

✓ There are many types of mentoring partnerships, the most common being one-to-one mentoring.

✓ Group mentoring is useful if you have a smaller pool of mentors. Flash mentoring is a once-off conversation with a mentor.

4

WHY TRAINING IS VITAL

Mentoring has been around for so long that you may be wondering why you would need to be trained to be a mentor or mentee.

From my experience with running and observing mentoring programs, I have noticed that mentors and mentees feel more confident to go out and begin their mentoring relationship after they have attended a mentoring training workshop. They know what their roles are and what is expected of them. Many participants who come to the workshop with the idea that they only want to be a mentor or a mentee realize that they can be both. They take away conversation skills that can be used in all areas of their life, not only mentoring.

Why train as a mentor and mentee?

The biggest learning for me over the years is that mentors and mentees who are trained seem to have **more successful relationships** than those who are not trained. If both the mentor and mentee attend the same training workshop, we pair them together for most of their conversations. The result is they report that **this accelerates their journey,** so they are able to kick-start their mentoring meeting having already built rapport and trust.

As a mentor, you have specific knowledge or experience that you are willing and able to share with your mentee. You are trusted to lead your mentee to a destination that they desire to reach by helping your mentee set goals for their journey. However, if you are ill-prepared for your role, your mentee will be able to pick up on this, which can lead to feelings of disappointment, frustration, and perhaps a breakdown in your relationship. The better prepared you are, the more effective you will be as a mentor. This is why it is so important to receive training before you embark on a mentoring journey.

As a mentee, you will get more out of your mentoring relationship if you are trained and feel prepared for your journey. You will understand your role as well as what is expected of you. This will lead to a more positive and fruitful experience for you and your mentor.

Knowing how to be a better mentor and mentee, as well as learning the skills needed for your conversations, will ensure you get the most out of your relationships.

David Clutterbuck, in his book *Making the Most of Developmental Mentoring*, says if both mentors and mentees receive training, nine out of 10 relationships will receive **significant learning**, compared to three out of 10 relationships if both mentors and mentees are untrained and four out of 10 if only the mentor is trained.

WHY TRAIN AS A MENTOR AND MENTEE?

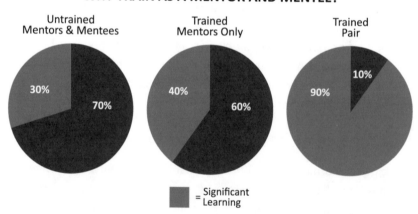

When speaking to businesses, I encourage them to incorporate training into their mentoring program, at the beginning as well as during the program. I also encourage them to include both mentors and mentees in the training to ensure that there is significant learning. If just left to their own devices, mentors and mentees really do not know what to do and relationships tend to fall apart within the first three months.

From my experience, untrained mentors tend to talk too much and give unsolicited advice, while untrained mentees do not prepare for meetings or take ownership of their mentoring journey.

I am passionate about training! I truly believe that as a mentor or mentee, you really do need to be equipped so that you can get the most out of your mentoring journey.

Key takeaways:

✓ Training increases your confidence in being a mentor or a mentee.
✓ You will get more out of your relationship if you are trained.
✓ You will be more prepared for your mentoring journey.

5

AM I READY TO BE A MENTOR?

As a mentor, you may be wondering whether you should embark on this journey or whether you have the confidence or experience to be a mentor. Here are some questions to answer to see if you are ready:

- Have you developed your own self-awareness?
- Do you enjoy helping and developing others?
- Have you examined your values, strengths, and superpowers?
- Would you like to make a difference in another person's life?
- Are you a good listener?
- Are you ready to positively challenge your mentee?
- Are you able to give constructive feedback?
- Is lifelong learning important to you?
- Do you want to learn from someone?
- Do you want to leave a legacy?
- Do you have stories and experience to share with someone else?
- Are you willing to commit the time to the process?

It's also good to ask yourself, **"Who has been a role model in my life?"** We often forget all the mentors we have had along the way, whether they have been a parent, a schoolteacher, a friend, a partner, a colleague, or a boss. We have mentors along our life journey, even if it is not in a formal relationship.

Then ask yourself, **"How did they make me feel?"** Often when we reflect on how we felt, we understand the traits and values that we need to embody to be a mentor ourselves.

Who do you want to model yourself on?

Benefits of mentoring for the mentor

Remember that I said the relationship is **mutually beneficial**, the mentor gets as much out of the relationship as the mentee? When I spoke to Carlos, who had mentored Ian the fruit farmer, and asked him what he enjoyed about the mentoring experience, he looked up into the corner of the room, his mind working, and said, "I was able to reflect so much on my career, what I had gone through and where I was currently. For me it was a period of huge self-reflection. I also learnt about a whole new industry. It felt so good to be able to share my learning with someone else."

The most common things I have heard mentors get out of their mentoring relationship is that it has afforded them the opportunity **to give back, to pay it forward, to make a difference in someone's life** and **to help someone**. This has probably been my biggest takeaway for when I have been a mentor myself. Other benefits are that you can reflect on your own journey and career, learn a new industry, learn new ways of doing things from someone else, be stimulated as your thinking is challenged, and celebrate in the success of seeing someone grow, develop, and reach their goals.

I have had so many people say to me that they don't think they will be a good mentor as they don't know very much. But that's not true. If you have some life experience, then you can be a great mentor. You only realize how much you actually know once you start to mentor. A CEO of a large, listed insurance company said to me after he had mentored an entrepreneur for 12 months: "Wow, I never realized how much I knew until I mentored this person."

These are some of the key benefits of being a mentor:

- **Learning:** Mentoring is a mutually beneficial experience for both the mentor and the mentee – the mentor usually learns as much as the mentee.
- **Giving back:** You can share your learning with others, making a

difference in another person's life or leaving a legacy.

- **Rewarding:** Mentoring is a rewarding experience, and you can take pride in your mentee's success and achievement.
- **Self-awareness:** You will develop more self-awareness in mentoring another person.
- **Enhance conversational skills:** By having frequent mentoring conversations, you can develop and enhance your own conversational and leadership skills.
- **Reflection:** You will reflect on your own career journey, what you have achieved, what you know, and what you have learned.
- **Networks:** You have the opportunity to extend your own professional and personal network.

Research at the University of South Florida by Tammy D. Allen, Elizabeth Lentz, and Rachel Day, published in the *Journal of Career Development*, shows that individuals who serve as a mentor to others report a greater salary, greater promotion rates, and stronger subjective career success than do individuals without any experience as a mentor to others. The results provide preliminary evidence supporting the notion that career benefits are associated with serving as a mentor to others.

Just to show that mentoring is not all about business mentoring, let's look at the success of it in prisons. Mentoring has been a very successful tool in integrating prisoners back into society. Mosaic's ex-offender mentoring program, part of The Prince's Trust in the UK, is helping prisoners aged between 18 and 30 years old find jobs once they leave prison and integrate back into society. A 2013 research project by The Reasons Why Foundation, interviewing mentors of ex-offenders in London, discovered that mentorships are not only beneficial for the mentee, but the mentors as well. Becoming a mentor made them feel empowered and emotionally rewarded from giving back, as well as experiencing an increase in self-esteem. Furthermore, both the mentors and mentees found the mentorship relationship allowed them to develop interpersonal skills and to build trusted relationships, and strengthened their openness to change.

During my time working on a global mentoring program, I had paired a CEO with an entrepreneur in a mentoring relationship. I had had to really persuade the CEO to become a mentor. He was reluctant to do so, saying he had no time. I followed up with the mentee and heard that they were meeting regularly, and it was going well. However, I had not heard back from the mentor. I was really hoping that he was enjoying the experience. A few months later, I went to an event and saw the mentor sitting at a table with his friends. As I approached the table to say hello, I heard him telling his friends, with his face lit up, that he was a mentor to an entrepreneur and never thought he would have enjoyed it so much. Everyone was keen to hear more about his experience of being a mentor. He was the centre of attention, having captured the interest of those around him, not telling them anything that was confidential, but more about what he was getting out of it. He was literally beaming from ear to ear! Yes, giving back feels good and making a difference in another person's life comes with personal rewards.

Don't consider being a mentor if...

- you don't have the time to commit to it – at least one hour a month or every six weeks;
- you think you have all the answers and need to tell your mentee what to do; or
- you are not good at listening and not prepared to improve your listening skills. As a mentor, you should spend 20% of the time talking and 80% of the time listening!

You need to know:

- You don't get paid to be a mentor, but you will receive a lot of self-growth and fulfilment.
- You will learn as much as, if not more than, your mentee.
- There will be a lot of self-reflection.
- You will find out that you know more than you think!
- You may not like your mentee at first, but you just need to believe in them.
- Being present is probably the most important thing that you need to do.

Key takeaways:

✓ Mentoring is a mutually beneficial experience. You will learn as much as, if not more than, your mentee.

✓ Mentoring is a way of giving back and making a difference in another person's life.

✓ Mentoring will lead to reflection of your own life and career. You will realize how much you do know.

6

AM I READY TO BE A MENTEE?

You may be wondering whether mentoring really is for you or maybe whether you are ready to be a mentee. Here are some questions to answer to see if you are ready to embark on your mentoring journey as a mentee:

- Would you like to spend time exploring your personal growth, career development, and purpose in life with someone who is objective?
- Would you like to have a safe place to discuss your vision, dreams, and aspirations with a mentor?
- Are you going through a transition or challenge in your life that you require support with?
- Are there skills you would like to develop in your current role or require for a new role?
- Are you struggling with a particular issue at the moment?
- Would you like to learn from someone who has experience and wisdom in the area in which you are seeking mentoring?
- Do you have goals that you would like to achieve and would like someone to guide you on your journey?
- Do you want someone to hold you accountable?
- Are you ready to be positively challenged?
- Are you ready to set goals that you can work towards with a mentor?
- Are you looking for someone to be a sounding board off which you can bounce your ideas and thinking?

- Is lifelong learning important to you?
- Are you willing to commit the time to the process?

Benefits of mentoring for the mentee

You as a mentee will learn from someone who has been there and done that. You will have a mentor who can be a sounding board, a guide, and a thinking partner, and someone who challenges your thinking. This is an opportunity to grow, reflect, and learn. It's a safe place where you can do deep thinking, explore your ideas, be open to new ideas, and ask advice. Your mentor will also hold you accountable and ensure you are moving forward towards your goals.

- **Learning:** You will learn from your mentor as well as being encouraged to do self-reflection along the way.
- **Clarity:** You will be able to gain greater clarity on your career and/or development issues.
- **Access to experience:** You will have access to someone who can share their learning, wisdom, stories, and experience with you.
- **Self-awareness:** You will develop deeper self-awareness during your mentoring journey.
- **Sounding board:** Your mentor will be your sounding board as well as a role model.
- **Reflection:** This is an opportunity to reflect on your own progress in reaching your goals.
- **Stretch:** You will be encouraged to set more ambitious goals than you would ordinarily set yourself.
- **Challenged:** It is an opportunity to be positively challenged by someone who sees the potential in you.

It's always heartening to hear about the impact of mentoring outside of business, impacting people from all realms of society. Here are two programs using mentoring to benefit their mentees in youth development and education:

- Earlier, I had mentioned that mentoring is so broad and can be used in all aspects of life. Mentoring has so many benefits to mentees in youth mentoring programs. In the Youth Mentoring Initiative, mentoring has been shown to increase their self-confidence, improve their sense of self-worth, improve their understanding of accountability and social responsibility, improve their communication skills, help them with dealing with their emotions, and improve their academics and social interactions with peers.

- A non-profit, Partners for Possibility (PfP), improves the quality of education in South Africa by capacitating school principals from under-resourced schools and enhancing their leadership skills through partnerships with business leaders. The results for the 177 partnership pairs who completed the program in 2018 show that the large majority of principals, the mentees, found the program to be substantially beneficial to their leadership role and to their schools.

I had a personal experience with hearing what impact mentoring had made on a mentee's life. In 2016 I boarded a flight to Singapore to attend a conference. As I was putting my bag down on my seat, I looked to see who was sitting behind me. There was a person I remembered who had been involved in the mentoring program I had run a few years before. At the time, I had trouble pairing him as he had really wanted a particular mentor and it took quite a bit of persuading for me to convince this mentor to take him on. (The mentor's reason was that he did not have the time.) Eventually, he accepted the mentorship, and I knew it had been a very successful relationship, but I had not heard much detail about it.

Neil was now seated on the plane behind me. After I had settled in, he stood up and said to me, "I'm not sure if I ever told you about my mentoring experience." I admitted he had not. "Well," he said very matter-of-factly, "mentoring changed my life." I just stared at him. What? Did he really say that? I felt goosebumps on my arms... "Tell me more." Neil continued, "I realized that I didn't want to run my business anymore and my wife was much better at it than I was, so I gave up running it and now spend all my time doing other things which I love, one of which is sitting on the board of my previous mentor's company. It truly changed my life for the better."

I sat back down on my seat thinking, "Mentoring changed someone's life! That is how powerful it can be."

Don't consider being a mentee if...

- you don't have the time to commit to it – at least one hour a month;

- you won't drive the relationship
- you won't take ownership of your learning or
- you don't want to put in the time to prepare for meetings.

You need to know

- Your mentor is giving up their valuable time for mentoring. This needs to be respected.
- Your mentor won't have all the answers but will be there to listen to you and ask questions to help you think more deeply.
- There will be a lot of self-reflection.
- You may not like your mentor at first, but you just need to believe in them.

Worksheet 1: Reflection exercise for mentees

Reflect on the following questions to find out if you are ready to be a mentee:

1. Would you like to spend time exploring your personal growth, career development, and purpose in life with someone who is objective?
2. Would you like to have a safe place to discuss your vision, dreams, and aspirations with a mentor?
3. Are you going through a transition in your life that you require support with?
4. Are there skills you would like to develop in your current role or require for a new role?
5. Are you struggling with a particular issue at the moment?
6. Would you like to learn from someone who has experience and wisdom in the area in which you are seeking mentoring?

7. Do you have goals that you would like to achieve, and would you like someone to guide you on your journey?
8. Do you want someone to hold you accountable?
9. Are you ready to be positively challenged?
10. Are you looking for someone to be a sounding board off which you can bounce your ideas and thinking?
11. Is lifelong learning important to you?
12. Are you willing to commit the necessary time to the process?

Key takeaways:

✓ Mentoring is a powerful experience that can truly impact your life.
✓ Your mentor is someone you can learn from and who will share their experience with you, while positively challenging you.
✓ Being a mentee is a commitment and you must be prepared to put the effort into the relationship.

PART 2:
LET THE FIREWORKS BEGIN – THE CATHERINE WHEEL MENTORING MODEL

"The quality of your mentoring journey
depends on the quality of your conversations,
which depends on the quality of the relationship
you have built with your mentor or mentee."
Catherine Hodgson

Most of us know that the Catherine Wheel is a type of firework that, when ignited, rotates in a wheel formation, creating sparks and flames – a dazzling wheel of spinning light.

When I was creating my model for a mentoring program, it transformed into a three-wheel layer of various colours. My name is Catherine, and I am known for being a firecracker with my abundant energy, so it seemed apt to adopt the name of the firework, the Catherine Wheel, for it.

Photo courtesy of Richard Rohrdanz

7

A ROADMAP FOR YOUR MENTORING JOURNEY

The Catherine Wheel is a roadmap. It is a step-by-step process that you can follow to get the most out of your mentoring experience. It gives you a structure.

The Catherine Wheel covers how to embark on your journey, how to build rapport and trust to create a solid foundation to your relationship, how to structure your mentoring conversations and then wrap up and end your journey.

The three wheels of the Catherine Wheel Mentoring Model

The model consists of three wheels.

The outer wheel, **The Journey**, usually lasting six to 12 months, comprises five steps: Embark, Connect, Commit, Review, and End.

The middle wheel, **The Relationship**, is so important to your mentoring experience. We will go into more detail in Chapter 13 on how to build rapport, develop trust, and continually review your relationship.

The inner wheel, **The Conversation**, shows the structure of your mentoring conversations. This provides you with a guideline for your conversations and we will go through The Conversation Flow in Chapter 18.

At the heart of the Catherine Wheel is a solid circle representing what is most important for your whole mentoring experience: trust, respect, confidentiality, and honesty. Without these your relationship will not get to the level where you will be able to have deep conversations with your mentor or mentee.

Let's find out more about the outer wheel: your mentoring journey.

THE CATHERINE WHEEL

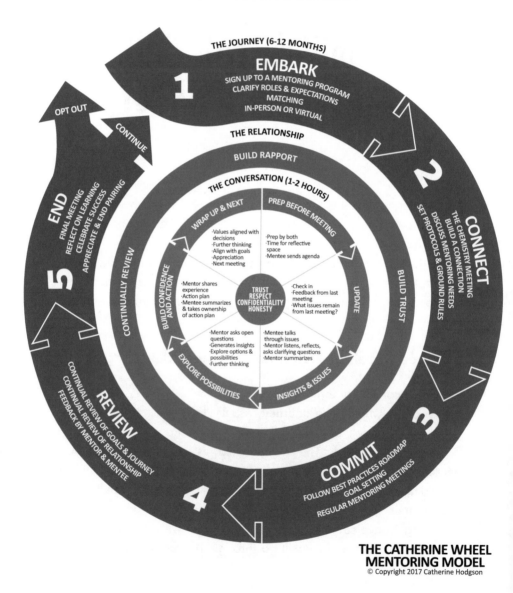

**THE CATHERINE WHEEL
MENTORING MODEL**
© Copyright 2017 Catherine Hodgson

8

THE OUTER WHEEL
– THE JOURNEY

The outer wheel is the journey – what you are about to embark on with your mentor or mentee. I would recommend at least six months for your mentoring journey; any shorter and you probably will not be able to get to achieving all the goals that you may have set for your mentee. Ideally, it would be best to embark on a 12-month journey of about 10 meetings to really experience a comprehensive mentoring journey. However, many mentors and mentees are reluctant to commit to 12 months, being unsure whether the relationship will work and if it doesn't, how to end it.

To overcome this obstacle, I would recommend committing to six months, and then, if both parties are getting value from the mentoring relationship and there is still work to be done and goals to be achieved, to renew it for another six months.

Step 1: Embark

Sign up to a mentoring program or find a mentoring partner

The first step on your journey is joining a mentoring program or reaching out to find a mentor or mentee. If you are fortunate enough to have access to a mentoring program in your organization, then find out more about how to join, either as a mentor or mentee or both.

THE CATHERINE WHEEL

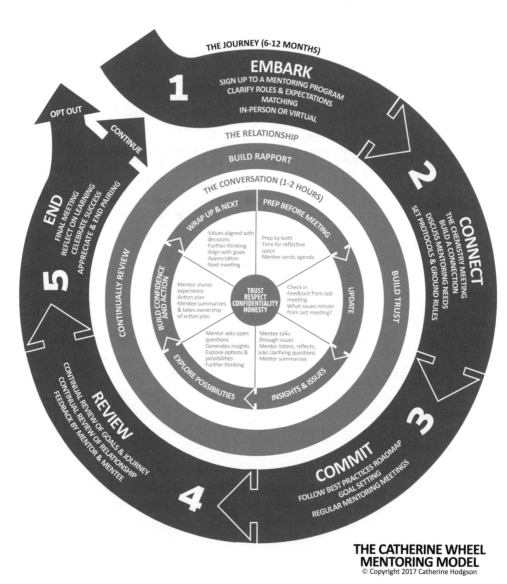

THE CATHERINE WHEEL MENTORING MODEL
© Copyright 2017 Catherine Hodgson

If you do not have access to any mentoring program, then have a look at some online mentoring platforms that you can join and partake in. There is a plethora of mentoring platforms now available, and many are open to anyone who wishes to sign up.

If this does not appeal to you as a mentee, then you may want to consider approaching someone to mentor you. I often get asked how this should be done. The one thing that you may fear is rejection and the embarrassment that goes along with it. I don't really know of anyone who would not be flattered to be asked to be a mentor, but some people may think that it is an onerous task to take on and they don't have the time available, or they may feel they are not competent to be a mentor.

A softer approach to asking someone outright to be your mentor is to ask someone if they would be able to meet with you for coffee as you would like to get their input/advice/opinion on an issue that you are trying to deal with. Most people have an hour they would spare if they were asked in this way. If you feel that the meeting went well and they have added value, then send them a thank-you message and a few weeks later ask if they are available to meet again. If the other person is also getting value from the meeting, then they will most likely want to carry on the conversations. Before you know it, you have a mentor, without it being official.

Clarify roles and expectations

As part of deciding that you would like to embark on a mentoring journey, it is important that you understand what your role would be as a mentor or mentee and what expectations you have of your mentoring partner.

You may be thinking of becoming a mentor but are not sure what your role will be or what is expected of you. Or you may not have considered being a mentor until now, but may realize, after reading this chapter, that you actually have a lot to offer.

When you first start out being a mentor, it's important to know your role, as well as what your mentee expects from you. If this discussion is not done upfront in one of your first mentoring meetings, then expectations could be unfulfilled. It's part of setting the **ground rules** for your relationship.

Role of a mentor

Your role as a mentor is to guide your mentee on their mentoring journey. You are their **thinking partner** who helps your mentee think clearly and expansively about challenges, opportunities, and issues that they may need to address. You are a sounding board, someone who positively challenges your mentee's thinking, while creating a safe place for your mentee to explore their own ideas. You will remain open to sharing your experience with your mentee as well as acting as an advisor, if required. You will also hold your mentee accountable and ensure they are moving towards their goals. You will commit to the process in terms of time and being present for your mentee.

Your role is as follows:

- Be a guide and a thinking partner, walking alongside your mentee on this learning journey.
- Encourage and support.
- Ask questions that result in the mentee identifying new ways of thinking, exploring new approaches, and seeing new perspectives.
- Create psychological safety – a safe space that encourages exploration and openness, is nonjudgmental, and also holds the mentee accountable.
- Be present and honest and strive to work with integrity.
- Communicate openly, sharing and reflecting back observations.
- Hold the focus of the sessions in line with the goals that the mentee sets for themself.
- Help the mentee to identify blind spots and assist them to deal with them effectively.
- Share your experience, wisdom and advice when asked or with permission.
- Provide feedback and ask for feedback.

YOUR THINKING PARTNER

Role of a mentee

A mentee will learn from their mentor, someone who has experience in the area in which the mentee may be seeking insight.

Your role is as follows:

- Drive the process and take ownership of your learning.
- Prepare for your mentoring sessions and commit to spend time in reflective thinking.
- Be committed to taking ownership of your action plans and implement them.
- Be present during the sessions, be honest and open.
- Provide feedback to the mentor.
- Ask questions and be open to being positively challenged.
- Embrace a growth mindset.

MENTEES DRIVE THE RELATIONSHIP

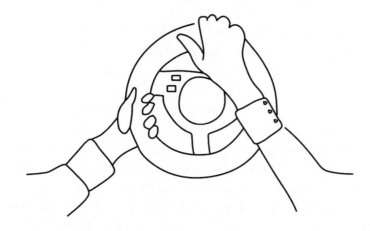

We will discuss these roles in more detail in the next two chapters where we look at the Seven Strengths of Highly Effective Mentors and Seven Strengths of Highly Effective Mentees.

9

THE SEVEN STRENGTHS OF HIGHLY EFFECTIVE MENTORS

We have looked at the roles of both the mentor and mentee in the previous chapter. Let's now focus a bit more on the mentor and look at some of the strengths that a mentor would need for their mentoring relationship.

I created **The Seven Strengths of Highly Effective Mentors Model** as I like to see things visually to make it more memorable and sticky. The acronym that I have for mentors is **P.R.E.S.E.N.T.** As a mentor, the most important strength you bring is to be **present**. For me, if you are fully present, then everything else will fall into place.

As a mentor, the most important strength you bring is to be present, aware of what is happening right now, not in the past or the future. The power of being fully present allows everything else to fade away, leaving only what you have to do in this moment.

The Seven Strengths of Highly Effective Mentors Model

THE 7 STRENGTHS OF HIGHLY EFFECTIVE MENTORS
P.R.E.S.E.N.T.

THE 7 STRENGTHS OF HIGHLY EFFECTIVE MENTORS MODEL
© Copyright 2020 Catherine Hodgson

Let's go through the seven strengths in more detail.

You, as a mentor, have the responsibility to offer the tools, guidance, support, and feedback that your mentee needs to thrive in their career and life. You may have travelled the same road as them and have now offered to be their guide along their journey.

P.R.E.S.E.N.T.

Present

In your mentoring meetings, the most important thing you can do is to be fully present – to be mindful. It is not easy to do this, so you will need to have this top of mind so that you try to remain present throughout. I like to do the following exercise before I facilitate my mentoring workshops to get everyone fully present for the time ahead. This is also a good exercise to do before you go into a mentoring meeting, and it only takes a few minutes.

On a piece of paper (yes, I said paper and pen, not keyboard or phone), write down all the things that could keep you from being fully present right now. What are you concerned about? What can you not get out of your head? What is on your mind? Write them all down. Now, when you look at that list, what feelings come to mind when you read it? Write down those feelings. Once you have done this, fold the piece of paper in half and put it away, out of reach. It will be waiting for you later.

What just happened? Physically writing down what could keep you from being fully present and then putting a feeling to it immediately lowers your anxiety when you think about it. We are often not in tune with our feelings, so learning to express them and name them helps us to realize that we do not need to take them on and carry them with us.

When I have done this exercise in workshops or meetings, I always have people comment that this exercise really helps them put their "monkey mind" on mute and helps them to focus and be present for the workshop. Try it and let me know how it goes for you at your next meeting.

As a mentor you will be investing time in your relationship. It does not take a lot of time, but you need to commit to it. Mentors are also self-aware, meaning they have done work on themselves and understand themselves. You know what your strengths and weaknesses are, you are in tune with your feelings and emotions, you know your triggers and you understand how you are perceived by others. Why, you may ask, do you need to be self-aware? Knowing yourself helps you to understand your own reactions, your own strengths and weaknesses, and thereby you can help others become more self-aware themselves.

Relationship

A highly effective mentor focuses on building the relationship first. You need to put the relationship before the task. That means spending time getting to know each other, building rapport and trust so that you can have the deep conversations that are needed. At the heart of the relationship and in order to build trust, you need to model confidentiality, and be honest, transparent, and respectful. It's definitely worth it to spend the time on your relationship upfront as it will reap huge benefits down the line with both of you feeling more comfortable to share openly with each other.

Another important trait is to be authentic. Even though you are the mentor, you don't need to have all the answers or pretend to have all the answers. Just be yourself. Remove any ego and be open to being vulnerable.

Encourages

As a mentor, you play a **supportive** role to your mentee. You are their guide along their mentoring journey. You believe in them and know that they have their own best answers within. As their biggest supporter, you encourage and validate them.

When I was working in corporate for a large cosmetics company, we underwent retrenchments throughout the company. We were all waiting to be called into the office of one of the directors and we sat anxiously, not knowing our fate. I was the first one called into the marketing director's office. I had been working for the company for a few years and had a very good relationship with my boss, the marketing director. I didn't know if, by being called first, I was going to be told that I didn't have a job any longer. I sat down across the table from him, hands sweating, and he suddenly smiled and said, "Catherine, you are going to stay because I believe in you and know that you will do everything to make this company successful." He believed in me. By saying this, he showed his trust in me, and I knew I would do anything to continue to work as hard as I could, because he was relying on me to do so. He was a great mentor to me, and we continued to have a strong relationship where I would work hard because I knew he believed in me.

You, as a mentor, will be holding your mentee **accountable** along the way as this helps them achieve their goals. Sometimes a person just needs someone to hold them accountable.

You may also be a **role model** for them as they see what you have achieved and want that for themselves. In organizations, it's important to understand that your mentee is going to be observing how you speak to others, how you react in certain situations, how you deal with solving problems or with your staff. If you are mentoring within your own organization, be very aware that you are a role model to your mentee.

Most importantly, though, you are a **sounding board** for them. Most of the time, mentees just need someone to listen to them so they can bounce their ideas off someone. How often are we able to talk freely while the other person just listens to us? Not often. Having someone be a sounding board for us is a gift. This also can help your mentee reach their own insights themselves.

In my own mentoring partnership, my mentor was a sounding board to me a lot of the time. He would listen as I would have a conversation with myself, bouncing my thinking off him while he really just listened to me. I also knew that he was encouraging me along the way, knowing that I would be okay and find a solution for myself.

All along, you are **empathetic**. The definition of empathy is the ability to share someone else's feelings or experiences by imagining what it would be like to be in that person's situation. It is trying to step into their shoes to try to understand the path they have walked. So often we see things from our own perspective, coming to solutions that would work for us but may not necessarily be the right solution for another person. By trying to understand where they have come from, how they think, what past experiences have helped form them, we can understand our mentee better. Asking them "How can I support you?" to help them move forward, rather than saying "I feel what you feel" is a way to be empathetic.

Shares

You have experience, wisdom, and stories, which you can share with your mentee. Your mentee may ask for your advice and you may wish to give it to them. You give advice not because you like to hear yourself talk, but because you really want others to benefit from the lessons you have learnt. You are their trusted advisor.

However, the following caution should be noted:

Only share your experience, stories, and advice once you have explored all your mentee's own thinking first.

You may not know the intricacies of their issue and offering advice can be dangerous. If your mentee does insist on receiving advice, then explain that you cannot take responsibility for any consequences of following the advice.

Rather share your stories instead. However, only do so once you have asked permission to do so, at the appropriate time and if it is relevant. One of the biggest breakdowns of a mentoring relationship is that the mentor talks too much, telling too many of their own stories. Be careful not to let your ego get in the way!

As a mentor, you may also want to introduce your mentee to your network. You will probably only feel comfortable doing so if trust has been established in your relationship. If you feel your mentee will benefit from meeting someone in your network, then feel free to make that introduction.

Explores

Be infinitely curious. Put aside your own opinions and answers for a while. Actively listen and then ask questions to get your mentee to do their own thinking. I know that many mentors are so enthusiastic to show their mentee the way forward that they stop being as curious as they should be. Your questions should inspire your mentee to think more deeply, and you should positively challenge them to stretch their thinking further than they would do themselves. Be prepared to be challenged yourself as your mentee may question some of your own thinking.

I'm often asked about challenging your mentee. To get the right balance of challenge, and for it to be experienced as positive rather than negative, have a discussion about it. At the beginning of the relationship, in the first couple of meetings, while you are setting up your ground rules, discuss the subject of challenging. You may ask your mentee: "How much challenge would you like in our mentoring meetings? Are you open to being **positively challenged**?" Your mentee can then think about it and tell you exactly how they feel about being challenged. The key word is "positively" challenge. You are asking them questions to make them think more deeply, more broadly and to be a little out of their comfort zone. The challenge should not be threatening, demeaning, or make the mentee feel stupid.

In my mentoring relationship with Rob, he would ask me questions that I often could not answer. He would also push me a bit further than I wanted to go, forcing me to think about something that I probably would not have wanted to think about before. For example, he challenged me to start thinking about what I would do after I had finished on the international committee as mentoring chair. At that stage, I was only wallowing in the grief of having to leave it and could not think about what lay beyond. He challenged me to look further. Similarly, in our business, I would get caught up in the details, yet he challenged me to be more strategic, to look at the bigger picture – our blue ocean strategy.

You as a mentor can do the same for your mentee.

Nonjudgmental

Set your own judgments aside. I know that is a very difficult thing to do as we are all so judgmental. It's hard not to be.

Judging is easy and doesn't require much thinking or reasoning. Our brains are wired to make automatic judgments about others' behaviours so that we can move through the world without spending much time or energy on understanding everything we see. Within the first seven seconds of meeting, people will have a solid impression of who you are – and some research suggests a **tenth of a second** is all it takes to start determining traits such as trustworthiness.

So, to prime yourself to be nonjudgmental, go into your meetings with an **open mind-set**, acknowledging that you do not necessarily know everything, and you are also open to learning. Open your head, heart, and gut to be receptive to what may unfold. You may need to spend a few minutes beforehand taking a few deep breaths or a meditation to become more present and focus on being nonjudgmental. Whatever works for you, do it to have an open mindset.

As a mentor, you are probably a **lifelong learner**. You are eager to learn from others and open to learning from your mentee. Although you are the mentor and will be their guide along the way, sharing your stories while the mentee learns from you, you will also want to learn from this mentoring journey. At the beginning of the relationship, ensure that you let your mentee know what you would like to learn too. They may have some skills that you would like to learn – share your thoughts with them. Be open to learning.

Two-way feedback

David Rock, founder of the NeuroLeadership Institute, says in his book *Your Brain at Work* that we must **ask for feedback**, rather than give feedback. This makes the feedback less threatening to the recipient. As a mentor, if you ask for feedback from your mentee, the chances are that they will ask for feedback too. Feedback should be **two-way** – both of you should be providing feedback that is positive and focuses on ensuring that it is relevant, providing learning and growth. Focus on giving compassionate feedback. More will be covered on feedback in Chapter 24.

Worksheet 2: The Seven Strengths of Highly Effective Mentors Exercise

Look at the Seven Strengths of Highly Effective Mentors Model below. As a mentor, write down or circle what you are good at. What are your strengths? What are your "superpowers"? Now, write down or circle in a different colour those things that you know you are not so good at. What can you do to improve them?

If you are a mentee, write down or circle those things that are important for you in a mentor.

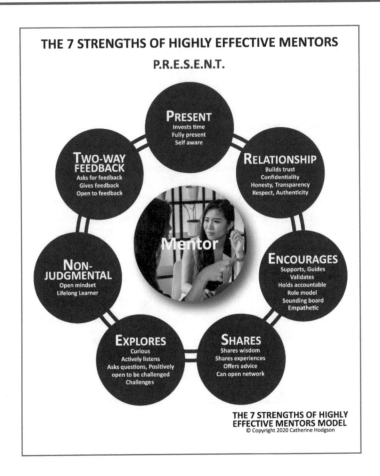

THE 7 STRENGTHS OF HIGHLY EFFECTIVE MENTORS

P.R.E.S.E.N.T.

PRESENT
Invests time
Fully present
Self aware

TWO-WAY FEEDBACK
Asks for feedback
Gives feedback
Open to feedback

RELATIONSHIP
Builds trust
Confidentiality
Honesty, Transparency
Respect, Authenticity

Mentor

NON-JUDGMENTAL
Open mindset
Lifelong Learner

ENCOURAGES
Supports, Guides
Validates
Holds accountable
Role model
Sounding board
Empathetic

EXPLORES
Curious
Actively listens
Asks questions, Positively
open to be challenged
Challenges

SHARES
Shares wisdom
Shares experiences
Offers advice
Can open network

THE 7 STRENGTHS OF HIGHLY
EFFECTIVE MENTORS MODEL
© Copyright 2020 Catherine Hodgson

As a mentor, my strengths are:
_____
_____
_____

As a mentor, my weak points are:
_____
_____
_____

What can I do to improve them?
_____
_____
_____

Key takeaways:

- ✓ Being P.R.E.S.E.N.T. is the most important strength you need to have as a mentor.
- ✓ Be your mentee's guide and greatest supporter.
- ✓ Listen, be curious, ask questions, positively challenge, and give constructive and compassionate feedback.

10

THE SEVEN STRENGTHS OF HIGHLY EFFECTIVE MENTEES

You, **as a mentor**, now know what strengths you need to have or develop. However, it is also important to know what is expected of your mentee and help them develop these strengths, which we are going to look at shortly.

You, **as a mentee**, now know what to look for in a mentor as well as what you would expect from them. However, it's just as important that you know what your role is and what your mentor would expect from you. After all, this is your mentoring journey, and your mentor is giving their valuable time to help you reach your goals. So, make sure you are the best mentee that you can be.

The Seven Strengths of Highly Effective Mentees Model

The most important thing a mentee needs to know is that they need to prepare for their mentoring journey and their mentoring conversations, hence the acronym **P.R.E.P.A.R.E.** for this model. The better prepared the mentee is for their conversations, the more they will get out of them.

P.R.E.P.A.R.E.

**THE 7 STRENGTHS OF HIGHLY
EFFECTIVE MENTEES MODEL**
© Copyright 2020 Catherine Hodgson

Let's go through the seven strengths of highly effective mentees.

Present

As a mentee you need to realize that mentoring is a commitment, and you will need to put in the time. Ask yourself, "How committed am I to this journey? Do I have the time to invest in it?" Your mentor has given up their time to be available for mentoring, so be respectful of their time.

Try not to cancel meetings unless it is an emergency. At the meetings, the most important thing you can do is to be fully present – to be mindful. You need to put aside anything that could be preventing you from being fully present: note it and put it aside.

Relationship

It's more important to build the relationship first, building rapport and trust, before diving into the issues and challenges that you may be facing. That means spending time to get to know each other, and building rapport and trust so that you can have the deep conversations that are needed.

It's not only up to your mentor to ask questions about you in order to build that trust. Get to know your mentor by asking questions as well. "What are you passionate about? What do you believe in strongly? What did it take to get to the position you are in now? What successes did you have along the way? What did you learn from your failures? What would you like to learn from this mentoring journey?"

By asking questions such as these, you are finding out what their values are, what makes them tick and what drives them. When you show interest in them, they will show interest in you. You will also find some common ground, which will help to build that rapport.

At the heart of the relationship and to build trust, you need to embrace confidentiality, to be honest, transparent, and respectful of each other. Remember to be authentic at all times.

Establishes goals

You should think about why you are wanting mentoring before your first meeting. Spend some time reflecting on why you signed up to be a mentee, what your values are, what your vision is and what you would like to achieve. Try to put this down in writing – can you put it into one sentence? If you do already know some goals that you want to achieve, bring these along to your meeting and discuss them with your mentor.

If you have not defined your goals yet, that is not a problem and can be done during a session with your mentor.

Proactive

The most important thing for you to do as a mentee is to be proactive – you **drive the relationship**, not your mentor. It is not up to the mentor to be chasing you to send an agenda, set up a meeting, and do the actions that you committed to doing. You should be setting up your meetings ahead of time, at least at the last meeting, preparing the agenda with some key points you would like to discuss in your meeting, and sending it to your mentor at least three days before your meeting.

Also spend time in **reflective space**, thinking what you would like to discuss and do some of your own thinking around the issue or topic. We will discuss more about reflective space in a further chapter. The better prepared you are, the more you will get out of the meeting. You only have a set amount of time, so make the most of it.

Asks questions

You are in this mentoring relationship to have your thinking stretched and challenged – be prepared for questions that could positively challenge you. During the first couple of meetings, you and your mentor should set ground rules for your relationship and conversations. Discuss with your mentor whether you would like to be challenged and how much challenge you would like. Through positively challenging you by asking you questions, your mentor will enable you to think more broadly and deeper. If you ever feel that the challenge is too much or negative, then ensure you let your mentor know.

Your mentor also wants to learn, so don't be afraid to ask them questions as well.

Reflects on feedback

Your mentor will be giving you feedback; try to be open to it. It should not be seen as criticism but rather serves to help you learn or shed some light on your blind spots. **Ask for feedback** from them and remember that they also want feedback from you.

When you are doing your update, give your mentor feedback, such as what has happened since you last met, what actions you were able to get to and what actions you were not able to complete.

Embraces a growth mindset

To have a growth mindset means being open to learning, flexible to changing your own mindset and to embracing the opportunity to grow. Go into your meeting with an open mindset so that you ensure you are constantly learning.

Worksheet 3: The Seven Strengths of Highly Effective Mentees exercise:

Look at the Seven Strengths of Highly Effective Mentees Model. As a mentee, write down or circle what you are good at – what are your strengths? Now, write down or circle in a different colour those things that you know you are not so good at. What can you do to improve them?

If you are a mentor doing this exercise, write down or circle those things that are important for you in a mentee – what would you like to see in your mentee?

THE 7 STRENGTHS OF HIGHLY EFFECTIVE MENTEES

P.R.E.P.A.R.E.

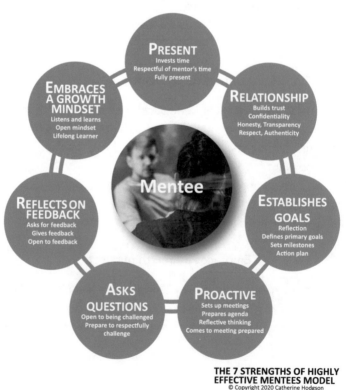

THE 7 STRENGTHS OF HIGHLY
EFFECTIVE MENTEES MODEL
© Copyright 2020 Catherine Hodgson

As a mentee, my strengths are:

_____
_____
_____

As a mentee, my weak points are:

_____
_____
_____

What can I do to improve them?

_____
_____
_____

Key takeaways:

✓ Clarify your role as a mentee and your expectations of your mentor at the beginning of your journey.
✓ You as a mentee need to P.R.E.P.A.R.E. for your mentoring journey and your sessions.
✓ Drive the relationship, take ownership of your learning, be committed, ask questions, give feedback, and embrace a growth mindset.

11
MATCHING

We are on step one of the outer wheel: **Embark**. You have decided to join a mentoring program, signed up, and learnt what your roles are as a mentor or mentee and what you would expect from your mentoring partner. You are now ready to be matched with a mentoring partner by your mentoring program, or you want to reach out and find a mentor or mentee yourself. This chapter will focus on how to do so, as well as the benefits and challenges of face-to-face versus virtual mentoring.

In an organization without an online mentoring platform there is usually a program manager or team of people who will do the matching of mentors to mentees. The matching is usually done based on a mentee's needs and wants, matched to a mentor's strengths and skills. This is relatively straight forward in small and medium organizations or in pilots of up 50 people. However it is not the easiest of jobs! When I had to match mentors to mentees, it was really hit or miss. Initially, I had mentors and mentees fill out an application form to join the mentoring program either as a mentor, a mentee or both. In the application form for mentees, we asked them what their needs were and what they were looking for in a mentor. For mentors, we asked them in which areas they could mentor and what their ideal mentee would look like. We then sent relevant application forms to the mentors for them to choose which mentee they would like to meet. That meeting was set up as an initial meeting to get to know each other to see if there was chemistry and if the match would be relevant.

It got harder to match the more applications we had in our mentoring program. At one point, when we had expanded the program around the world and still didn't have an online platform, I remember sitting on my bed with applications printed out and trying to put pairs together for programmes in other countries. I soon realized that this method of manually matching was not sustainable and we would need to look for an alternative method.

I learnt that some of the guesswork in matching could be removed if we used a mentoring platform. We shopped around for a suitable one, bearing in mind that there was a limited number available at the time. We wanted a platform where we could get involved in making it our own for the organization. After a while we found one that suited the organization's needs.

So how were we going to match mentors to mentees?

We looked at matching mentors to mentees based on their values as well as needs and strengths. You may be asking why we were matching on values. We reached out to coaching and mentoring experts and realized why we would need to take a person's values into account: it seems that if values are more closely aligned, then the chances of the relationship being successful increases significantly. Therefore, we asked participants to list their top five values and they could see how many of the values matched their mentoring partner.

I do not believe that values need to be completely aligned, as diversity in thought leads to interesting conversations. Also, someone who is like us is sometimes not the best person to push us out of our comfort zone. However, I have seen that if a pair's values are polar opposites, then the relationship really does struggle. For instance, if your mentee regards bribery in business as part of what they do but you as a mentor feel it goes against all your values, it may be more difficult to build a strong trusting relationship with that person.

When we were setting up the online platform, we also looked at the areas in which the mentee is needing mentoring (for instance, marketing, finance, personal development, or leadership) and then broke that down into more defined categories. They were then matched to mentors who had strengths, experience, and skills in those areas.

If you have decided to become a mentee and are joining a mentoring program, here are some tips for you, if you are able to choose your own mentor.

Five tips to help you choose your best mentor

Mentor matching can be tricky, but with a matching platform that problem is halfway solved for you. If you are on a mentoring platform, you will be shown your best mentor matches, using the criteria you inputted when you filled in your profile and mentoring needs.

If you are not on a mentoring platform, you need to still consider what you would like from a mentor. Here are some tips on what to consider before you connect with a mentor:

1. Consider what skill sets you require of your mentor

This may be obvious; however, it is important to look at the mentor's profile (on a platform or their LinkedIn profile) to see what skills the mentor has and how applicable they are to what you are requiring from your learning. Look at their industry skills, management skills, communication skills – are they skills that you would like to learn? If you are not on a matching platform, then write down what skills you require from your mentor.

2. Look at the mentor's experience level

You preferably want someone who has had experience in the area in which you are needing mentoring. How many years have they had in that area? Although we may think this may equate to true experience and understanding, sometimes it does not, so we need to look carefully at what they have done in that area. Is their experience up to date? Look at their LinkedIn profile to see what they have been up to lately.

3. Consider if your values align

What are your values? Have you reflected on what is important to you and listed your top 10 values? Do these align with your mentor's? They do not need to align completely but discern if there is anything there that could cause a conflict with you. If you are not on a matching platform, then in your first meeting you can ask them what their values are, or you can get an idea of what they care about by looking at their LinkedIn profile, if they have one, or any articles they may have written.

4. Hierarchy

Your mentor does not always need to be someone older than you. If they have the experience that you are requiring to learn, then they could mentor you. However, it is important that your mentor is not the person you report to directly. The reason is that sometimes it is difficult to be completely open and transparent with a person you report to directly.

5. Industry and department

It's important to look at what industry and department your potential mentor is from. For example, if you are looking to learn management skills, then the industry or department is not important as management mentoring is very similar across the board. However, if you are looking for guidance in a certain role or to climb the corporate career ladder, then looking for a mentor in the same industry or department is very important.

Mentoring is highly personal, and you will not know if the person is a good match for you until you have had a few sessions and got to know each other a bit better. Then you will be able to assess if the mentoring process is adding value to your life and your career. You will just need to take the plunge and reach out to connect with the suggested mentors – however, take consideration of these five points before you do so.

Five tips to help you choose your best mentee

You may have signed up to a mentoring program or platform, eager to mentor someone as a way of giving back, share your experience and yourself learn more. You may be wondering if you should reach out to a mentee or wait for someone to connect with or contact you. Here are a few things that you can do to start making a difference in someone's life.

Introduce yourself

You wouldn't arrive at a party and not greet the hosts and introduce yourself to other guests. The same goes for joining a mentoring program or platform. Let people know that you are there, that you have arrived. Introduce yourself to the community by sharing who you are, what you want to get out of the mentoring journey (why are you there?), what your strengths are (your superpowers) and what you could share with others (what is your area of expertise?).

Before reaching out to a mentee consider the following:

1. Skills

Look at what skills the mentee is wanting to learn. Do you have those skill sets? Would you feel comfortable guiding a mentee to learn those skills?

2. Experience

What is the mentee wanting to learn? Do you have the necessary experience in that area? Would you be able to offer the mentee value in that area?

3. Values/strengths

If the mentoring platform shows values, then look at the mentee's values and how they align with or differ from your values. Is there any area that you may struggle with? If values are not shown, check to see if there are strengths that are highlighted.

4. Hierarchy

You do not need to be older than your mentee, as long as you have experience in what your mentee is looking to learn. However, ensure that the potential mentee does not report directly to you. If you are more senior than your mentee, try to make them feel as comfortable and safe as possible by removing all hierarchy from your interactions.

5. Industry and department

It's important to look at what industry and department your potential mentee is from. For example, if they are wanting to learn skills in management, then the industry or department is not important as mentoring in management is very similar across the board. However, if they are looking for guidance in a certain role or to climb the corporate career ladder, then looking for a mentor in the same industry or department is very important.

If you have just joined the program, get active straight away rather than waiting for someone to contact you. You can start making a difference in someone's life. After all, is that not why you joined?

Face-to-face versus virtual mentoring

As part of Step 1 on the Catherine Wheel, you will also consider whether you will be embarking on a face-to-face (in-person) mentoring relationship or a virtual relationship.

A face-to-face mentoring relationship where you meet in-person is easier for most people. One can "feel" the connection more easily and pick up cues by observing body language and facial expressions. However, it also has its disadvantages in that it often can become a longer meeting, the time it takes to get to and from a meeting needs to be factored in, and you are limited to a mentor or mentee who is in the same city or area as you.

Virtual mentoring does have its advantages and it is becoming more popular. After the pandemic, our world became a lot more virtual, and so did mentoring. Many of us were a bit afraid to embark on a virtual mentoring journey with someone we had never met in person, but today this does not feel so daunting or scary. We feel so much more comfortable with virtual interactions that sometimes virtual meetings just seem easier. Let's look at the pros and cons of virtual versus in-person mentoring, and what needs to be put in place for a virtual mentoring session. I will then tell you about my experiences with virtual mentoring.

Benefits of virtual mentoring

- You can connect with someone in another country or continent. You are not restricted to being in the same geographical place – so the world is your oyster.
- You can connect with someone in another company whom you probably would never have had access to before.
- Meetings tend to be shorter – I usually recommend one hour for a virtual session and two hours for in-person. It's more tiring connecting virtually and more difficult to concentrate, hence the shorter time recommendation.
- No travel time is wasted. You don't need to sit in traffic, find parking or commute to the mentoring session.
- You can have more than one mentor or mentee as there is usually a larger pool available on an online mentoring platform.
- Remote mentoring is good for diversity and inclusion, as more

people from different countries, departments, teams, and cultures can be included in the program.

- Hierarchy concerns are reduced as often virtual meetings are less intimidating than face-to-face meetings.
- Using a virtual platform that both parties are familiar with makes meetings easy to set up.

Challenges of virtual mentoring

It is sometimes difficult to pick up on cues that you would otherwise pick up in-person. Because the visual view of body language is limited, you may miss obvious body language cues from your mentoring partner. You usually can only see the person's head, so you can only pick up their facial expressions. You also cannot "feel" their energy, unless you pay attention to the tone of their voice, the cadence of their voice, their eye movements, and so on.

- Privacy can be a problem. An agreement needs to be made that all conversations are confidential and held in a space where nobody can overhear you. You need to discuss if you are putting your call on speakerphone or not. These discussions are part of the ground rules that would need to be set upfront to avoid any privacy issues.
- There are many distractions in front of us when we are on a virtual call. You may be tempted to look at your phone or send a message or email while the other person is speaking. The other person can pick this up immediately and you need to be careful that trust is not lost due to this.
- Culture and language are a potential issue. With virtual mentoring, you may have a mentoring partner in another country who is from a different culture and your first language is not theirs. It can therefore be much more difficult to converse virtually than in-person. Things need to be slowed down a lot more and there may need to be more clarifying questions.
- There may be reasons the other person, due to poor internet connection or culture, may not wish to put their camera on. This makes it more challenging as you cannot pick up visual cues and concentrating is harder.
- Being on a call virtually is tiring and you may lose focus much more easily than being face-to-face.

- Connectivity and technical problems remain the number one issue for virtual calls. Not everyone has good connection all the time and we have all experienced technical difficulties on calls. This can disrupt the flow of the conversation as well as your thinking.
- It is more difficult to establish chemistry with someone you do not know virtually versus in-person. If rapport and trust are not built at the beginning of the relationship, then you will not get to the conversational depth that you require for mentoring.

How to make virtual mentoring work

For virtual mentoring to work well, you need to put the following in place:

- **Privacy:** choose a place that is private, where nobody can overhear your conversation or that of your mentoring partner. If someone does walk into the room, have a hand signal or word that you can use to halt the conversation.
- **Build rapport and trust:** spend time building rapport and trust at the beginning of your relationship. Do this in the first two meetings. Get to know each other. Share your values, your strengths, your challenges. Be open to being vulnerable. Keeping your cameras on will help to build that rapport more quickly. Have a conversation about how both of you feel about keeping your cameras on.
- **Set ground rules** in your first meeting. How often will you meet, how long, what are your expectations around confidentiality, openness, honesty, and so on.
- **Connectivity and technical issues:** talk about possible connectivity and technical issues and work around them upfront. Maybe you need to switch your camera off to get a better connection. Maybe you need to move to another space for better connectivity. If you do decide to meet with no cameras on, then ensure that you are there on the call and not tempted to step away for a few minutes.
- **Actively listen:** don't listen only to the words they are saying, but consider their facial expression, their tone of voice, their cadence of talking, the emotion in their voice, what their eyes are doing and what they are not saying. This all helps you understand the other person better.
- **Overcome distraction:** if you are getting tired or distracted, take a break or make your meetings shorter.

- **Cultural differences:** discuss your cultural differences openly. What works for one person may not work for another. One person's interpretation of something may mean something completely different to another person. Discuss sense of humour and jokes. How will you tackle these challenges and get around them without offending the other person?
- **Structure:** having a structure in place helps with the flow of the conversation. Ensure you have an agenda and check in with each other as you go along.

If you do feel comfortable with a virtual relationship, then it is a great experience. I've had a few virtual mentoring partnerships, and I'll tell you about two of them.

My first virtual partnership was with a CEO from Mexico who was looking for a mentor with experience in the beauty industry. Early in my career, I worked for a corporate in their perfume and toiletries divisions, so I was familiar with manufacturing in the beauty arena, even though it was more than 25 years ago. We spent time getting to know each other, learning about each other's families, where we both lived, how we started our businesses, and the usual "getting to know you" conversations. We set up a meeting once a month for one hour and set the ground rules. There were a few key takeaways for me from this mentoring relationship.

1. The language was a real barrier. English was his second language and I struggled to understand everything he said.
2. I felt as though I missed out on seeing his factory and premises. Although he showed me the products in his office, I felt as though I didn't fully understand his business.
3. We were not as structured in our conversations as we should have been. In a virtual relationship, I believe your mentoring sessions benefit from a structure. We tended to float around without me knowing exactly what he wanted to get out of each session. Now I know that having an agenda in place and a structure such as the Catherine Wheel would have given me more structure to guide him through the conversation.
4. We did not set goals for his mentoring journey.
5. We didn't spend enough time building our relationship before getting down to the issues. We probably should have spent two

sessions really trying to get to know each other and building rapport and trust. Doing a few exercises with him would have helped. Our time spent getting to know each other was more contractual than really being open to being vulnerable.

6. He did not leave each session with an action plan.

The second experience that I want to share with you had a great impact on the way I mentored going forward.

I attended a coaching course, which was the first that was run fully online as we had just entered the pandemic. I was with a cohort of coaches from Dubai, mostly women and just a couple of men. Over the course of nine months, I only saw the faces of the women a few times. At first, I was irritated that the trainer did not force everyone to have their cameras on and I struggled to hold myself back from saying something. Luckily, I didn't, as it dawned on me only a couple of sessions into the program that this was due to their culture – how naïve of me! Once I had realized this, I accepted it and saw it as a learning for me to be aware of cultural differences and how quickly we can make judgments.

Over nine months we were paired off with a partner and had to practise coaching conversations once a week with each other. My regular coaching partner said that she was more comfortable keeping her camera off during our sessions as she liked to walk around the room while being coached. I wondered how I was going to deal with this as well as being able to do coaching properly. Everything that I had been training other people to do when mentoring another person and building rapport and trust had just gone out the window. How was I going to build rapport if I could not see her? How was I going to pick up body language and facial expressions? I took a deep breath and went with the flow, switching my camera off as well.

What happened was one of the greatest learnings that I received from the course. I now no longer had to look at my screen and see my face at the same time. So often we spend time looking at ourselves and wondering about our hair, our facial expressions, our backgrounds. Without this distraction, I started to really listen … listening to her tone of voice, her emotions in her words, her pauses, her breathing, and her steps. I often closed my eyes and went into a world of intense attentive listening. I started to listen better because I was not relying on my sight anymore and I became more attuned to my other senses and intuition.

When she coached me, I kept my camera off as well. I found that I was no longer having to see how I looked. I could walk around the room, which helped a lot with my thinking. I could look outside and not have to look at a computer screen and I could even lie down. It felt liberating and I was able to think better.

At the final coaching program session with all the participants, our celebration, everyone put their cameras on. This was the first time that I saw my regular coaching partner. It was like reading a book and afterwards seeing the movie version. What a gift I had received from this coaching partner!

Hybrid relationships

Some of the most successful pairings have been when you can combine virtual and face-to-face sessions. Many people who start mentoring using an online platform have virtual sessions; then they want to meet their mentoring partner face to face. Having one or two mentoring sessions in person really helps to build better rapport and trust, if you can do so.

Key takeaways:

- ✓ To find your best mentor, consider what skills you require, look at the mentor's experience level, what their strengths are, and what industry they are from.
- ✓ To find your best mentee, consider what skills they want to learn, what experience they are wanting to gain, what their strengths are, and what industry they are from.
- ✓ Virtual mentoring can be highly effective if ground rules are set beforehand.

12
CONNECT

You are now moving to step two, **Connect**, on the outer wheel of the Catherine Wheel. You have now been matched or you reached out to someone to meet you for your first mentoring meeting. This is the meeting at which you will decide if you are the right person for your mentoring partner. You want to "test the chemistry" to see if you are the right fit.

Below is a roadmap that I developed to help you see the steps you go through and what needs to be done once you are matched. It follows the outer wheel of the Catherine Wheel, but it is more detailed.

You can see from the roadmap that you are heading for your first mentoring meeting.

Your first meeting with your mentoring partner should be focused on **building the relationship by building a connection** with that person.

How to build a connection

Meeting someone like your mentor or mentee for the first time can be a bit daunting. You may have connected with someone on an online mentoring platform, or maybe you were matched with a mentoring partner you do not know. You now have your first meeting scheduled and you are not sure what to expect. As a mentor, you should be the one to lead first, to set the atmosphere and tone for the conversation. So how do you do that? How do you connect with someone quite quickly, as you don't have a long meeting set up?

THE CATHERINE WHEEL

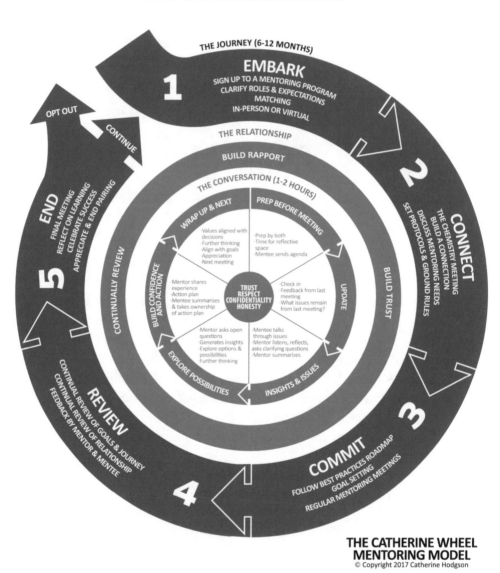

**THE CATHERINE WHEEL
MENTORING MODEL**
© Copyright 2017 Catherine Hodgson

To build a connection we usually **find some common ground**. Think of yourself at a dinner or cocktail party when you meet someone for the first time. You try to establish commonality such as the people you both know, friends you have in common, if your children are similar ages or go to the same school. We are subconsciously looking for some common ground. When we find that common ground, we connect with that person as we see that this person is like us. It is easier to make a connection with people who are like us.

ROADMAP FOR YOUR MENTORING JOURNEY

1. YOU'RE MATCHED!
Mentees set up the first meeting – date, time and place.
Reflect on what you would like to discuss and what you want to get out of your journey.

2. THE CHEMISTRY MEETING
Usually one hour in length.
Ensure meeting is held in a confidential place.
Set ground rules for your mentoring journey.

3. BUILDING RAPPORT AND TRUST
Spend time getting to know each other.
Ask: What are your values? What are you passionate about? What successes have you had? What have you learnt from your failures?

4. GOAL-SETTING
Mentees to reflect on aspirations and goals.
Mentors can help to establish goals for the mentoring journey.
Goals should be achievable with some stretch.
Goals should align with your values.

5. PREPARING FOR MEETINGS
Mentees spend time reflecting on what they would like to bring to the next mentoring meeting. The more prep you put into your meeting, the more you will get out of it.
Mentees send the agenda a few days before the session.

6. REGULAR MEETINGS
Set up your meetings in advance. Ensure meetings are regular, at least every 4 – 6 weeks apart to ensure you do not lose momentum.

7. ACTION FOR NEXT MEETINGS
Have a written action plan at the end of each meeting which mentees can work on before the next meeting.

8. REVIEWING THE RELATIONSHIP
Review your relationship regularly – be open and honest. The deeper the trust, the deeper the conversation.
Reflect on and discuss:
What can I do differently?
What can my mentor/mentee do differently?

9. REVIEWING GOALS
Review the goals regularly and check that they align to the mentee's values.
Goals do not need to be static and can change along the way as you get more clarity from your journey – be open to the changes that need to be made.

10. ENDING OR TRANSITIONING THE JOURNEY
Prepare for your final meeting. Reflect on what you have achieved.
Celebrate your successes.
Appreciate and thank each other.

ROADMAP FOR YOUR MENTORING JOURNEY
© Copyright 2023 Catherine Hodgson

We see them as a friend rather than a foe – something our ancient brain is doing all the time…looking for threats.

So, in your first meeting, try to find a connection to things you may have in common – spend the time seeking them out.

Next, **share something that the other person may not know about you.** By doing this and by being a bit vulnerable, you are showing the other person that you are opening yourself up to them. As soon as a person sees this, there is a connection as they can see that you are trusting them with information that is important to you. A mentor will usually need to model this opening up and being vulnerable for their mentee to follow suit.

In his book *The Trusted Advisor*, author David Maister says that to build a strong relationship, you do the things that you would do in a romantic relationship. You try to be understanding, thoughtful, considerate, sensitive to feelings, and supportive.

The chemistry meeting

We have spoken about building the connection, now this is the meeting where you need to put it into practice. I call it your "chemistry" meeting. Why chemistry? Well, it's the meeting to see if there is a connection between you and if you both want to embark on a mentoring journey together.

This may feel daunting, and you may be wondering how it should be conducted. Remember that the **mentee needs to drive the relationship,** so it's up to the mentee to reach out to the mentor to set up that first meeting. Don't wait too long to set it up – get that date in the diary! Ensure that the meeting will be held in a confidential space so that the conversation can flow freely.

The purpose of your first meeting is the following:
1. To get to know each other – build a connection.
2. To discuss your mentoring needs.
3. To decide on your meeting protocols and ground rules.

Once your meeting is set up, some prep work is required so that you get the most out of your first meeting. The better prepared you are for your meetings, the more you will get out of them.

94

Prepare for your chemistry meeting

How do you prepare for building rapport and trust?

As we have seen in the previous chapter, sharing something personal and being open to being vulnerable will help to build rapport and trust.

Worksheet 4: Prepare for your chemistry meeting

Reflect on the following questions and make some notes. In brackets is who should do this exercise.

- What are five things that I value most? (Both mentor and mentee) (Go to the exercise on identifying your values in Resources, Part 5.)

_____

_____

_____

- What are my strengths? My superpowers? What am I good at? (Both mentor and mentee) There are many tools that can be used for this such as online "strengths finder" tests, or this free one from High 5: https://high5test.com.

_____

_____

_____

- What energizes me? What do I love to do? (Both mentor and mentee)

_____

_____

_____

- What am I prepared to share with my mentoring partner that opens me up to being vulnerable? (Both mentor and mentee)

  _____

  _____

  _____

- What difficulty have I experienced in my life/career that has taught me a meaningful lesson? (Mentor)

  _____

  _____

  _____

- What are my aspirations? In my personal life? In my career/business? (Mentee)

  _____

  _____

  _____

- What do I want to improve on in my life/career? (Mentee)

  _____

  _____

  _____

Worksheet 5: Key questions to ask my mentor

Once you have reflected on these questions and made notes, write down three key questions you would like to ask your mentoring partner in the first meeting.

Three key questions I would like to ask my mentor:

1. _____
   _____
   _____
2. _____
   _____
   _____
3. _____
   _____
   _____

The chemistry meeting

Once you have prepared for your meeting, you will meet with your potential mentor or mentee.

The first thing to do is to discuss what you have reflected on in the exercises above. This will help you to build rapport and trust. The next is to discuss your reason for mentoring. This exercise can be done beforehand as preparation, or just discussed in your meeting.

Discuss your reason for mentoring

It is important that you reflect on why you are wanting mentoring and what you would like from your mentor.

Worksheet 6: Your mentoring needs
Reflect on the following questions and make some notes.

* What do I want to get out of this mentoring process?
  (Both mentor and mentee)

_____
_____
_____

- What do I want to learn? (Both mentor and mentee)

  _____

  _____

  _____

- What is my role as a mentee? (Mentee)

  _____

  _____

  _____

- What do I expect from my mentor? (Mentee)

  _____

  _____

  _____

- What do I want to learn from my mentor? (Mentee)

  _____

  _____

  _____

- What can I offer my mentee? (Mentor)

  _____

  _____

  _____

- What is my role as a mentor? (Mentor)

  _____

  _____

  _____

Meeting protocols and ground rules

Ground rules should be established in this first meeting. Discuss the following:
- How often will we meet and for how long? What are we both prepared to commit to on this mentoring journey?

- Frequency of meetings? Suitable times? Length of meeting?
- Where will we meet – virtually (using what platform) or in person?
- Virtual: ensure that both parties are familiar with the platform if it is virtual. If one is not used to the platform, then give them a tour around the platform during your first session so they feel comfortable using it.
- In-person: ensure that you choose a place that is private, confidential, and where both of you feel comfortable to share and be vulnerable. If your mentor chooses to have the meeting in their office, try not to sit at the mentor's desk, but rather next to each other or in chairs away from the desk. Remove all feeling of hierarchy.
- **Agreement on confidentiality, honesty, and openness.** This is core to your mentoring relationship and it's important you discuss this upfront as well as at the beginning of each session, reiterating that confidentiality. How open am I prepared to be? What do I expect from my mentee? My mentor?
- **Commitment to the time it will take.** Agree on what to do if we have to cancel or change sessions. Discuss if you are both committed to this relationship. What could get in the way? How will we deal with it?
- **How to contact each other and how often.** We cannot presume that we can just pick up the phone at any time to contact our mentoring partner or send them a message. Boundaries need to be put in place. What are appropriate times and days to contact each other? Are evenings and weekends out of bounds except for emergencies? Discuss this upfront to avoid any awkward situations.
- **How will we give feedback to each other?** How do we want to receive feedback? How do we feel about giving feedback? How often?
- How often should we **review our relationship?**

Head space: It's also important that you are in the right head space. Plan so that you have time before your meeting to focus on being present and open with your mentoring partner.

The chemistry meeting agenda

I have put together an agenda to help guide you through your first meeting. This meeting is the most difficult one as it's usually the first time you will be meeting your mentor or mentee. Having an agenda to guide both of you will take the pressure off and you won't need to worry if you are asking the right questions. I have made a 60-minute agenda as this is best practice for this first meeting. The agenda is a guideline you can use, or go with your own one.

 **MEETING AGENDA 1**

The chemistry meeting agenda
(60 minutes)

1. BUILDING RAPPORT AND TRUST (20 MINUTES)
Get to know each other and build on this rapport and trust in further meetings. • Introduce yourself and give a little background – personal, family, career, interests. • What do we have in common? • Share something that the other person may not know about you.
2. AGREEMENT FOR ENGAGEMENT AND SETTING GROUND RULES (10 MINUTES)
What do you both agree on for you to engage with each other going forward? This agreement needs to be reviewed at each meeting. Draw up a list together. • Safe haven and confidentiality • Commitment to the journey • Honesty and openness • Being present • Actively listen • Desire for both to learn from each other • How to give feedback and how often • Challenging each other • Reviewing our relationship – how do we do it and how often? • What will we do if the other person does not commit to this agreement going forward? • How often should we meet and for how long? • Who drives the relationship and sets up meetings? • What boundaries need to be put in place? • How do we contact each other outside of this meeting? • What time commitment is expected for this mentoring journey? • Are we both prepared to commit to the time required?
3. ROLES AND EXPECTATIONS (10 MINUTES)
Discuss with each other the roles and expectations of a mentor and mentee. • What is my understanding of what a mentee should do?

Continued
• What are your expectations of a mentor? • What is my understanding of what a mentor should do? • What are your expectations of a mentee?
4. ASPIRATIONS AND GOALS (15 MINUTES)
Discuss your aspirations for your mentoring journey. Both to share. • What do you aspire to get from this mentoring journey? • Do you have any challenges, issues, or dilemmas that you are wanting to bring to the mentoring conversations? (Not to go into detail, but to share top level and then decide what to bring along for next meeting.) • Do you have any goals that you have been thinking about? • Do you want to list any primary goals that you would like to work on and any secondary goals? • How would you define those goals in one sentence or a few words?
5. WRAP UP AND APPRECIATION (5 MINUTES)
Closing the first meeting. • Set up a date, time, and place in the calendar for your next meeting. • Exchange any other contact details you may not already have shared. • Reminder for the mentee to send the agenda or list of discussion points a few days before the next meeting. • Appreciate each other.

Post chemistry meeting

After this meeting, the mentee should send a thank you message to the mentor, thanking them for their time.

You can both now reflect on how it went and whether you would like to continue with your assigned mentoring partner. If you do have some concerns about them, reflect on whether these concerns can be overcome. Can you give it another meeting or two so that you can build more rapport and trust? This person does not need to be like you. If they are adding value to your life or career, then that is good.

However, in some cases, a mentoring partner just does not work out and your mentoring champion or program manager will need to be contacted so that they can look for another match for you.

I was asked to meet with someone who was seeking mentoring. After spending an hour with her, I realized that I would not be the best person to be her mentor and suggested that she seek out a qualified coach (back then, I had not qualified to be a coach). Sometimes, you just know that you are not the right fit for the person, or you cannot offer the other person what they may expect from you. When you have that gut instinct, rather step aside than try to make it work.

Key takeaways:

✓ The purpose of your first meeting is to get to know each other, build rapport and trust, discuss your reason for mentoring, and decide on your meeting protocols.
✓ You will get a good feel after your first meeting for whether you want to continue with your mentoring partner.
✓ Don't rush into setting goals and dealing with issues in your first chemistry meeting.

13

THE MIDDLE WHEEL
– THE RELATIONSHIP

"Take the time to build trust – it is the
foundation of your mentoring relationship."
Catherine Hodgson

You now understand what happens in your chemistry meeting and how
to connect with your mentoring partner. But to take the conversation
deeper for your ongoing mentoring sessions, you need to know how to
really build trust in your relationship.

The relationship is the middle wheel of the Catherine Wheel and
probably the most important of all the wheels. **Your mentoring
relationship is key to your conversations and needs to be built,
nurtured, and continually reviewed.**

Being in a successful mentoring relationship means being connected
with that person. For that connection to be strong, so that your
conversations can go deep, you need first to focus on building rapport,
which we have spoken about in the previous chapter, connecting with
your mentoring partner. Trust develops as time goes along.

THE CATHERINE WHEEL

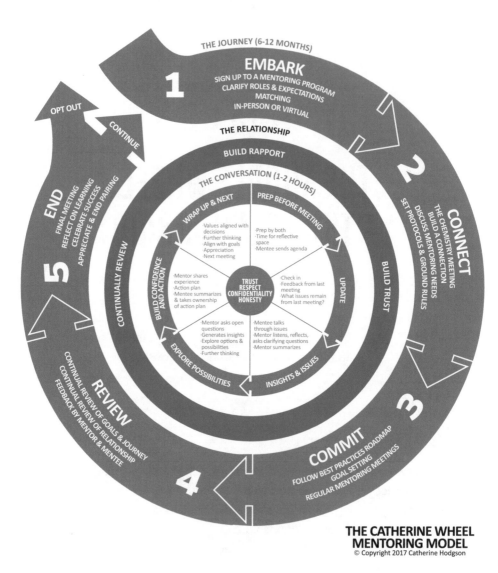

**THE CATHERINE WHEEL
MENTORING MODEL**
© Copyright 2017 Catherine Hodgson

Building trust takes time

We are usually able to assess within a few seconds straight after meeting someone whether we like them. We can usually feel whether we have a connection with someone, or if we can respect them.

ROADMAP FOR YOUR MENTORING JOURNEY

1. YOU'RE MATCHED!
Mentees set up the first meeting – date, time and place. Reflect on what you would like to discuss and what you want to get out of your journey.

2. THE CHEMISTRY MEETING
Usually one hour in length.
Ensure meeting is held in a confidential place.
Set ground rules for your mentoring journey.

3. BUILDING RAPPORT AND TRUST
Spend time getting to know each other.
Ask: What are your values? What are you passionate about? What successes have you had? What have you learnt from your failures?

4. GOAL-SETTING
Mentees to reflect on aspirations and goals.
Mentors can help to establish goals for the mentoring journey.
Goals should be achievable with some stretch.
Goals should align with your values.

5. PREPARING FOR MEETINGS
Mentees spend time reflecting on what they would like to bring to the next mentoring meeting. The more prep you put into your meeting, the more you will get out of it.
Mentees send the agenda a few days before the session.

6. REGULAR MEETINGS
Set up your meetings in advance. Ensure meetings are regular, at least every 4 – 6 weeks apart to ensure you do not lose momentum.

7. ACTION FOR NEXT MEETINGS
Have a written action plan at the end of each meeting which mentees can work on before the next meeting.

8. REVIEWING THE RELATIONSHIP
Review your relationship regularly – be open and honest. The deeper the trust, the deeper the conversation.
Reflect on and discuss:
What can I do differently?
What can my mentor/mentee do differently?

9. REVIEWING GOALS
Review the goals regularly and check that they align to the mentee's values.
Goals do not need to be static and can change along the way as you get more clarity from your journey – be open to the changes that need to be made.

10. ENDING OR TRANSITIONING THE JOURNEY
Prepare for your final meeting. Reflect on what you have achieved.
Celebrate your successes.
Appreciate and thank each other.

ROADMAP FOR YOUR MENTORING JOURNEY
© Copyright 2023 Catherine Hodgson

We also get an immediate sense if we do **not** trust them. However, we very rarely walk away after a few minutes saying that we fully trust someone. We may feel that this person is someone who we could be able to trust or find trustworthy.

To trust someone requires effort on both sides. It takes time. It takes experience with that person. Trust needs to be earned. It's not something that happens instantly. Therefore, as a mentor or mentee, we need to put time into building the relationship and the trust.

When there is a lack of trust, people cannot relate to each other in a way that produces innovative and strategic thinking.

Our brain is wired to detect threats – this is our primal instinct. When we are in a state of distrust, we feel threatened and that we need to protect ourselves. However, if the interaction feels safe and we feel comfortable, our body produces oxytocin and dopamine, both "feel-good" hormones. These make us feel open, safe, and connected. Our executive brain, the pre-frontal cortex, opens up and allows us to think more clearly, being able to access empathy, innovation, and higher decision making. We connect with others more deeply and can trust the other person.

How to build trust in a relationship

Trusting ourselves first is key. We need to trust ourselves before we can trust others. To trust ourselves we first need to understand ourselves, know our own strengths and weaknesses, our core values, what we are good at, and what triggers us. How do we react in various situations when are we at our best and when are we at our worst? Do we trust ourselves to get things done? Do we trust ourselves to commit to something and follow through with it? Doing personal work on ourselves is key to trusting ourselves first.

How do we then build trust? Trust needs to be earned and deserved. The other person needs to see they can trust you based on evidence. Often, we need to give it in order to get it. By tuning in to the other person and what their needs are, and showing that you can be trusted, you can slowly start to build a trusting relationship.

When I think of building trust, I go to the acronym **T.R.U.S.T. – Transparency, Relationship, Understanding, Shared Success, and Truth Telling** – which I first learnt with Judith E. Glaser when I studied *Conversational Intelligence*®. However, I have changed "Shared

Success" to "Stay Reliable" for discussing trust in a mentoring relationship.

Transparency

You need to be **open and transparent** to build trust. You cannot be hiding things from your mentoring partner, withholding information, only giving them what you think they need to know. In a mentoring relationship, if you are not transparent with your mentoring partner, they will not be able to completely understand you or your challenge or issue.

It also means being open to being vulnerable. As a mentor, you may not think of showing vulnerability to your mentee. We often have this image of what a mentor should be, someone who knows it all and is a trusted advisor. However, by sharing your weaknesses, your failures, the difficulties you have experienced in your business and life, as well as your fears, you allow the other person to see you as a real person. They will know that even as a mentor, you have faced difficulties too, so it's okay for them to show you their failures, fears, weaknesses, hopes, and dreams. As soon as you **show vulnerability**, the other person will be more open to being vulnerable as well.

Brené Brown has shed much light on vulnerability in her TED Talk, "The Power of Vulnerability", as well as in her books, *Dare to Lead* and *Daring Greatly*, allowing us to see it as courage rather than a weakness.

Relationship

To build trust, you need to put the **relationship before the task**. This means spending time getting to know each other before jumping straight into the issue or problem.

It's so tempting to go straight into the issue rather than first finding out more about the other person. Even in a business meeting, I tell my staff first to spend time with their client having some "small talk", finding out one or two things about them personally, and then following up this conversation at their next meeting. For example, if they share with you that their dog Lucy is sick and had to have an operation that week, and you know it means a lot to them, make a note about it, and ask about Lucy before you begin your next meeting. This helps to connect you and shows that you are a person who is genuinely interested in them.

Spend the first mentoring meeting, your chemistry meeting, asking questions to fully understand how your mentoring partner thinks, their background, their strengths, their values, their fears, what got them to where they are today. Ask them about their vision and aspirations. Only once you really understand the person can you better understand the issue at hand.

A mentor told me that he spent the first two meetings with his mentee just trying to get to know her and understand the way she thinks and the way she runs her business. This helped when it came to tackling the issues that she was facing and in which she needed mentoring. He told me that he would not have been able to have the depth of conversation, or for her to be as open as she was with him, had he not taken the time to build the trust beforehand.

Understanding

Of course we think we know what understanding means! If you say to someone that you understand them, then you are hearing what they are saying, interpreting their meaning and understanding them, right? Actually, not really…

Understanding is not about understanding the other person, it is **standing under the other person's reality.**

To truly understand someone, we also need to **"stand under"** that **person's reality,** to stand under the same umbrella. We need to ask ourselves, "How can I step into the other person's shoes, to see the world through their eyes? How can I stay open and nonjudgmental? How can I feel what they are feeling? How does my reality differ from their reality? How can I bridge the gap between our realities with words and actions?"

Every person comes to the conversation with their own personal experiences, memories, stories, interpretations, values, and beliefs. These experiences, memories, values, and beliefs may be very different to your own. Hence your realities may be completely different to the other person's realities. Be especially aware of this if you are mentoring across cultures, religions, gender, languages, and countries. We often presume that how we think is how another person thinks, too. This is your opportunity to see that your way of seeing something is not the only way.

I know this may be a very difficult thing to do. We make judgments about others without really knowing the other person's whole story, where they come from, what has happened in their lives, and the reasons they are doing what we may be judging.

Think about how you can **suspend judgment.**
- Do you have a right to judge that person?
- Stop all your own thinking and be open to listening to the other person with an open heart.

I know it's not easy. Everyone is judgmental and it's hard not to be. It's the way our brains are wired – we make judgments within 0.01 seconds of meeting someone. However, if we are consciously aware of it, then we can suppress it. I myself am guilty as charged. Sometimes just having someone call it out to you makes you aware again of putting your judgment back in the box where it belongs.

What happens in our bodies if we can truly "stand under" the other person's reality? Both of you will experience a rush of oxytocin in your bodies. Oxytocin, often known as the cuddle hormone or love hormone, is released when a mother is breastfeeding, when people snuggle up or bond socially, and it is a "feel-good" hormone. It is released in our bodies when we connect with someone. Even connecting with our eyes, giving or receiving a hug, a handshake or a kiss will release oxytocin in our bodies and make us feel good. Although it does not stay in our body for long, it helps create a bond between people and makes us feel connected.

When we truly step into another person's shoes without judgment, we can experience the rush of oxytocin. We then feel connected.

Next time you are listening to someone, step into their shoes and stand under their reality – that way you will truly understand what they are saying.

Stay reliable

Do what you say you are going to do. If you tell your mentoring partner that you are going to do something, then do it, or let them know why it has not been done. I often like to think of a mentor as being the **mentee's unbiased non-executive board member.** They need to be able to rely on you and trust you. They are needing someone reliable on their mentoring journey.

Be that someone!

If I am mentoring someone and say that I am going to send them a contact number, an article, or a podcast, I try to do it within 24 hours of our meeting. This way it's not forgotten, and I don't find myself scrambling to do it the day before we meet. Doing it straight away shows that you really care about them.

Truth telling and testing assumptions

Yes, you need to tell the truth to build trust. But you also need to **test what assumptions you are making about another person**, see where the reality gaps lie and then work on bridging the gaps. All too often we quickly make assumptions about other people. But if we are open with them, listen intently, ask discovery questions, and become genuinely curious, then we can bridge those reality gaps. To do this you need to reflect to the other person what you are hearing so that you are both on the same page. Don't just assume you understand what they are saying. By doing this, you will be showing the other person that you are genuinely listening to them.

Once you have spent the time building rapport and trust, the connection that you have made will allow for deeper conversations where learning can be fostered.

If trust is broken

It may take a long time to build trust, but it can be broken down in a minute. What can you do if your trust with your mentoring partner has been broken?

I coached a client where this had happened. Confidentiality had been breached and the relationship had broken down due to the one party not feeling comfortable to share things openly with the other. The conversations were now shallow and both parties were not getting much out of their mentoring relationship. I asked if they were both willing to work on building up the trust again and continuing with their relationship.

With them both willing to do so, I suggested the following:

1. Talk about the incident honestly and openly, emphasizing your feelings and emotions about the situation.
2. Give each one time to talk about it. Don't dominate the conversation.
3. Listen to each other. Be aware of the emotion the other person is expressing.
4. Repeat back to them what you heard to ensure you have heard correctly.
5. Usually there is blame involved. If you are to blame, then admit your mistake and apologize. Be the first one to do this rather than waiting for the other person to do so. I know it's difficult, especially if you feel that you are in the right. But even apologizing for being part of the trust breaking down goes a long way towards repairing a relationship.
6. Ask how the other person would like to move forward.

7. Then, once you both agree to move forward, take the time to build the trust up again. It does take a while to do so.

We've all experienced relationships where trust has been broken. The adage that time heals is true and we can repair it, even if there may be a few cracks. But both parties need to be open to it.

Key takeaways:

✓ Build rapport and connection first by finding things you have in common with the other person and sharing things they may not know about you.

✓ Build trust so that you can have the depth of conversation that is needed in your mentoring relationship.

✓ Earning trust takes time. Be open and honest, put your relationship first, step into the other person's shoes, stay reliable by doing what you say you are going to do, and test the assumptions that you may make about other people.

14

COMMIT

You now understand how to build rapport with your mentoring partner and how to foster trust. It's time to look at the next step on your mentoring journey and go back to the outer wheel.

So far, we have covered **Step 1: Embark** and **Step 2: Connect** of the outer wheel. We will now move to **Step 3: Commit** on your mentoring journey. Steps 4 and 5 will be left for later after we have discussed your mentoring conversations.

Step 3: Commit

You have now committed to the mentoring sessions that you will have on your journey. The mentoring sessions should ideally take place once a month, but some mentoring pairs meet more frequently in the beginning to get things moving. It all depends on what suits both of you. Your mentoring journey will last about six to 12 months, but this depends on the mentoring program that you are joining. For a six-month mentoring journey, I suggest a minimum of six mentoring meetings and for a 12-month journey, a minimum of 10 meetings.

Overview of timing

Below is a sequence of timing for you to understand this journey a bit more fully.

THE CATHERINE WHEEL

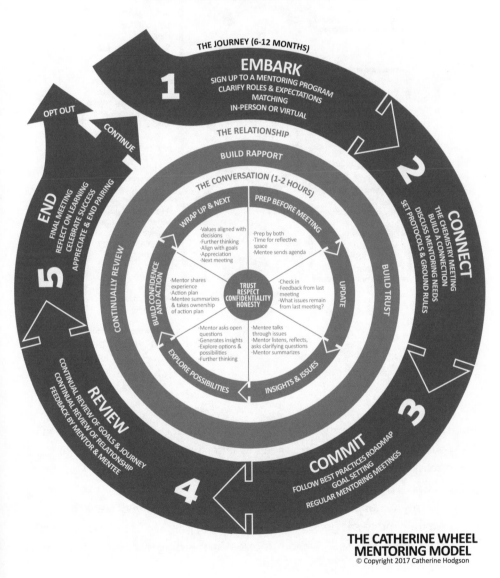

THE CATHERINE WHEEL
MENTORING MODEL
© Copyright 2017 Catherine Hodgson

6-MONTH MENTORING JOURNEY
MONTH

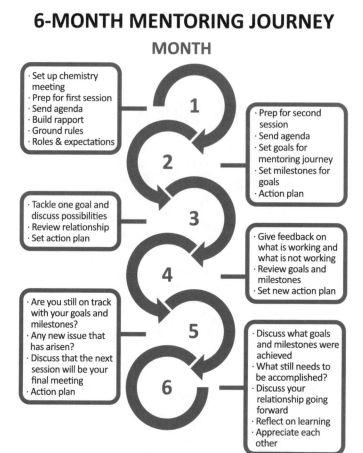

- Set up chemistry meeting
- Prep for first session
- Send agenda
- Build rapport
- Ground rules
- Roles & expectations

1

- Prep for second session
- Send agenda
- Set goals for mentoring journey
- Set milestones for goals
- Action plan

2

- Tackle one goal and discuss possibilities
- Review relationship
- Set action plan

3

- Give feedback on what is working and what is not working
- Review goals and milestones
- Set new action plan

4

- Are you still on track with your goals and milestones?
- Any new issue that has arisen?
- Discuss that the next session will be your final meeting
- Action plan

5

- Discuss what goals and milestones were achieved
- What still needs to be accomplished?
- Discuss your relationship going forward
- Reflect on learning
- Appreciate each other

6

6 MONTH MENTORING JOURNEY
© Copyright 2021 Catherine Hodgson

Goals

The next step is to move on to setting goals and this can be done in your second meeting. One meeting (after your chemistry meeting) to discuss purpose, vision, values, and goals, as well as setting actual goals, is sufficient.

In my experience, I have found that many mentoring pairs do not take the time to set goals for their mentoring journey. They tend to dive straight into the issue without looking at the bigger picture of where they want to go.

Setting goals is important to do once you have built rapport and understood your reason for mentoring. If goals are set, you have something to work towards and progress can be measured. However, don't get too hung up on setting SMART goals straight away. (SMART is an acronym that stands for Specific, Measurable, Achievable, Realistic, and Timely.) These can narrow your focus too soon.

The first thing you need to do is help your mentee to step back. Get them to look at the bigger picture before rushing into listing the goals. Below is a diagram showing how we need to start at the bottom of the pyramid and work upwards. Spending some time in reflection first is crucial for a successful outcome.

4 STEP GOAL PYRAMID

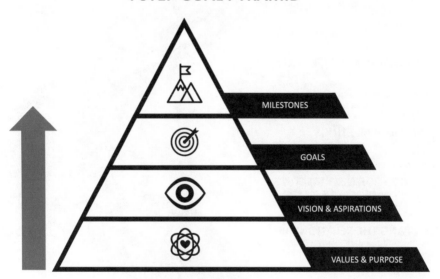

Reflection

Before rushing into goal-setting, spend some time in reflection to see the bigger picture. As a mentor, you would help your mentee do this. Ask them to sit somewhere on their own. Think about their **values and wider purpose**. What is the story that they tell themselves and others? What do they want their story to be? It's not just about SMART goals. They need to go further in their thinking, and then bring this back in to tangible goals. As a mentor, you could ask them the following questions, or, as a mentee, you can reflect on these questions yourself.

ROADMAP FOR YOUR MENTORING JOURNEY

1. YOU'RE MATCHED!
Mentees set up the first meeting – date, time and place. Reflect on what you would like to discuss and what you want to get out of your journey.

2. THE CHEMISTRY MEETING
Usually one hour in length.
Ensure meeting is held in a confidential place.
Set ground rules for your mentoring journey.

3. BUILDING RAPPORT AND TRUST
Spend time getting to know each other.
Ask: What are your values? What are you passionate about? What successes have you had? What have you learnt from your failures?

4. GOAL-SETTING
Mentees to reflect on aspirations and goals.
Mentors can help to establish goals for the mentoring journey.
Goals should be achievable with some stretch.
Goals should align with your values.

5. PREPARING FOR MEETINGS
Mentees spend time reflecting on what they would like to bring to the next mentoring meeting. The more prep you put into your meeting, the more you will get out of it.
Mentees send the agenda a few days before the session.

6. REGULAR MEETINGS
Set up your meetings in advance. Ensure meetings are regular, at least every 4 – 6 weeks apart to ensure you do not lose momentum.

7. ACTION FOR NEXT MEETINGS
Have a written action plan at the end of each meeting which mentees can work on before the next meeting.

8. REVIEWING THE RELATIONSHIP
Review your relationship regularly – be open and honest. The deeper the trust, the deeper the conversation.
Reflect on and discuss:
What can I do differently?
What can my mentor/mentee do differently?

9. REVIEWING GOALS
Review the goals regularly and check that they align to the mentee's values.
Goals do not need to be static and can change along the way as you get more clarity from your journey – be open to the changes that need to be made.

10. ENDING OR TRANSITIONING THE JOURNEY
Prepare for your final meeting. Reflect on what you have achieved.
Celebrate your successes.
Appreciate and thank each other.

ROADMAP FOR YOUR MENTORING JOURNEY
© Copyright 2023 Catherine Hodgson

- What energizes you?
- What do you want to achieve for yourself? For others?
- What is your purpose?
- Is it aligned to your values?

Next, go up one level on the pyramid and reflect on your **vision and aspirations**. As a mentor you can ask your mentee these questions in your goal-setting session:
- What do you want for yourself?
- Where do you see yourself/your business/your career in the future?
- What is your Mount Everest?

Taking a first-hand look at the **bigger picture**:

When I first started my own business at the age of 30 with my husband, we had our annual meeting with our auditors to go through the year-end financials. A senior partner of our auditing firm would meet with us once or twice a year. He had met with my husband's parents in their business for the past 20 or so years and was seen as a trusted advisor to the family. Rodney was the age of my husband's parents. He was short, had white hair and glasses, but was not your typical accountant. He had a sense of humour, was a charmer of the ladies in a very respectful way, and had an acute understanding of our business and the intricacies of relationships within family businesses. He was my husband's mentor and became mine as well over the years.

In one meeting, when we were looking at the figures for the business that I ran, he looked up from the financials and said to me, "You need to get out of the engine room and go and stand on the bridge for a while. You need to start spending more time thinking about your business."

Rodney was straightforward and got to the point. He always just said it how it was. Until then, I had been working non-stop, involved in every aspect of the business, driving it forward and hardly stopping to see where we were going. We were very busy, and I was driving it, but without a strategy or plan of where we were heading. It was true. I was shovelling coal in the engine room and hardly had time to poke my head above the deck.

Rodney then asked me where I could go to do some thinking about the business. He said, "Go anywhere, but it needs to be out of the office. Go and sit in a sauna or something."

That meeting had a big impact on me, and I left it reflecting on what he had said. I was so caught up in the business, as well as our young family, that I didn't have any time left to think where I wanted to take the business.

So began my journey of taking time out of my business to think more strategically about it. In fact, I'm not sure I did a lot of thinking in a sauna, as he suggested, but it did give me an excuse to get out of the office and the house. I think I did most of my thinking with my running shoes on, either jogging or going for a walk. He triggered a point, though: that I did need to step back from the business and think bigger. I needed to step away, create a vision, and decide where I wanted to take the business, and what I wanted from it. It gave me the chance to breathe and step out of the engine room and onto the bridge occasionally. And yes, it really did help me take our business further.

Rodney was a wise mentor. I will be forever grateful for his words when I needed them most!

Requirements of goals

Before setting goals, it's important to understand the **characteristics of your goals**.

1. Inspiring

You and your mentee should be excited about working towards these goals. Check that your mentee is feeling energized to achieve these goals. I've been asked in my mentoring masterclasses how all goals can be inspiring. Maybe a goal is to close one's business, or maybe it is to end a partnership, or something that does not seem to be inspiring at all. Even though these goals may have some negative connotation, how can these goals be reframed so that the mentee **wants to** achieve them and **is motivated** to do so?

As a mentor, you may need to ask your mentee to reframe their goal. So, instead of "I need to close my business because it's not what I want to do any more or not performing well", the goal can be reframed as "Finding a successful closure for my business and celebrating what we achieved".

Questions to ask your mentee:
- How inspiring or motivating is this goal for you on a scale of 1 to 10?
- Does this goal contain a vision for the future?
- Is this goal motivating for you?
- How do you feel about achieving this goal?

Your mentee should score this around eight and above for them to want to achieve it. If they score it lower than that, then ask them if this is the right goal for them to pursue right now.

2. Challenging and achievable

The goals set for your mentee should be challenging yet achievable. Your mentee will grow from the process if there is a bit of a stretch to the goal. Increase the challenge of the goal, with permission, if you feel it is not challenging enough.

If you, as a mentor, feel that a 5% growth for their business can easily be achieved without much effort, ask them if they can achieve a slightly higher percentage growth. It may be just the challenge they need.

Questions to ask your mentee:
- How much more stretch could there be in this goal, while still being achievable?
- Do you need any more challenge with this goal?
- Do you have a sense that this goal is achievable within a time frame?

3. Measurable and time-based

The goal should be measurable, if possible, so you both know when it is achieved. Make the measure part of the goal statement. Also put a time frame in place for the goal to be achieved. You can link the goal to a measure of currency, a percentage, or a person. For example: "Increase sales by 60% over the next 12 months."

Questions to ask your mentee:
- How will we know when you have achieved this goal?
- How can we put a measure to this goal?

4. Succinct

The goal should be able to be stated in one sentence. Ensure that it is not rambling and that your mentee cannot lose focus of the goal.

Questions to ask your mentee:
- Can we say this in one sentence?
- What would the headline of news be for this goal?

For example, a personal goal may be: "To use my writing skills in the next 12 months to inspire and educate others in my community to make change about their use of plastic."

A manager may have a goal: "To be an inspiring leader to my team so they feel self-motivated to achieve 100% of their goals."

We can get inspiration from the mission statements of some large companies, such as the following:
- Tesla: "To accelerate the world's transition to sustainable energy."
- PayPal: "To build the web's most convenient, secure, cost-effective payment solution."
- TED: "Spread ideas."
- LinkedIn: "To connect the world's professionals to make them more productive and successful."
- JetBlue: "To inspire humanity – both in the air and on the ground."

I know the goal you set for your mentoring journey may not be a big mission statement like these. However, you can try to make it as short, succinct, and inspiring as these, whatever the goal is.

5. Reviewed regularly

The goal should be reviewed often and can be changed or adjusted along the way. Although these are the primary goals, sometimes goals do need to be changed. Both of you need to discuss that the goals should be reviewed regularly and that you are both flexible to changing the goals if necessary.

Primary goals

These are the goals you will focus on in your mentoring sessions. I usually recommend you aim for three primary goals for your mentoring journey.

Here are some examples of primary goals.
- Improve my relationships with my team by 50%.
- Sign up three new customers in 12 months.
- Increase sales in my division by 30% in the next year.
- Spend quality time with my family every weekend.
- Book and enjoy my dream holiday within the next eight months.
- Spend quality time with my parents at least once a month.
- Attain financial freedom within the next 12 months.
- Run my first half marathon within six months.
- Swim 40 laps three times a week at the gym.
- See my book on Amazon in 24 months.

Secondary goals

You may also want to set **secondary goals**. These goals are not as important as your three main goals, but you would still like to work towards them. This is completely optional and based on how long your mentoring journey is. Go through the original list that you created and see if there are any items on that list that you would like to add as secondary goals.

Now you can start to look at setting goals. The reason we do this is that jumping straight into goal-setting narrows your focus and prevents you from thinking and dreaming big. You also need to make sure you know what your values are so that your goals are aligned with your values and vision. If they are not aligned, the chances of you achieving those goals are limited.

Key takeaways:

- ✓ Step back and look at the big picture first – your mentee's purpose, values, vision, and aspirations.
- ✓ Understand the requirements for goals: inspiring, challenging and achievable, measurable and time-based, succinct, and reviewed regularly.
- ✓ Set three primary goals and some secondary goals if necessary.

15

SEVEN STEPS TO GOAL-SETTING

Setting goals is so important for the success of your mentoring journey that it is important to spend the time necessary on it to ensure the goals are the right ones for your mentee.

However, don't let your mentee get so attached to their goals that they are not open to changes that may need to be navigated along the way. Know that goals are set, but they are not set in stone. They may need to be adapted and changed as life happens. Be open to being flexible and discuss this upfront.

To help you with the process of goal-setting, here is a seven-step process for getting to three primary goals.

Your mentee should ideally have up to three primary goals. To identify what those goals are, you can follow a **seven-step process: explore, filter, identify, needs analysis, blockages, milestones, action plan.**

7 STEPS TO GOAL-SETTING

👀 STEP 1

EXPLORE
Explore different areas suitable for mentoring

🔍 STEP 2

FILTER
Filter up to 3 areas most relevant for mentoring

⊙ STEP 3

IDENTIFY
Define up to 3 goals - SMART
(Specific, Measurable, Achievable, Relevant and Time-bound)

🤲 STEP 4

NEEDS ANALYSIS
What is needed to achieve these goals?

🔺 STEP 5

BLOCKAGES
What can get in the way of achieving these goals?

🚩 STEP 6

MILESTONES
What milestones need to be set?

📋 STEP 7

ACTION PLAN
Timeline and action plan for each

The **first three steps – Explore, Filter, and Identify –** are really important to ensure that the goals are relevant for mentoring, and that they are written down succinctly, preferably in one sentence. The diagram helps you see how these steps work:

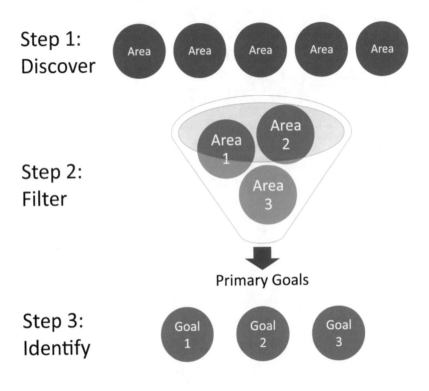

Step 1: Explore

As a mentor, you are going to take your mentee through a process of looking at all the major things they are dealing with in the different areas in their work or personal life.

As a mentee, you can do this exercise by yourself before your mentoring session. Write the issues down on a list. Keep it at a high level and do not get into details yet. This will prevent you from getting side-tracked and it reduces the noise in your brain so you can stay focused.

If you are doing it together and your mentee does start to go into detail, you can say to them, "Can we get into the details later as we don't need them right now?"

Questions to ask:

- What do you want to accomplish in the upcoming months?
- What are some things that you would like to learn or do?
- What comes to mind in terms of work or life that you are dealing with right now?
- What else would you like to achieve in your work or personal life?
- What else have you always dreamed of doing?
- What would you like to see in your life that currently is not there?
- Do you have a vision or purpose that you would like to work towards?
- Are there any issues in these areas that you are facing?

If ideas start to run out and there are silences for a long time or if your mentee says that they are finished, you can ask, "What else comes to mind?" or "Is there anything else you have not considered yet?"

When making the list of ideas, keep the list succinct and to the point. Try to get at least 10 areas written down.

At the end of this exploratory process, you will have a list of everything the mentee is dealing with. From this list, you can now look at the next stage of filtering.

Step 2: Filter

The next stage is to filter the list that you and your mentee have created and reduce it to three areas that are most relevant to them for mentoring. You don't need to have the final goals here, just reduce this list to three.

You will need to read the list to your mentee and check they are happy with everything on the list before trying to reduce it. You can use a numbering system such as 1 for important and urgent, 2 for important but not urgent, 3 for not important or urgent. You can also use a system of yes/no/maybe next to each item to see whether it is relevant for mentoring.

Use whatever system works for both of you in order to reduce the list to three items that would be relevant to work on in your mentoring sessions.

Questions to ask your mentee:
- What areas from this list are significant to you?
- What areas are you already satisfied with and don't need any mentoring?
- What areas are similar and can be combined?

- Let's go through the list and put a yes/no/maybe next to each item to see whether it is relevant for mentoring.

At the end of this filtering process, you should have at least three areas in which your mentee would like mentoring.

Read these three items back to your mentee to ensure these are the three areas they would like to focus on. If you only have one or two areas, then that is also acceptable, especially if your mentoring journey is not very long (six months or less), or if the one area is very big and you know there may be more than one goal coming from the one area.

Step 3: Identify

The third stage involves identifying and clarifying the primary goals. Each goal is to be written down in one sentence.

Start by asking your mentee their vision for the areas that they have narrowed it down to. Don't go into details as you need to keep them focused on a big vision and goal. You need to listen carefully to them and help them to formulate their goals. Interact with them and, if necessary, help them to think bigger.

Questions to ask your mentee:
- What is your vision in this area?
- What emotion do you feel when you think of this?
- What could be an inspiring goal for this area?
- Could the goal be "x" and how does that feel for you?
- It sounds like you are saying…
- What would you like to be different in this area "x" months/weeks from now?
- Can you put that into one sentence? Is that inspiring for you?
- What is the measure of success for each goal?

At the end of this step, you should have three goals that are succinct, one sentence long, and inspiring for your mentee to achieve. Check that the goals are written down.

Writing them down forces you to visualize your goals and increase your commitment to them.
- Can you write the goal down in a positive way that inspires you?

- Can you write each goal succinctly in one sentence?
- How does that goal feel to you?
- What emotion comes to you when you look at each goal?

To ensure that you are on the right track with your goal statement, check each one against these requirements. The goals should not be about fixing something, but rather should be motivating and focused on the future.

Questions to reflect on:
- Are these goals positive and motivating to you?
- How inspiring are they on a scale of 1 to 10?
- How challenging are they to you on a scale of 1 to 10?
- Do these goals need a bit more stretch for you?
- Are these goals achievable?
- Are they time-based?
- What is the measure of success for each goal?
- How will you know when you have achieved this goal?

Now that you have your goals written down, ensure that these goals are positive, motivating, inspiring, and measurable.

Step 4: Needs analysis

Now you can help your mentee think about what needs to be done to achieve each goal. Identify where they are now, what their vision is for each goal, and how to get there.

Questions to ask your mentee:
- What is your vision for this goal?
- What skills do you need to achieve this goal?
- What resources do you need?
- What information or knowledge do you need?
- What help, assistance, or collaboration do you need?

Step 5: Blockages/obstacles/assumptions

In this step you will find out what could **get in the way** of your mentee achieving their goals.

Questions to ask your mentee:
- What obstacles may lie in the way of you achieving this goal?
- What could block you or hold you back from reaching these goals?
- What assumptions are you making about achieving these goals?
- Are these assumptions true?
- Who could hold you accountable to help you achieve these goals?

Often a mentee makes assumptions that can hold them back from achieving their goals. Sometimes these assumptions are not true and need to be looked at in more depth. Once these blockages are removed or dealt with, realizing their goal becomes clearer.

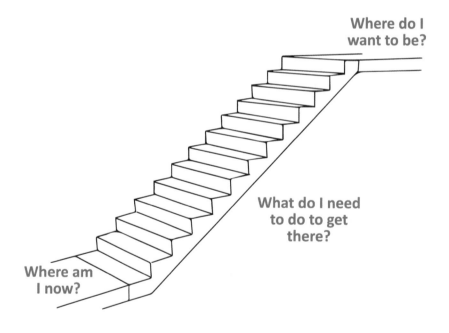

Where do I want to be?

What do I need to do to get there?

Where am I now?

Step 6: Milestones

It is important that milestones are set so that progress can be measured. Start putting milestones against each goal, as well as a timeline.

You will need to ask yourself, or your mentee, where they are now in terms of their goal and where they would like to be. **They need a starting point for their goal and then a vision of where they want to be.** The plan is then created on what they need to do to get there and measurements along the way. This will help them to think about what milestones are needed along the way.

Questions to ask your mentee:
- Where are you now with this goal?
- What is the reality of where you are now in relation to the goal?

This helps you understand the starting point and allows you to understand the goal a bit better. You will then ask your mentee for their vision for this area.

Questions to ask your mentee:
- Where do you want to be?
- What is the outcome you would like to achieve?

Ask open questions to get your mentee to think big, to dream, and to envision what this goal would be like if it was achieved.

You can then explain to your mentee that they need milestones along the way.

Questions to ask your mentee to help set milestones:
- What do you need to do to work towards your first goal? Second goal? Third goal?
- Can we put a milestone to that and what do you want to call it?
- When do you think you will be able to achieve that?
- What could you do next towards achieving this goal?
- What could you do after that?

Put timing in place for each step or milestone.

Remember to celebrate the milestones achieved along the way. Each milestone is a big accomplishment for your mentee.

Step 7: Action plan

Once you have the milestones written down, you need to start looking at how to get to each milestone. This is where planning comes into play.

Questions to ask your mentee:
- What do you need to do to get there?
- Can we explore some possibilities and options for achieving this milestone?
- How long will that take you?
- Can you put a timeline to each milestone and then to each goal?
- What support do you need?

At the end of these seven steps, your mentee should have up to three goals with milestones and an action plan for each.

Secondary goals can also be set up if your mentee has many goals on their list. You may need to help them prioritize which are the primary goals and which can be secondary goals.

Ensure that they have no more than three primary goals, though, otherwise it will be too difficult to achieve them given the timeline of your mentoring journey.

Worksheet 7: Goal-setting

GOAL-SETTING WORKSHEET

Explore different areas that you are dealing with in your work and personal life.		

STEP 1 DISCOVER

Filter the list and reduce it to three areas that would be relevant to mentoring.		
Area 1	Area 2	Area 3

STEP 2 FILTER

Define and clarify three primary goals.		
Goal 1	Goal 2	Goal 3

STEP 3 DEFINE

What is needed to achieve these goals?		

STEP 4 NEEDS ANALYSIS

STEP 5 BLOCKAGES

What can get in the way of you achieving your goal?		
Goal 1	Goal 2	Goal 3

STEP 6 MILESTONES

Write down milestones with a timeline and then an action plan for each milestone.		
Milestone & Action	Milestone & Action	Milestone & Action

STEP 6 ACTION PLAN

Milestone & Action	Milestone & Action	Milestone & Action
Milestone & Action	Milestone & Action	Milestone & Action

Once you have completed setting up your goals, you are ready for your regular mentoring conversations so you can work towards achieving these goals.

Key takeaways:

- ✓ Use the seven-step process to set goals: Explore, Filter, Identify, Needs analysis, Blockages, Milestones, Action plan.
- ✓ At the end of the process, you should have up to three primary goals with action plans and milestones.
- ✓ Remember to review the goals regularly. However, goals are not set in stone. Remain flexible and open for them to change along the way if necessary.

16

THE INNER WHEEL
– THE CONVERSATION

"Mentoring is all about the conversation.
This is the heart of your mentoring journey."

Catherine Hodgson

We have covered the first three steps of the outer wheel, the **Journey** of the Catherine Wheel, and we will cover steps four and five later in the book. We have also explored the middle wheel, **The Relationship**, and how to build rapport and trust.

We are now going to dive into the inner wheel, **The Conversation**, which is how to have your regular mentoring meetings.

The inner wheel – The Conversation

Let's face it, mentoring is just a conversation between two people, one of whom is the mentor, the other the mentee. The Conversation is therefore the most important part of mentoring, because it **is** mentoring.

The inner wheel of the Catherine Wheel is **The Conversation**, consisting of six segments. In the centre of this is a core representing the values that need to be held sacred in any mentoring conversation: **trust**, **respect**, **confidentiality**, and **honesty**. If these values are not adhered to by both parties, then your relationship is doomed to fail, and your conversations will be shallow and of little value.

We will go through each of these segments of **The Conversation** wheel, going into detail of how you need to prepare for your meetings, give updates and feedback, as well as enter a conversation flow that includes the next three segments: **Insights and Issues**, **Explore Possibilities**, and **Build Confidence and Action**.

Finally, you will learn some recommended ways to wrap up The Conversation.

THE CATHERINE WHEEL

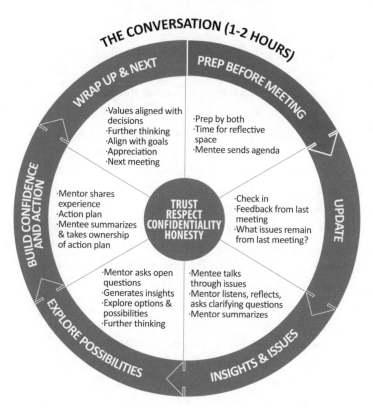

THE CATHERINE WHEEL
MENTORING MODEL
© Copyright 2017 Catherine Hodgson

Prep before the meeting

I believe that preparing for your mentoring conversation is as important as the actual conversation, which is why it is included in the conversation wheel. I also know that this is an area that often gets forgotten or neglected. However, the better prepared you are for your meetings and the more time you spend preparing for them, the more value you will get out of each conversation. The saying **"The more you put in, the more you get out"** applies here.

You may be wondering what you need to prepare and how to prepare for your meeting. If you are a mentor, you may wonder why you need to prepare at all. I'm going to take you through both sides so that you can understand how each needs to prepare for the meeting to get the most out of it.

Reflecting

It's important for you to spend time reflecting before your meeting. So, I'm going to ask you this question to think about now:

"Where do you have your best ideas and thoughts?"

By that I mean your most creative, innovative thinking, on your own.

Where do you go or what are you doing? Do this now… take a minute to pause, close your eyes and ask yourself that question right now.

If you are thinking that your best ideas are when you are showering, walking, exercising, in nature, falling asleep, driving, or something similar… then you are in good company.

What I look out for is if anyone says they have their best creative thoughts at work. In my experience, almost no one has their most creative thoughts when they are at work or behind their desk.

Why, then, do we think we or our staff can do their best and most creative thinking when they are driving their desk? If you are going to a strategy meeting, brain-storming session, or creative hub meeting, then go to the place where you do your best thinking first. Spend time there reflecting on what needs to be thought about. Tell your staff or colleagues to do the same before the meeting. The same goes for a mentoring meeting. Before your meeting, spend time in that place or doing what helps you think best. You will be able to bring more innovative thinking to your next mentoring meeting.

You may be wondering why you get your best thoughts in these places. It's usually when you're doing something repetitive, such as walking, running, swimming, driving, or showering – something that you do not have to think about doing. It's automatic. When you are partially occupied doing these things, you allow your brain to start thinking about other things. You are not focusing on the issue, but allowing ideas to wash through, which can start to lead to innovative thinking. For your best ideas to come through, you usually need to be in a positive frame of mind as well. This usually means that you have more serotonin, dopamine, and oxytocin in your body, which allows your prefrontal cortex, your executive brain, to be able to do its thinking. People who are depressed, sad or tired do not usually come up with their most creative thinking when they are in that state. They often have too much cortisol in their body, which can shut their prefrontal cortex down.

When you are needing to prepare for your meetings, go to the place where you do your best thinking. Let your issues wash over you without dwelling on any particular one. You may just have some great insights.

Pressing issues

All of us have issues that are unresolved and that we store in our head at any one time. The concept of significant unresolved issues arose from David Clutterbuck's unpublished research in the 1990s on what issues mentees brought to their mentors for discussion. It emerged that most people in professional and managerial roles, who were mature, stable in personality, and mentally healthy, could cope with between 25 and 35 significant unresolved issues before they noticed a severe impact on their ability to cope.

With all these issues swirling around in your head, you may be wondering which issue to bring to a mentoring session, if any. When you go to your reflective space, let these issues wash over you and see if you latch onto any one of them. Is this an issue that your mentor will be able to help you with?

The following exercise will help you reflect on your most pressing issues and hopefully one will surface as an issue to bring to the next mentoring session. Get a pen and do Worksheet 8 right now.

Worksheet 8: Your top five pressing issues

Write down your top five most pressing issues. What is keeping you awake at night? What can you not stop thinking about? What comes to mind first, without thinking too hard about it? It could be business related, family, or personal.

1. Write down what comes to you first – up to five issues.
2. Look at your list and rate these issues according to urgency on a scale of 1 to 5 (1 = least urgent, 5 = most urgent). Put a number next to the issue.
3. Rate according to the importance of the issue to you in achieving your overall goals or purpose (1 = least important, 5 = most important). Put that number next to your urgency number. For instance, you may have a goal of running the next London marathon. Then getting fit would rank as 5 in order of importance for you to achieve this goal.
4. Now add up the urgent and important numbers, and then rank your list from highest to lowest. Circle the highest number – that is your most urgent and important issue.
5. Out of these issues, what is causing you the most stress? Are there any that you would like to bring to the next mentoring session?

You can give this exercise to your mentee to do before their session with you, so that they then have time to think about the issue and what they would like to get out of their next mentoring meeting with you.

Mentee prep

How should I prepare for my meetings?

As a mentee, you should spend at least 30 minutes, preferably more, preparing for your mentoring meetings. Ensure you are fully prepared so that you get the most out of your mentoring meeting.

Do some reflective thinking, going to the place where you do your best creative thinking.

Make some notes on the following 4 points:

1. **Action plan**: Go through the action points you compiled from your last meeting and make notes on your progress on each action point.
   - Are there any issues that have come up from the action plan?
   - Did anything hold me back from completing my action plan?
   - Do I want to carry any of the action-plan items forward to the next meeting?
2. **Journal:** If you have kept a journal, go through your journal, reflecting on what has happened in your life/career/business since your last meeting.
3. **Goals:** Look at the goals and milestones that you wrote down from your initial meeting and reflect where you are now in terms of those milestones and goals.
4. **Notes:** Make some notes using the following questions to help you with your agenda:
   - What has happened in the weeks since our previous meeting?
   - What has been challenging for me since we last met?
   - What do I want to bring to the next meeting?
   - What issues or challenges am I facing right now?
   - How can my mentor help me with any of these issues or challenges?
   - What do I want to work on to move closer to my milestones and my goals?
   - What would I like to learn from my mentor?
   - What questions do I want to ask my mentor?

You are now ready to put together an agenda for what you would like to discuss in your next mentoring session.

Send a calendar invitation to your mentor and an agenda or a list of discussion points at least a few days before your meetings.

Agenda for monthly/regular mentoring meetings

I believe in sending an agenda or discussion points to your mentor as this really helps them know how to feel better prepared for the meeting.

It allows them time to find any articles they would like to share with you, or material they would like to give you, before the meeting.

When I was a mentee, my mentor would have to remind me a week before to send through an agenda. I was not very good at preparing for my meetings, but realized only afterwards, when I had mentees myself, that an agenda really does help. It also should not be the responsibility of the mentor to remind their mentee to send the agenda. I feel bad that my mentor had to constantly remind me!

This is what a typical mentoring agenda could look like, but it is only a guideline for you. You also may like to put down discussion points and then have this outline as a backup to follow.

 MEETING AGENDA 2

Regular Mentoring Meeting Agenda
(60 minutes)

Mentoring Meeting Agenda

1. UPDATE: (10 MINUTES)
• Reminder of confidentiality • Check in and update of what has happened since last meeting • Action points from last meeting
2. ISSUES AND INSIGHTS: (20 MINUTES)
• Current reality • Issues/challenges/topics to discuss • Desired outcomes • Review goals
3. EXPLORE POSSIBILITIES: (15 MINUTES)
• Explore options to achieve outcomes • Strategies to achieve goal • Mentor sharing
4. BUILD CONFIDENCE AND ACTION: (10 MINUTES)
• List actions
5. WRAP UP AND NEXT: (5 MINUTES)
• Next meeting • Appreciation

Mentor prep

You may be asking "Do I need to prepare anything before my meetings?"

As a mentor you do need to prepare for your meetings, and it should involve the following:

- Read over your notes from the previous meeting to familiarize yourself with the conversation.
- What actions did your mentee agree to take or reflect on?
- Are there any actions that you committed to taking before the next meeting? Have you done them?
- What thoughts do you have from the agenda that your mentee has sent to you?
- What experience or knowledge do you have to share with them with regard to what they want to discuss?
- Ensure that you have enough time before your meeting to be in the correct head space for your meeting – don't rush in from another meeting without having a gap to do some reflecting first. This will ensure you are calm and present for your mentoring meeting. Ask yourself: "What can I do to ensure that I am in the right head space and mindset for my upcoming meeting? How can I become present and stay mindful?"

You may have heard about your three brains: the head, heart, and gut brain. Marcia Reynolds, master coach and author of *The Discomfort Zone*, says that we should focus on opening up our head to be curious, our heart to be generous, and our gut to be courageous before our meeting.

Here is a simple visualization exercise that you can do before a mentoring meeting, tapping into your head, heart, and gut, to help you become fully present. If you feel like practising it right now, read this visualization in Worksheet 9 slowly, closing your eyes after each point and following the instructions. You will be amazed how refreshed you feel afterwards.

Worksheet 9: Visualization exercise

1. Sit in a chair to remain alert, feet firmly placed on the ground. Close your eyes or shift your gaze downward.
2. How does your body feel? Do you need to shift your position to feel more comfortable?
3. Be aware of the chair you are sitting on and your contact with it. Be aware of your feet on the floor.
4. How are you feeling emotionally? Do you feel calm? Relaxed? Stressed? Tired? Impatient? Accept that emotion.
5. Relax and take a deep breath in through your nose to the count of four, hold and release slowly to the count of four. Repeat three times, focusing on your breath.
6. Feel your body relaxing. Notice any spots of tension in your body. Breathe in again and focus on those spots, releasing the tension from your body.
7. Resume normal breathing in and out.
8. Picture a ray of light, bright and warm above your head. It is shining down, the rays moving into your head. You can feel it now shining in your brain. Your brain is open to receive this warmth. Any thoughts you have, judgments and opinions are now being dissolved by this warm light. Bask in this warmth.
9. Your mind is now free of thoughts. You have a completely open mind, ready to learn. You are infinitely curious.
10. Take a deep breath in and as you breathe out, say the word "curious" to yourself.
11. The light is passing through your head, down your neck and into your chest. The light is now shining its warmth on your heart. Place a hand on your heart.
12. You are thinking about someone you love, a person,

pet, physical or spiritual being or a place that you love to be, a place that makes you feel happy and where you feel safe. You feel love. You are grateful. You are joyful. You are generous. You are safe. Your heart is so big you feel it could burst. You are feeling the light warming it and making that love expand. Bask in that warmth and love.

13. Take a deep breath in and as you breathe out, say the word "love" to yourself.

14. The light now travels downwards towards your belly. Your belly starts to feel warm from the light. Place a hand on your belly.

15. Think of a time when you were not afraid, when you did something that was brave, when you were courageous and proud of yourself. Your belly is warm as you think about this. If you were feeling any anxiety or fear beforehand, it has now disappeared. Bask in the warmth in your belly.

16. Take a deep breath in and as you breathe out, say the word "courage" to yourself.

17. The light now travels down your legs, to your feet and out through your toes. You are left feeling full and satisfied.

18. Revisit your head and say the word "curious". Revisit your heart and say the word "love". Revisit your belly and say the word "courage".

19. Take another deep breath in and slowly out.

20. Open your eyes and come back to the room.

Did you have any difficulty with this visualization? Did one area feel uncomfortable to focus on? Were you able to access the other areas more easily? Sometimes, people find that they have difficulty with one area, which is an area that they do not give enough attention to or that they find it more difficult to access. If, for instance, you can do the head or gut but find the heart more difficult, then you know that listening to your heart is probably not what you do very often.

Marcia Reynolds says that people who tend to be helpers listen more easily from their heart than their gut. Risk-takers, who move quickly on instinct, find it easier to listen from their gut than their heart.

In your everyday conversations, try to practise receiving from your most vulnerable place and to listen from your head, heart, and gut. This will help you open up and align your entire nervous system when you are mentoring.

The most important thing you can do as a mentor is to be fully present during your mentoring conversation. Focus on how you can achieve this and how you can stay present throughout.

Key takeaways:

- ✓ Find where you do your best thinking and ensure you spend time there, reflecting on your upcoming mentoring session and any issues you would like to bring to your meeting.
- ✓ You, as a mentee, need to prepare before your meeting by sending your mentor an agenda or key topics to discuss, going through your action plan from your last meeting, and checking where you are in terms of achieving your goals.
- ✓ As a mentor, you need to ensure you are in the right head space before arriving at your meeting.

17

UPDATE

We have covered all the preparation for the meeting and how to do it. We are now moving on to the actual mentoring meeting, and the first segment of the conversation, which is the update.

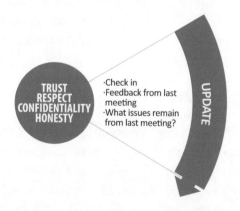

**THE CATHERINE WHEEL
MENTORING MODEL**
© Copyright 2017 Catherine Hodgson

There are six points you would ideally cover in your update:

Update on what has happened since last session

The first thing to do in your mentoring session, as a mentee, is to update your mentor on what has happened since you last met. Now, it's tempting to get stuck in this stage for far too long. I know because I used to get stuck here with my mentor. I took so long updating him that we spent a large part of the time looking at what had happened rather than focusing on the present issues on hand. However, this is an important phase that cannot be overlooked as it provides feedback for both of you.

Update on action plan

The mentee gives feedback on whether **they actioned their action plans** from their last meeting, what still remains and what may have got in the way of them completing those actions. This gives the mentor great insights. Some issues from the last meeting may not have been covered adequately as you may have run out of time. These should also be highlighted. Discuss whether the mentee wants to bring them up in this meeting.

Update by mentor

In my meetings with my mentor, I also used to ask him about what had happened in his life since we last met. Often Rob would share things with me about what he was doing, and I would take an interest in his life and goals as well. Make the feedback two-way!

Check in emotionally

It's a good idea to check in where you both are, emotionally. One day I arrived at my mentoring meeting feeling quite down and not my usual enthusiastic self. Rob immediately picked it up and said he could sense I was not feeling myself today. He asked whether I would like to talk about it. Showing that you are responsive to other people's emotions goes a long way to building trust. For me, it was a relief that he had noticed, and I was able to tell him what was on my mind. You can simply say to each other, "What emotions are you feeling right now before we begin our session?"

Being present

Another question that I often ask at the beginning of my sessions is,

"What could be preventing you from being fully present today?" I ask my mentee to write down on a piece of paper anything that comes to mind. I then ask them to read it to themselves and write down what emotion comes to mind when they read it. After they have written down their emotion, they are asked to fold up the piece of paper and put it away – it will be waiting for them after the session.

Just doing this simple exercise allows you to put aside things that may be preventing you from being fully present. We are also often not very in tune with our emotions, so writing our emotions down and being more in tune with them allows us to reduce the anxiety that issues may be causing us.

You don't need to do this full exercise, but merely acknowledging where each of you is emotionally sets up the session for full presence, empathy, and trust.

Ground rules

Remind yourselves of the ground rules that you set at the beginning of your mentoring journey. Remind each other that confidentiality is key! Also discuss how long the meeting will be and what time you will finish (so that you are both on the same page).

Key takeaways:

- ✓ Update your mentor on what has happened since your last meeting.
- ✓ Update your mentor on what actions you were able to complete from your action plan.
- ✓ Don't get stuck in your update.

18

THE CONVERSATION FLOW

I like to think that conversations have a flow to them – they are like a river, winding along towards an estuary with the water flowing at different speeds along the way. Sometimes the river follows in a straight path and sometimes it's a bit windy. Sometimes there are rocks that the water needs to flow over and sometimes there is smooth sand.

Your mentoring conversation is similar. It has a definite beginning and end. Often you don't know in which direction it is going to go. It may take some twists and turns along the way. Sometimes the conversation flows easily and sometimes it takes longer to overcome obstacles that get in the way, and you need to look for new routes, new possibilities, and a way forward.

The **Conversation Flow** is a model to show how you can guide another person through an issue or challenge to help them come up with their own insights, which can lead to action. It is part of the Catherine Wheel. We will explore three steps in the conversation wheel: **Step 1: Issues and desired outcome**, **Step 2: Explore possibilities**, and **Step 3: Build confidence and action**.

The Conversation Flow Model below reflects this highlighted portion of the Catherine Wheel Mentoring Model.

The red arrows show a U curve, which shows the energy flows. We start at a normal energy level. When we start to think of issues we are dealing with, our energy goes from outward energy to inward energy, as we are now using up brain power to process our thinking.

THE CATHERINE WHEEL

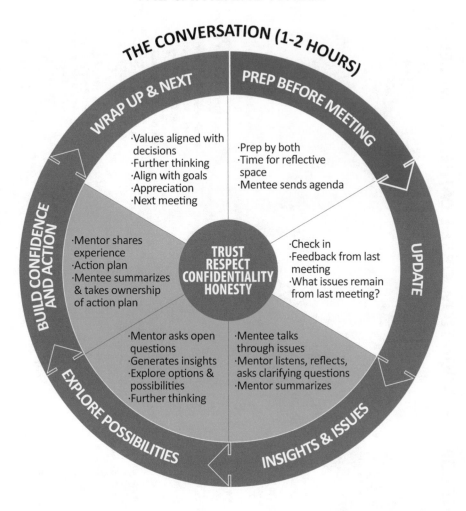

THE CATHERINE WHEEL
MENTORING MODEL
© Copyright 2017 Catherine Hodgson

In David Clutterbuck's unpublished research in the 1990s, he explains that if a person is walking and starts to think about their issues, their walking pace starts to slow as their thinking goes inwards. However, as soon as an insight is revealed – that "Aha!" moment – our energy goes from inward to outwards and we pick up the walking pace again.

Insights energize us.

THE CONVERSATION FLOW OF THE CATHERINE WHEEL

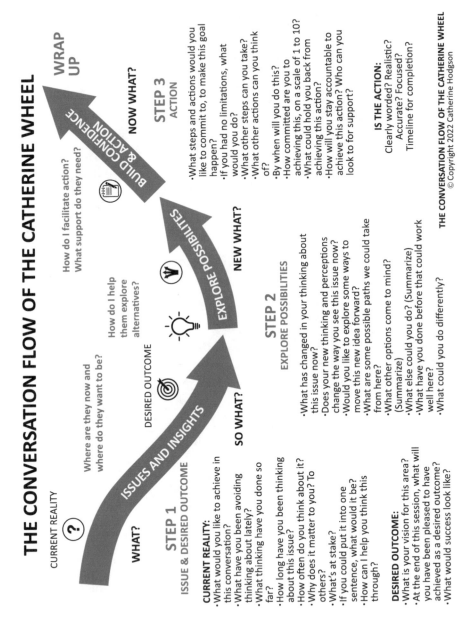

CURRENT REALITY

Where are they now and where do they want to be?

WHAT?

STEP 1
ISSUE & DESIRED OUTCOME

CURRENT REALITY:
- What would you like to achieve in this conversation?
- What have you been avoiding thinking about lately?
- What thinking have you done so far?
- How long have you been thinking about this issue?
- How often do you think about it?
- Why does it matter to you? To others?
- What's at stake?
- If you could put it into one sentence, what would it be?
- How can I help you think this through?

DESIRED OUTCOME:
- What is your vision for this area?
- At the end of this session, what will you have been pleased to have achieved as a desired outcome?
- What would success look like?

DESIRED OUTCOME

How do I help them explore alternatives?

SO WHAT?

STEP 2
EXPLORE POSSIBILITIES

- What has changed in your thinking about this issue now?
- Does your new thinking and perceptions change the way you see this issue now?
- Would you like to explore some ways to move this new idea forward?
- What are some possible paths we could take from here?
- What other options come to mind? (Summarize)
- What else could you do? (Summarize)
- What have you done before that could work well here?
- What could you do differently?

EXPLORE POSSIBILITIES

NEW WHAT?

How do I facilitate action?
What support do they need?

BUILD CONFIDENCE & ACTION

NOW WHAT?

STEP 3
ACTION

- What steps and actions would you like to commit to, to make this goal happen?
- If you had no limitations, what would you do?
- What other steps can you take?
- What other actions can you think of?
- By when will you do this?
- How committed are you to achieving this, on a scale of 1 to 10?
- What could hold you back from achieving this action?
- How will you stay accountable to achieve this action? Who can you look to for support?

IS THE ACTION:
Clearly worded? Realistic? Accurate? Focused?
Timeline for completion?

WRAP UP

THE CONVERSATION FLOW OF THE CATHERINE WHEEL
© Copyright 2022 Catherine Hodgson

Using the conversation flow, a person can generate their own insights by asking themselves the right questions. However, going through this process with someone else, such as your mentor, will help you generate insights quicker and may help spark new insights and thinking. A mentor will tend to push you further than you will push yourself in questioning your thinking.

Generating insights

Let's take a closer look at how to guide a person through the conversation flow model to help them generate insights.

One of the most exhilarating experiences you can have as a mentor is to see your mentee experience an insight. This is one of the ultimate goals in any mentoring relationship.

An insight is seeing something differently to how you saw it before. The capacity to gain an accurate and deep understanding of someone or something. A new path. A new way of thinking. It's like someone has revealed a whole new way of seeing something. Once you have seen it, it can never be unseen.

Insight can be defined as: "**(the ability to have) a clear, deep, and sometimes sudden understanding of a complicated problem or situation**", according to the *Cambridge Dictionary*.

It can often be experienced by a mentor as a sudden "awakening" of the mentee. Their eyes may widen, they may say "Aha!" or "Yes"! Think of "**Eureka!**", the famous exclamation attributed to Archimedes, when he is said to have jumped from his bath and run through the street naked after his insight into how to measure the volume of objects by submerging them in water.

You will pick up a shift in energy. An increase in energy. It could be a big insight, where your mentee is "awakened" to a whole new way of thinking, or it could be a smaller insight, but still an insight, nonetheless.

What is happening in the brain when this occurs? Only in the past decade have the powerful tools of cognitive neuroscience been applied to the problem. Tools such as the electroencephalogram (EEG) and functional magnetic resonance imaging (fMRI) are being used to unravel the neural mechanisms that underlie creative insights. Neuroscientist John Kounios and his colleague Mark Beeman developed a task that allowed them to study insight in the laboratory. They studied volunteers solving puzzles using an EEG and saw that their right temporal brain lit up when they "saw" how to solve it. However, before it lit up, there was a burst of high frequency activity in the right visual cortex. The same effect on the EEG can be achieved by simply closing one's eyes, which people often do during intense mental effort.

In a mentoring meeting, you as a mentor may observe your mentee looking up to one corner of the room, looking down or closing their eyes

– thinking over their issue and trying to solve it. I have observed people looking down or to the side with their eyes darting back and forth. My husband says that when I'm thinking, my eyes dart back and forth so much it makes him dizzy!

When you see this happening, be silent. Pause. Allow this thinking to happen. It may lead to an insight.

Why generate insights?

You may be wondering why it is so important for a mentor to help their mentee generate their own insights. Isn't it easier to just tell them what to do or share your own thoughts with them? Why can't you just give them some good old advice instead?

The reason you want your mentee to have their own insight is that they will take ownership of it. They need to go through the process of coming up with their own insight as that will be the best one for them. Once they have an insight and can see things in a different light, they can then move on and explore possible solutions for their issue. Having a mentor share their own ideas or give them advice too soon will stop the mentee's own thinking. The mentee must explore their own thinking first. They know the intricacies of their issue, the background, and the details. They therefore will probably come up with the best solution for themselves.

Is it time to shift gears?

Let's go back now and see how you can best support your mentee to have their own insight.

Your mentee may arrive at your mentoring meeting with an issue or dilemma that they need to deal with. Or you may be working with them and guiding them on ways to reach their next milestone towards their goal. Your job as a mentor is to listen first and then ask questions to prompt your mentee to do their own thinking.

Let's go back to the Conversation Flow Model.

Step 1: Issues and insights

What is your mentee's current reality?

As a mentor, ask yourself: "Where is your mentee now and where do they want to be?"

By listening to their issue first, you should be able to uncover what their current reality is. If not, then ask them. A few questions to help them would be:

- What is keeping you awake at night? What is on your mind?
- What would you like to achieve in this conversation?
- What would you like to talk about today to help you reach your next milestone?
- What have you been avoiding thinking about lately?
- What thinking have you done so far?
- How long have you been thinking about this issue?
- If you could put it into one sentence, what would that be?

THE CONVERSATION FLOW OF THE CATHERINE WHEEL

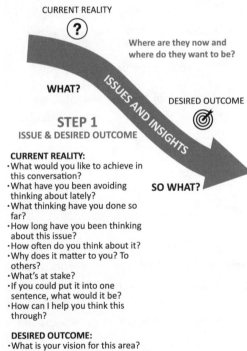

CURRENT REALITY

Where are they now and where do they want to be?

WHAT?

ISSUES AND INSIGHTS

DESIRED OUTCOME

STEP 1
ISSUE & DESIRED OUTCOME

SO WHAT?

CURRENT REALITY:
- What would you like to achieve in this conversation?
- What have you been avoiding thinking about lately?
- What thinking have you done so far?
- How long have you been thinking about this issue?
- How often do you think about it?
- Why does it matter to you? To others?
- What's at stake?
- If you could put it into one sentence, what would it be?
- How can I help you think this through?

DESIRED OUTCOME:
- What is your vision for this area?
- At the end of this session, what will you have been pleased to have achieved as a desired outcome?
- What would success look like?

THE CONVERSATION FLOW OF THE CATHERINE WHEEL
© Copyright 2022 Catherine Hodgson

It is crucial that you clarify what the issue is before you go ahead with the process. Ensure that your mentee can put the issue into one sentence, that you understand it, and that you can reflect it back to them. Sometimes, a mentee comes to the meeting with many issues. You will need to ask questions to clarify which one they would like to discuss in this meeting. You may ask, "I'm hearing that you have this issue and that issue. Which one would you like to focus on today?"

A significant chunk of time may be spent in this area. It is okay to spend time here to clarify the issue, as you don't want to go down a whole line of questioning about the wrong issue. This can waste valuable time.

A mentee may come to the session with a stated issue, but after you have explored if this is the issue they want to discuss today, you find that there is really another issue that may need to be discussed first.

Don't get bogged down here with too much detail. You may not need to know the intricate details of the issue. You only have so much time allocated, so use your time wisely. Stay a bit higher level rather than getting stuck in the details.

Importance of the issue

Find out what the implication of this issue is for them, their health, their relationships, their business, their family, their colleagues, or their career – whatever is important to them.

- Why does it matter to you?
- Why does it matter to others?
- What's at stake?
- What are the implications of not dealing with this issue?

It's important here that the mentee knows what the implications are of not dealing with this issue. This line of questioning also allows them to look at the bigger picture – "What is the implication for others?" Sometimes a mentee is so caught up with themselves and the issue that they don't realize the impact it has on others. Help them to see this.

Desired outcome

During this step, understand what your mentee wants to achieve in the mentoring session. What is the outcome they are striving for? Clarifying the outcome will give you direction on where the conversation needs to go and what questions you will need to ask. You will also be setting a goal for the mentoring session, so that you both feel that something has been achieved at the end of it. Ask questions such as:

- What is your desired outcome?
- What is your vision for this area?
- What do you want from me during this session today?
- At the end of this session, what will you have been pleased to have achieved as a desired outcome?

By listening, reflecting back what you are observing and hearing, summarizing, and asking questions, you will be helping your mentee do their own thinking. Allow for pauses, for silences. You do not need to fill in all the gaps in the conversation. During these quieter times, your mentee can do their own thinking and you are allowing them the space to do so. If you are firing questions one after the other, the mentee will not have much time to think. Allow for pauses and reflection.

Step 2: Explore possibilities

THE CONVERSATION FLOW OF THE CATHERINE WHEEL

NEW WHAT?

STEP 2
EXPLORE POSSIBILITIES

- What has changed in your thinking about this issue now?
- Does your new thinking and perceptions change the way you see this issue now?
- Would you like to explore some ways to move this new idea forward?
- What are some possible paths we could take from here?
- What other options come to mind? (Summarize)
- What else could you do? (Summarize)
- What have you done before that could work well here?
- What could you do differently?

The questioning that you have done until now, exploring your mentee's **current reality** and **desired outcome,** will have helped your mentee clarify their own thinking. Your mentee may not yet have come up with an insight. An insight may be big or small, but it is a new way of thinking and a new way of seeing something.

If your mentee does have an insight and you see the change in energy, harness it. What does this mean? As soon as they have had an insight, their energy will increase and there will usually be a plethora of new ideas. Start exploring the ideas with them. Make a laundry list of possibilities and ideas. This energy only lasts for a short period of time, so make the most of it to explore new ideas together.

Ask them questions such as:
• I noticed a shift in energy – can you tell me about it?
• Has any of your thinking now changed?
• Have you had any new thinking about this issue?
• Would you like to explore some ways to move this new idea forward?

If your mentee has not had any new insights, then help them explore possibilities by nudging them to do so.

• What are some possible paths we could take from here?
• Can you come up with a laundry list of ideas that come to mind? (A "laundry list" means that you are expecting them to push themselves beyond three ideas.)
• What other options come to mind? (Push them some more.)
• What else can you do? (Push them even more.)
• What have you done before that could work well here?
• What ideas would your wife/partner/boss/kids come up with for you?
• What could you do differently?

When new ideas are generated, **summarize** them at various points for your mentee. This will help them clarify their thinking. We need to summarize them to ensure that we have heard them correctly and for our mentee to hear them listed back. They may then alter those possibilities, or it may trigger new ideas for them.

This is also the time when you, as a mentor, can ask permission of your mentee to share your own ideas. For instance, you can ask, "Would this be a good time to share my own ideas with you?" or, "I had a similar experience in this area; would you like me to share it with you?" Only share your ideas or thoughts if they are going to be helpful to your mentee. Put your ego aside. This is not the time to tell long stories. Your thinking should help your mentee with their own ideas and thinking.

Step 3: Take action

Once you have walked through **Step 2** of **The Conversation Flow**, you should be armed with a list of possibilities.

As a mentor, you want to build your mentee's confidence and ensure they act. The questions you should ask yourself are, "How do I facilitate action? What support do they need?"

THE CONVERSATION FLOW OF THE CATHERINE WHEEL

How do I facilitate action?
What support do they need?

WRAP UP

BUILD CONFIDENCE & ACTION

NOW WHAT?

STEP 3
ACTION

•What steps and actions would you like to commit to, to make this goal happen?
•If you had no limitations, what would you do?
•What other steps can you take?
•What other actions can you think of?
•By when will you do this?
•How committed are you to achieving this, on a scale of 1 to 10?
•What could hold you back from achieving this action?
•How will you stay accountable to achieve this action? Who can you look to for support?

IS THE ACTION:
Clearly worded? Realistic?
Accurate? Focused?
Timeline for completion?

THE CONVERSATION FLOW OF THE CATHERINE WHEEL
© Copyright 2022 Catherine Hodgson

Harness their energy while it is up and get them to write out an action plan for themselves. Pin them down to specific actions by asking questions such as these:

- What steps and actions would you like to commit to, to make this goal happen?
- If you had no limitations, what would you do?
- What other steps can you take?
- What other actions can you think of?
- By when will you do this?
- What could hold you back from achieving this action?
- How will you stay accountable to achieve this action?
- Who can you look to for support?

On a scale of 1 to 10, ask them how committed they are to achieving this action. I have found that if it is below 8, the chances of them achieving it are slim. A score higher than 8 means they are committed to getting it done. If the list is very long, ask them to prioritize things so they are not overwhelmed and not able to achieve anything. Then ensure they put some action dates next to each action.

The last thing before wrapping up is asking your **mentee to summarize** their actions for you. Why do you need to do this? The mentee then takes ownership of their actions and the chances of them achieving them will increase.

You need to ask:

- Is the action clearly worded?
- Is the action realistic?
- Is the action accurate?
- Is the action focused?
- Is there a timeline for completion?

The mentee then walks away with a completed action plan to work on before your next meeting.

Practical example

This is a shortened conversation between a mentor and a mentee that demonstrates the workings of the Conversation Flow. The mentee is a general manager for a company in which she manages a team of 15 staff members. She has been paired with a mentor to help her with team-building and leadership skills.

Mentor: What would you like to bring to this session today?

Mentee: I want to discuss how to talk to my team so they will respect and listen to me.

Mentor: Where are you now with this issue and where would you like to be?

Mentee: Where I am now is that I feel I talk to them, but they don't listen to me, they often do exactly the opposite of what I asked them to do, and I feel that they don't respect me. They talk over me; they have conversations where I feel they are talking about me, and I don't know how to gain their respect. Where I would like to be is to be seen as a respected leader.

Mentor: What would you like from me during this session?

Mentee: I would like you to listen to me, share some of your ideas with me on how I can gain some respect, maybe share some of your own experiences with me and help me see any blind spots that I may have.

Mentor (*summarizes*): What I'm hearing is that you would like to gain more respect from your team. This would translate to them listening more to you. At the moment you do not feel respected by them, and you would like to be seen as a respected leader. You would like me to listen to you and for me to share some of my ideas and experiences with you. You are also inviting me, perhaps, to positively challenge you, so you become able to see some of your blind spots. Have I summed up everything?

Mentee: Yes, that sounds good. I know I may not get to where I want to get today, but I want to start working on this, even if it takes a while to reach my goal.

Mentor: Talking about goals, this fits into your goal of wanting to improve your leadership skills and building your team.

Mentee: Yes, it will help me with achieving my milestones that we set a few meetings ago.

Mentor: Are you ready to move on to the next section of unpacking this a bit more now? *[You are now making a segue from Step 1 of the Conversation Flow to Step 2, Exploring Possibilities, and asking permission of your mentee to move forward.]*

Mentee: Yes, I'm ready and excited.

Mentor: What thinking have you done so far in how you can gain more respect from your team so they will listen to you?

Mentee: Well, I may be a bit forceful some of the time. I always think that I know what they should do, and I tell them what to do.

Mentor: How do they react to you when you tell them what to do?

Mentee: They tend to turn away and not look at me. They don't show me any respect.

Mentor: How do you react if someone comes in and tells you forcefully what you should do?

Mentee: I don't like being told what to do. I prefer it when someone asks me questions.

Mentor: Do you ask your team questions before you tell them what to do?

Mentee: No, not usually. I know what they should do, so it's easier for me to just tell them.

Mentor: How do you think they would respond if you asked them what they thought rather than telling them what to do?

Mentee: They would probably be surprised – but they would probably like it. It may be good to try asking them what they would do, instead of me just telling them what to do. Then we could have more of a discussion about it.

Mentor: Who would take ownership of that, then?

Mentee: Well, I suppose they would. I guess that if they take ownership then they would do it and not feel like I have told them what to do. I never thought of that.

Mentor: What is your tone of voice when you tell people what to do?

Mentee: Often I am a bit aggressive, I suppose. I get irritated that they have not done something and that I have to tell them in the first place. So my tone is quite forceful.

Mentor: How would it feel for you to be spoken to by your boss in a forceful and aggressive tone?

Mentee: Oh, my boss never talks to me like that! In fact, I would be offended if he spoke to me like that! [*Mentee looks up to the corner of the room and smiles.*]

Mentor: I see that you have a smile on your face. Has anything changed in your thinking about this issue now?

Mentee: Yes, I see that I am approaching this in completely the wrong way. By talking to my team like this, I am not respecting them. So how can I expect them to respect me?

Mentor: What could you do differently?

Mentee: I think I need to change my whole attitude towards them. I need to see them as thinking human beings who can come up with their own ideas, rather than me thinking I need to think for them. I need to show them respect.

Mentor: How can you show them respect?

Mentee: I could listen to them. I could ask them questions.

Mentor: And what else could you do differently?

Mentee: I could change my tone of voice. I could be gentler, yet firm. I could remove my irritation and have a two-way conversation rather than a one-way monologue. I could show more interest in them.

Mentor: Anything else you can think of?

Mentee: No, that's all I can think of.

Mentor: Would this be a good time for me to share some of my ideas with you, as well as share a relevant story? [*Ask permission to do so.*]

Mentee: Yes, please do.

Mentor: … [*Shares his ideas and experience.*]

Mentor: Are you ready to move on and look at some actions you can take once you leave this session? [*You are asking permission to move to Step 3: Action.*]

Mentor: What steps and actions would you like to commit to after this session?

Mentee: I would like to take this new approach when I next think of telling my team what to do.

Mentor: What other steps can you take?

Mentee: I'm going to listen to my team more and ask them questions. In fact, in my individual meetings with the divisions, I am going to spend more time listening and asking them questions before sharing my own ideas.

Mentor: Anything else?

Mentee: Come to think of it, I never ask them how they are doing or ask them any questions about their families or what they are going to do on the weekend. I am going to start doing that.

Mentor: Those sound like wonderful ideas. By when will you do all this?

Mentee: Tomorrow I am going to go around and ask them all how they are doing and a question or two about their families. By next week I will have had all my division meetings, so I will listen to them and ask questions in those meetings, and then share my ideas with them. By our next meeting in a month, I hope to have had individual meetings with everyone and to have practised this new approach.

Mentor: Is there anything that could hold you back from doing this?

Mentee: Only my head and ego. But I think I can put my ego aside and get out of my head and into my heart.

Mentor: It sounds like you are committed to this. Do you need any other support?

Mentee: If you have any articles or TED Talks that you think are relevant to this topic, then please send them through to me. I know that I have a lot to learn.

Mentor: I will send you some articles I have that I think you may find useful. Can you sum up your action plan for me, then, so we are both on the same page?

Mentee: … [*Sums up action plan.*]

Mentor: On a scale of 1 to 10, how likely are you to do these actions?

Mentee: 10 out of 10. I will do them.

Mentor: That's real commitment, I'm so excited that you are doing this and believe it will transform the way you lead. Let's wrap up then if you are ready to do so.

[*They wrap up the meeting.*]

As you can see from the conversation, a lot can be achieved very quickly without getting into all the details. As a mentor, you do not need to know all the details in order to nudge your mentee along the Conversation Flow. You do not need to ask too many questions. You let your mentee talk and come up with their own solutions. The most important thing as a mentor is to listen, nudge, ask questions, reflect back what you've heard, summarize, and let your mentee come up with their own actions.

This seems very easy in theory, but often it is not as clear as this. Sometimes your mentee may find it difficult to clarify their issue, or they also may not be able to come up with possibilities. However, having a framework gives you a general idea of what you should be covering and how to nudge your mentee along.

Steps to being more insightful

1. Spend time in reflective space.
2. Define the issue and desired outcome.
3. As a mentor, listen with curiosity.
4. Ask more thought-provoking questions.
5. Allow for pauses and don't be afraid of silence.
6. Harness the energy once an insight has been experienced.
7. Look beyond the obvious (explore possibilities).
8. Let your mentee do their own thinking before asking permission to share your ideas.
9. Don't be afraid to reframe the problem.
10. Move to action and let the mentee take ownership.

Key takeaways:

- ✓ There are three steps to the Conversation Flow. Step 1: Issue and desired outcome; Step 2: Explore possibilities; Step 3: Action.
- ✓ The mentor summarizes after Step 1 to ensure they understand the issue before moving to Step 2.
- ✓ The mentee summarizes after Step 3 to take ownership of their action plan.

19

WRAPPING UP THE CONVERSATION

How to end a mentoring session

Let your mentee know that the session is coming to an end. Ensure that you make it an exciting exit and your mentee is walking away feeling energized.

You can say to your mentee, "We are now going to complete the session. I will go first…"

WRAP UP & NEXT

·Values aligned with decisions
·Further thinking
·Align with goals
·Appreciation
·Next meeting

TRUST
RESPECT
CONFIDENTIALITY
HONESTY

THE CATHERINE WHEEL
MENTORING MODEL
© Copyright 2017 Catherine Hodgson

Then be authentic and specific with completing. Don't go into too much detail, just a couple of sentences. For instance: "I'm really excited about the actions you have set for yourself and are going to take away with you. I think these will help to move you towards your goal. Is there anything you would now like to say to complete this session?" (The mentee will then probably mirror you and complete on their part.)

This next exercise can be done at the end of each session.

Worksheet 10: W.R.A.P. exercise

If you are on a virtual call, share your screen with your mentee and show them the acronym W.R.A.P. You answer the questions one by one, and your mentee then does the same.

- WHAT CONCERNS have surfaced or remain?
- Is there anything that was RESOLVED after our session today?
- Has there been a new AWARENESS after our session today?
- What do you PLAN to do as a result of today?

Worksheet 11: L.E.A.R.N. exercise

The L.E.A.R.N. acronym may also be suitable.

L. What has been your biggest LEARNING today?
E. What are you most EXCITED about?
A. What are you most ANXIOUS about?
R. What RESONATED with you today?
N. Is there anything that you still NEED?

Close with appreciation

It's very easy to say a quick thank you and rush off to your next meeting after your mentoring session. But don't exit before you have done a proper appreciation. Make it sincere and thoughtful. Let the other person know what you especially appreciated from the session.

For instance, as a mentee you might say, "The story that you shared with me about your experience in the area that I was struggling with was very helpful. It made me see my situation in a different light and has given me food for thought. Thank you for sharing that with me."

How do you think your mentor would feel about that appreciation? Pretty good, I'm sure!

As a mentor, you might say, "Thank you for sharing your challenge with me. I'm sure that was difficult for you, and I appreciate you being so open with me and trusting me with your story."

Lastly, ensure that you have the next meeting set up before you say your goodbyes.

Many people ask me if the mentee should share with the mentor a list of their actions by email after the session. It really is up to both of you to decide whether you want to do that. If the mentee has them written down and the mentor has made a note of them, it is not necessary.

This is how one would use the Conversation Flow of the Catherine Wheel while going through the meeting agenda:

Key takeaways:

✓ Ensure your meetings end with a definite wrap up. Use your own exercise or one of the exercises in this chapter.
✓ Be sincere and authentic when you appreciate each other.
✓ Ensure you have a date for your next session before you leave.

 **MEETING AGENDA 3**

Regular Mentoring Meeting Agenda using The Conversation Flow
(60 minutes)

Mentoring Meeting Agenda

1. UPDATE: (10 MINUTES)
• Check in • What has gone well for you since our last conversation? • What successes have you had? • What achievements have you had? • What issues remain from the last meeting? Admin • When will we close this meeting today? • Can we remind each other about our agreement for engagement and the confidentiality?
2. ISSUES AND INSIGHTS: (20 MINUTES)
CURRENT REALITY • Where would you like to focus this session today? • What would you like to work on today? • What would you like to achieve from this conversation? • What would you like to build on from the last session? • What have you been avoiding thinking about lately? • What thinking have you done so far? • Can you put it into one sentence? • How can I help you think this through? DESIRED OUTCOME • What is your vision for this area? • How does it fit into your overall goals? • At the end of this session, what would you have been pleased to have achieved? • What is your desired outcome? • What do you want to happen? Why? THE MENTOR SUMMARIZES • Summarize the key issue and the desired outcome.

3. EXPLORE POSSIBILITIES: (15 MINUTES)
• Would you like to explore some ways to move this new idea forward? • How do you think we might move this insight forward? • What are some possible paths we could take from here? • What other options come to mind? (Summarize) • What else could you do? (Summarize) • What have you done before that could work well here? • What could you do differently? MENTOR SHARING: • Mentor can now offer to share experiences, wisdom and offer suggestions if asked. • Would you find value in listening to some possibilities that I've thought of? • Would you like me to share some of my own experiences with you around this issue? • Which questions would you like to ask me to assist you?

4. BUILD CONFIDENCE AND ACTION: (10 MINUTES)
• What steps and actions would you like to commit to, to make this goal happen? • What other steps can you take? • What other actions can you think of? • By when will you do this? • How committed are you to achieve this on a scale of 1 to 10? • What could hold you back from achieving this action? • How will you stay accountable to achieve this action? • Is the action clearly worded? Realistic? Accurate? Focused? Does it have a timeline for completion? • Summarize the actions written down.

5. WRAP UP AND NEXT: (5 MINUTES)
• Is the action aligned to the person's goals and values? • Any further thinking? • What issues have surfaced or still remain? • What insights have you had? • What ideas are you taking away? • What intentions do you have as a result of today? • When will we meet again? Date, time, place

6. APPRECIATION
Appreciate each other sincerely and graciously.

PART 3: KEY MENTORING SKILLS

We have covered the nuts and bolts of what mentoring is; how to be a mentor and mentee and get the most out of your mentoring journey; how to follow a structure; how to build rapport and trust in your relationship; how to set goals; as well as how to have a mentoring conversation.

We are now going to move onto some key mentoring skills that you need for your mentoring conversations.

20

THE TOP SEVEN MENTORING SKILLS

These skills are familiar to all of you but might not be top of mind when it comes to having a conversation.

There are seven main mentoring skills that you require to get the most out of your conversations. I know that it is impossible to work on all of them all the time. It takes time to develop and become proficient at them. But read about all of them and then, during each session, work on **one of them**. Go into your mentoring session focused on honing one of the skills and slowly build up your muscle for each of them. I do believe that these skills can be learnt – with practice, you can become extremely good at them. You just need to be conscious of putting them into practice.

We will also look at where these skills are most important in the Catherine Wheel – what skills are most needed and when.

Conversations are the one thing that we have almost every day. I find it amazing that many of us were not taught conversation skills at school or college. It is one of the most important and fundamental abilities that everyone should be taught from a very young age.

These key skills will stand you in good stead, not only in your mentoring relationships, but in your personal and professional lives as well. So many participants of my Mentoring Masterclasses say at the close of the workshop that they are going to use these skills in their conversations with their spouses or children. Many realize that they are not very good at some of these skills and, with some polishing and keeping them top of mind, they can transform their conversations at home and at work.

Top seven mentoring skills

We are going to go through these seven key mentoring skills: **listening, reflecting, summarizing, questioning, feedback, advice, and storytelling.**

First, though, on a scale of 1 to 10, how good/proficient do you think you are at each of these skills?

TOP 7 MENTORING SKILLS

TOP 7 MENTORING SKILLS
©Copyright 2022 Catherine Hodgson

Worksheet 12: Key mentoring skills proficiency

Don't skip this! Do this exercise now on a piece of paper. Put a tick next to each statement that you feel reflects your skill.

Listening:
- I find it hard to just sit and listen – my mind keeps wandering.
- I listen but I'm also listening to another conversation next to me.
- I listen but find that I wait for a pause so I can share my story with the other person too.
- I listen without interrupting at all and notice people's body language as well.
- I find it easy to listen and people often tell me I'm a good listener.

Reflecting:
- I never reflect back to people what I hear or see.
- I sometimes reflect back to the other person.
- I find myself often reflecting back what I hear or see.

Summarizing:
- I never summarize after I have heard what the other person has said.
- I sometimes summarize what I have heard.
- I always summarize what I have heard to make sure I understand what the other person is saying.

Questioning:
- I hardly ever ask questions.
- I find it difficult to ask questions, unsure of what to ask next.

- I sometimes ask questions when I feel the need to.
- I'm very curious and ask questions all the time.

Feedback:
- I never give feedback and find it very difficult to do so.
- I give feedback but feel uncomfortable doing so.
- I give feedback all the time.
- I don't like receiving feedback.
- I don't mind receiving feedback.
- I see feedback as a learning opportunity.

Advice:
- I always tell people what to do and love giving advice.
- I sometimes tell people what to do.
- I hold back on telling people what to do and rather ask questions.
- Giving advice makes me feel good.

Sharing experience:
- I don't like sharing my experience with others. I'm a private person.
- I don't mind sharing my experience with others.
- I love sharing my experience with others.
- I never ask permission to share my experience with others – I just do it.
- I always ask permission to share my experience with others.

Keep a record of your answers. Do this exercise again at the end of Part 3.

21

MINDFUL LISTENING

Being able to listen seems like a skill we all have, but what most hits home for people in the Mentoring Masterclasses I facilitate is that it's the one skill that we are usually not very good at. Developing good listening skills makes a fundamental difference in your relationships. You may know the saying, "We have two ears and one mouth, so that we can listen twice as much as we speak." It certainly applies to mentoring.

I would say that **listening is the most important mentoring skill of all**. Being a good listener can transform your relationships forever.

How do we become better listeners?

To truly listen is to be completely present. Yes, it's that mindfulness word again. But it's true – just ask your significant other! How many times have you been at a cocktail party and the person you are talking to is looking over your shoulder to see whom they are going to talk to next? How does that make you feel? To give someone your undivided attention is to show that person your utmost respect – you are giving them a beautiful gift of your attention.

It's not about listening to ask the next question. It's not about listening while waiting to speak so you can quickly also share your experience, without considering if it's relevant or not. It's not about listening and then finishing the other person's sentence for them because you think you know what they are going to say. It's not about listening with the focus on yourself and not on the person you are listening to.

Steven Covey said that most people do not listen with the intent to understand, they listen with the intent to reply.

Is that what you do too?

Listening is a completely selfless experience.

To listen beautifully is to be completely selfless. It's not about you. It's not your story. It's removing your feelings, criticisms, prejudices, judgments, experiences, and thoughts from the table – for now. It's all about putting the focus on the other person. Listening without intent, listening to understand what the other person is really trying to say, listening to what they are not saying – looking at body language, tone, and incongruencies. *That* is truly listening.

Once you have made eye contact, relax and be yourself. You don't need to stare your conversation partner to death, making them feel intimidated. Just relax into it and be normal. Try to remain attentive. What does this mean? The definition of "to attend" is to be present, give attention, apply or direct yourself, pay attention, remain ready to serve.

We need to screen out any distractions such as background noise and activity. Put your own thoughts aside, your own feelings, judgments, or biases.

To practise being good at listening, imagine a spotlight on a stage. Now imagine that spotlight is taken off you and is shining on the person with whom you are having a conversation – the spotlight is firmly on them. This is the way to listen. The focus should be on the other person who is speaking, without you thinking about your own issues, making your own judgments, and forming questions in your own head. It is listening with your whole being – your head, heart, and gut. You are focusing on the other person and being wholly present. I know this takes a lot of practice as we are accustomed to go inside our own head and start formulating opinions and questions, switching off our listening, and often missing a whole part of what the other person is saying.

In her book *Conversational Intelligence*, and having analysed research in neuroscience, Judith Glaser says that we go "inwards" every 12–20 seconds to process the information being fed to us, reaching for our own memories and stories. This is natural and we cannot stop it. However, what we can stop is being caught up inside our head for more than a few seconds and not popping out again. Have you ever been to a dinner party and being so caught up in your own head that you miss a minute or two of someone telling you a joke, only to find everyone around you laughing while you missed the punchline? Pop out. Don't get caught inside your head. Really focus on being present.

Be their thinking partner

In her book *Time to Think*, Nancy Kline says that we can improve the quality of another person's thinking by giving them the quality of our attention. This is powerful stuff. Just imagine... the more attention you give another person, and the better you listen to them, the more you will help improve their thinking. Imagine listening to your mentoring partner in this way – giving them the space to do their own thinking.

Nancy Kline also talks about creating the right climate for the other person to think well – she calls this the 10 components of a thinking environment: attention, equality, ease, appreciation, encouragement, information, feelings, diversity, incisive questions, and place. If we are aware of all these 10 components during our conversations, then we will help facilitate better thinking in the other person.

1. **Attention.** Listen with respect, interest, and fascination.
2. **Equality.** Treat each other as thinking peers. Give equal turns and attention.
3. **Ease.** Give the other person a sense that you have time for them.
4. **Appreciation.** Practise a 5:1 ratio of appreciation to criticism.
5. **Encouragement.** Do not compete with them for airtime.
6. **Feelings.** Allow sufficient emotional release to restore thinking.
7. **Diversity.** Use difference as a positive factor.
8. **Incisive questions.** Remove assumptions that limit ideas.
9. **Place.** Create a physical environment that says, "You matter."
10. **Information.** Enquire sufficiently to understand the issue from the other person's perspective.

Putting listening into practice

I was in the kitchen one evening, preparing dinner, when my daughter came to me crying that she had just had a big argument with her boyfriend. Usually, my first reaction would have been to give her a hug and then tell her exactly what she should say or do. However, that day I had just attended a Nancy Kline workshop on thinking and listening skills. I therefore changed my default behaviour and decided to test what I had just learnt from Nancy that day.

I sat down on the couch, faced her, looked into her eyes, and asked my daughter to tell me all about it, giving her my undivided attention. When she finished, I gently said, "Tell me more" and out came a whole lot more! After repeating that same sentence a few times, not saying anything in-between except nodding and listening, my daughter came up with her own solution on what to do. She drove to the boyfriend's house to go and talk to him in person.

An hour or so later she was home and came straight back into the kitchen, where she gave me a big hug and said, "Mom, thank you for just listening to me." I had not come up with any solutions and not told her what to do – she did not need that. All I did was give her my utmost attention.

Why not try this with your loved ones at home? Next time your child, spouse, or partner comes to you with something that demands your attention, don't default to your usual way of maybe not really listening to them, or offering them advice. Take the time to focus on them, give them your undivided attention. Show them that you care and that you are genuinely interested in what they are telling you. Listen with your whole being. Then see what happens… magic!

The five steps to mindful listening

As a mentor, you can develop your listening skills – just like building a muscle, it takes practice. You may be a very poor listener, but being aware of your listening ability opens up the opportunity for you to improve it. I'm going to introduce you to a powerful model showing you different levels of listening. In my experience, people can relate to this way of looking at how they listen, and they can then set their intentions to listen better in the future. This model sheds light on our listening skills.

Before we go through these steps, I would like you to reflect, right now, on how you usually llisten to others when you are one-to-one. Answer these questions: Do you regard yourself as a good listener? How strong is this skill for you? Are you open to improve your listening skills?

When you read through the following steps, keep in mind if any of these relate to you. Think of the situations you find yourself in, or with whom you are having these conversations.

Step 1: Disruptive listening

This listening is highly selective, with the listener identifying words, phrases and ideas that can be seized upon and used against the person talking. The person listening is not really listening. They may be listening to disagree. You are familiar with people who always want to argue or be "the devil's advocate?" They may interrupt you, finish your sentences or talk over you. Sound familiar?

Be very aware if you are prone to interrupting people who are speaking. Interrupting sends a variety of messages to the other person. It could be interpreted as saying:

- "I'm more important than you are."
- "What I have to say is more interesting, accurate, or relevant."
- "I don't really care what you think."
- "I don't have time for your opinion."
- "This isn't a conversation, it's a contest, and I'm going to win."

Finishing another person's sentences can also trigger the other person. Don't be a sentence-grabber! If the other person is speaking slowly and your brain is racing ahead, you may be tempted to speed them up by finishing their sentence for them. By doing this, you are assuming where the other person wants to go, instead of waiting to see where they want to go. If I find myself wanting to do this, I often stop myself and hold the word or end of the sentence that I was going to say, and then see what word they actually choose. More often than not, it's a completely different word than I would have chosen. So hold off and let the other person finish their own sentences themselves.

THE FIVE STEPS OF LISTENING

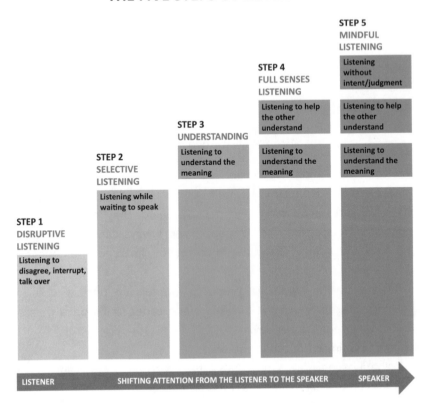

Step 2: Selective listening

This is when the listener is listening but waiting for their own chance to speak. The listener seems to be listening but in reality is thinking about the next question to ask or a story that they can tell, without fully listening to the other person. The listener hears what they want to hear, picking up a few words, and then hooks onto a story that they cannot wait to tell the other person about. As soon as the person finishes speaking, they hop in and tell their own story – not even thinking how this may sound to the other person. They have now hijacked the conversation, putting the focus on themselves rather than the other person.

Imagine someone asked you about your vacation and as you are telling them about it, you pause and the other person jumped in to tell you all about their vacation, which wasn't even related to yours. How would that make you feel?

Step 3: Understanding

This is listening to understand the meaning of what the person is saying. This level of listening involves the listener trying to understand what the speaker is saying and the meaning of the words. We may think that this should be the goal of listening – to understand what they are saying. However, we are still only focusing on the words that are being said.

In these three steps above, the focus is mostly on the listener and not on the speaker. If you can picture two people on a stage with a spotlight focused on the listener rather than the speaker, this is what you would see for steps 1, 2 and 3.

We now move to step 4. If you can, imagine the spotlight moving from the listener to the speaker, so that the speaker is now in the spotlight. This is what happens in steps 4 and 5 of listening: the focus shifts from the listener to the speaker.

Step 4: Full senses listening

This step involves understanding the meaning of what the speaker is saying, but also listening beyond the mere words. We are listening to what they are saying, the emotion behind their words, their tone of voice, their body language, their facial expressions, and what they are *not* saying. This shifts the attention from us to the speaker. This level of listening helps another person become more aware of their own thinking process, the meaning they attach to their words, and the emotions that colour their perceptions.

When we speak to someone on a virtual call without a camera on, we can tell a lot about how the person is feeling by the tone and cadence of their voice. Face to face with a person, we can detect a variety of emotions from a person by their body language and facial expressions. You can notice enthusiasm, boredom, irritation, or joy very quickly by noticing the expression around their eyes, the set of their mouth, the slope of their shoulders or the frown on their forehead. You can't ignore these clues. When listening, remember that words convey only a small fraction of the message a person is telling you.

Step 5: Mindful listening

This level involves understanding the meaning of what they are saying, their emotions, the tone of their voice, body language, and facial expressions plus **listening without intent or judgment. The listener has removed their ego. They are not focusing on or even thinking about where the conversation is going.** They are listening at such a level that the person who is speaking has the conversation that they really need to have with themselves. The listener is confident that the question will come to them when it is needed. It is being comfortable with silence... even long, awkward silences.

Most people's default listening level is at step 1, 2 or 3. Very few of us listen at step 4 or 5 unless we consciously think about listening at this level, or we have had lots of training on how to listen well, or we are a qualified coach or seasoned mentor. However, I believe that listening can be learnt and improved on. Once we become conscious of it, we can become much better listeners. We just need to be intentional about listening mindfully.

Worksheet 13: Five steps to mindful listening

Exercise: Look at the five steps to mindful listening. Ask yourself the following questions and write them down:

Which step do you currently listen at? Where is your default listening?

_____

What listening step would you like to listen at?

_____

What can you do to listen at a higher listening level?

_____

Which person or people do you struggle to listen to?

_____

What can you do to listen to them at a higher level?

_____

Silence does not need to be filled

One day I met my mentor for our regular meeting. After we had said hello and sat down, without me saying a word, he had picked up that I was stressed and tense. Once he had acknowledged his feeling about me, he sat in silence and waited for me to speak. The silence did not need to be filled. I was able to gather my thoughts without fear of being interrupted and be completely open in our subsequent conversation. He opened the door and then allowed me to speak by giving me his undivided attention.

Giving your mentee your undivided attention, without interruption, allows them to think more deeply, to open up more confidently, and to expose more than they otherwise would have exposed. A mentor needs to remove his own ego to be fully open to listening to his mentee. Only once the listening is done can the questioning begin.

Giving space

During my mentoring sessions, when I got to a place where I felt stuck or could not answer a question, my mentor would often say that he just needed to pop to the bathroom, and he wanted me to carry on thinking about the question or issue. He did this often and I'm not sure if it was because of the numerous cappuccinos we drank during our session, a weak bladder, or if he was giving me time to think without feeling pressured. It really did help, whatever the reason.

To just step away, giving your mentee space and time to think, is helpful and takes the pressure off the mentee.

Tips for listening well

Show your mentoring partner that you are listening well by doing the following:
1. Be intentional about listening.
2. Maintain eye contact. Look at them in the eyes, if your culture allows you to do so and you feel comfortable. You do not need to stare at them non-stop, just be normal.
3. Don't fidget or furiously write notes.
4. Put your phone off or on silent and put it out of sight.

5.   Look interested and think about being curious.
6.   Clear your mind of your own thinking and remove the incessant inner dialogue.
7.   Put all judgment aside.
8.   Try not to interrupt them, finish their sentences, or talk over them.
9.   Be okay with silence.
10. Keep your great advice to yourself for now.
11. Keep an open mind.
12. Find an anchor for yourself to come back to when you find your mind wandering. Use your breathe to do so or find something else to come back to.

What does poor listening look like?

Poor listening skills might include: looking at your watch or phone, interrupting the other person, avoiding eye contact, looking bored or impatient, tapping your foot or fidgeting, or finishing their sentences.

Listening in the Catherine Wheel Mentoring Model

In **the Conversation** wheel of the Catherine Wheel, where should we be listening the most? All the way through! For the mentor, they should be listening 80% of the time and talking 20% of the time. One of the biggest cause of breakdowns of a mentoring relationship is the mentor talking too much! Both parties should be aware of their listening skills throughout their conversation.

Key takeaways:

✓ Listening is the most important mentoring skill.
✓ Listening can be learnt and improved on. We can all learn to become mindful listeners.
✓ Be your conversation partner's thinking partner.

22

REFLECTING
AND SUMMARIZING

You may have started with listening as the first skill to work on. You will now move on to working on reflecting and summarizing as the next two key skills to improve.

Reflecting

Reflecting is a skill that we often forget to use as it does not come naturally to most of us. To reflect, we need to either use the same words (paraphrasing) or use our own words, but ensure the words we use are what we are hearing. You may ask why we need to do this. It shows that we are listening to the other person and trying to understand what they are saying.

Remember that **understanding resides with the listener until it is reflected back to the speaker.**

Reflecting is about reflecting the words your partner is saying, but also the things that you are noticing. Let's start with how to reflect the words. Listen to key words they are saying, or reflect back the last few words of their sentence:

"So what you're saying is..."

"What I'm hearing is…"
"It sounds like…"
"Here's what I'm hearing you say…"

Be aware of using your own words – your reflection must not sound judgmental, and it may not be what they are meaning. Try to use their own words when reflecting.

For example, the person may have said, "I'm upset because she did not let me know about her decision." You may have reflected, "It sounds like you are disappointed that she didn't tell you." By changing "upset" to "disappointed", it may come across as being judgmental. It may be better to just reflect, "So what I'm hearing is that you are upset she didn't tell you."

Then also reflect what you are noticing, seeing, and feeling. Reflect emotions to help the other person see their thinking. Emotions usually indicate that something else needs to be said. Ask yourself, "What emotions are they expressing? When do their emotions shift? What values, desires, fears are fuelling their emotions?" Reflect what you see.

"I noticed… I heard… I sense…"

Be aware of what you are observing and what it could mean to them. Notice the following:
- Tears (You can ask, "What are those tears telling you?")
- Nervous laughter
- Looking away
- Inserting "But" into an agreement
- Defensiveness
- Hesitation ("What are you afraid to say or avoiding saying?")
- Offer **observations** when they deflect, hesitate, or show resistance
- Notice **energy and emotional shifts**, tone of voice, pace of speech, inflection, and body language
- Notice any incongruence in what they are saying and the emotion you are seeing them display

Many people are not aware of, or in tune with, their emotions. Pointing out emotions is a way of making people more self-aware and it can often lead to an insight.

If you say, "I noticed that you looked down and seemed sad when you talked about that person", this could make the person aware that they felt an emotional attachment to that person that they were not aware of. "I noticed that every time you talk about that person you frown, and your mouth tends to tense up". Reflecting can lead to insight for the other person.

However, be aware of not getting attached to their emotion. As a mentor, we cannot take on their emotion as well. We can be empathetic, but taking on the emotion is not helpful to your mentee. Not taking on their emotion is called **non-reactive empathy**. As a mentor, you need to breathe in and let go.

Reflecting may feel strange to do at first, but with practice, it will become a habit and start to feel more natural. For the speaker, it is like playing a video back to them. We can really see ourselves in another person's eyes.

Summarizing

At some point in the conversation, the listener needs to summarize what they have heard. This is a crucial step, and it is important for you as a mentor to develop this skill. Summarizing allows you both to step back from the conversation and review what has been covered so far. It also allows you both to check your understanding of the issue.

As a listener, you need to summarize so that you ensure that you have understood the story or the issue correctly, before moving on to questioning. This also reassures the speaker that you have been listening. This may also be the time when the speaker can correct you if you did not understand exactly what they were saying to you.

Summarizing does not necessarily serve to condense what has been said so far, but rather serves to put a pause in the conversation so you can check in with each other and ensure you are both on the same page.

So how do you summarize?

Do not interrupt the other person. Choose the correct time to summarize when there may be a need to consolidate both of your thinking, or the mentee's thinking, thus far. "What have we learnt so far?"

Ask for permission, such as, "Is now a good time for me to summarize what I have heard?"

Summarize what was actually said, any emotion you felt from the mentee, as well as where you are going, the outcome.

When you summarize, you are using your own words and shortening the story that you have heard, highlighting the key points.

The conversation flow and when to summarize

There are key times in the conversation when the mentor and mentee need to summarize.

When does the mentor summarize? The mentor should summarize after step 1, before transitioning to step 2. The mentee would have discussed what they would like to talk about in the mentoring meeting, if there is an issue to discuss, or perhaps ways to move forward towards their next milestone. The mentor would have asked questions to clarify anything they need to understand and ensure that the mentee has had the time to talk through their issue. The mentor then summarizes what they have heard, to ensure they have heard correctly before moving to the next step of exploring possibilities.

THE CONVERSATION FLOW OF THE CATHERINE WHEEL

CURRENT REALITY

?

ISSUES AND INSIGHTS

DESIRED OUTCOME

EXPLORE POSSIBILITES

BUILD CONFIDENCE & ACTION

WRAP UP

STEP 1
ISSUE & DESIRED OUTCOME
Where are they now and where do they want to be?

STEP 2
EXPLORE POSSIBILITIES
How do I help them explore alternatives?

STEP 3
ACTION
How do I facilitate action? What support do they need?

CURRENT REALITY:
What would you like to achieve in this conversation?
DESIRED OUTCOME:
What is your vision for this area?

What are some possible paths we could take from here?
How can we reframe this?

What steps and actions would you like to commit to, to make this goal happen?

WHO DOES WHAT?
Mentee talks through issue.
Mentor listens, reflects, asks clarifying questions.
Mentor summarizes.

WHO DOES WHAT?
Mentor asks open questions to facilitate insight.
Mentee explores options.
Mentor shares experience, own thinking, further options and stories.

WHO DOES WHAT?
Mentee comes up with action plan.
Mentor adds further thinking.
Mentee summarizes action to be taken.

THE CONVERSATION FLOW OF THE CATHERINE WHEEL
© Copyright 2022 Catherine Hodgson

A mentor may find that after they have summarized, the mentee says, "No, that is not what I mean." It's important that you are both clear about what the issue or topic for discussion is before you move ahead into looking for possibilities.

When does the mentee summarize? At the end of step 3, the mentee should summarize the actions that they are committing to follow through with before the next meeting. Why do they do this? So that they take responsibility for their action plan. If the mentor comes up with the action plan, the chance of the mentee taking ownership is low.

Reflecting with questioning

I discussed reflecting and summarizing as part of active listening. If we take this one step further, out of this reflection a question will arise. John Dewey's work in 1910 referred to this, and many other coaches have built on it since then.

Marcia Reynolds, in her book *The Discomfort Zone*, says that we all need an external disruptor to prompt us to take out and evaluate our stories.

We all carry stories in our heads that we believe are true. These are often referred to as the movies of our mind. To really evaluate and look at these stories, we need an external disruptor, such as a mentor or a coach to help us do this. It is very difficult to do this on our own.

As a mentor, you are an external disruptor for your mentee, to help them see the stories that they have created in their mind.

By using reflective statements, you help a mentee see the stories they have created. Reflective statements include summarizing, paraphrasing, acknowledging key points and phrases, and sharing what emotions and shifts they express.

When we use reflective statements, people hear their words, see how their beliefs form their perceptions, and face the emotions they are expressing. Then we follow up with a **confirming question** ("Is this true?") or an **exploratory question** (starting with Who, What, When, or How) to help the person dissect their thoughts. This prompts them to stop and examine their thinking.

A person may be having difficulty speaking to their boss about an issue they are experiencing. They say that their boss would think they were stupid if they took the issue to him. It may show that they are incompetent.

Reflect these words: "What I'm hearing is that you think your boss would see you as stupid and incompetent if you took this issue to him."

Your mentee may confirm this or say, "No, what I meant is that I don't think I can speak to him about these issues as our relationship isn't open enough."

You also notice that they look down, or they have a small tear in their eye. Reflect what you see: "I see that talking about this is upsetting you as you looked down and it seems to be causing you some emotion."

They may say: "I'm actually feeling sad that we don't have the relationship that I hoped we would have, which is open and honest."

You say, "Is this true that you cannot take this issue to your boss because your relationship is not open and honest, rather than that you would think your boss thought you were stupid and incompetent?"

They may say: "Yes, it's true – it's occurred to me that we need to build trust in our relationship."

Voila! The mentee has now gone from seeing their issue as being that they cannot take their problems to their boss because their boss thinks they are stupid, to realizing that the relationship needs to be built and trust needs to be established for it to be more open and honest. This was done just by reflecting to them their words as well as what emotions you saw, as well as asking them a simple question.

Reflecting with questioning

Notice and use key descriptor words to reflect back to them.
Recap and encapsulate their perceived challenges and desired outcome.

Reflect what you are seeing, hearing, noticing and sensing.

Help them see their stories - by holding up the mirror to them.

Follow with a confirming and or exploratory question relating to your reflection. "Is this true?" "What, how..."

If you notice an insight, ask then to articulate it. "What is emerging for you now?"

"So you are saying..." "You got quiet (or loud) when..." "There seems to be something behind your hesitation..."

MY STORIES

?

Grab some sticky notes or a piece of paper and do this exercise now!

Worksheet 14: Skills to practise in your conversations

Go through the set of verbs below. Which skills do you need to improve in your conversations? Write each one down on a separate piece of paper or sticky note. For example, you may decide that being present, listening, asking, and empathizing are four key focus areas that you need to improve. Write each of these on a separate piece of paper or sticky note.

- Accept, don't judge
- Be present
- Listen
- Reflect
- Clarify
- Summarize

- Ask
- Empathize
- Share

In your next conversation, focus particularly on that one area that you wrote down. If you have genuinely achieved it, then put that sticky paper to one side and for your next conversation, focus on another area that you have written down. If you did not manage to achieve it, then focus on that skill again for your next conversation.

Commit to putting those sticky notes somewhere visible so they are a reminder for you to continue to focus on building these skills.

Key takeaways:

✓ Understanding resides with the listener until it is reflected back to the speaker.
✓ Reflect what you hear, see, and feel.
✓ Summarizing helps the other person feel understood and ensures you understand what they are saying.

23

DEVELOPING CRITICAL QUESTIONING SKILLS

The fourth critical mentoring skill is how to ask questions. This is often a skill that people feel uncomfortable with. Mentors often fret over which question to ask next that they stop listening and then fail to ask the right question. I want to take all the pressure off you. If you are just fully present and listen well, following that up with reflecting and summarizing, you will soon see that the questions will come easily to you.

I will take you through a list of questioning techniques and you can then start working on each of them, moving down the list as you get more skilled at them. You will find that you require different techniques in different circumstances. Just play around with them. They include the following:

Types of questions:
- Open vs closed questions
- Narrow vs broad questions
- Leading questions

Questioning techniques:
- Probing questions
- Challenging questions
- Powerful questions
- Unlocking questions
- Pause questions
- Never-fail questions

Why do we become less curious as we grow older?

Some studies suggest four-year-olds ask 200 to 300 questions a day. Warren Berger, author of *A More Beautiful Question*, says **at the age of four, children ask more than 400 questions a day.** Between the ages of two and five, the average child will have asked about 40 000 "why" questions, simply because they do not know. But by the time we reach 44, **adults only ask around six questions per day,** mainly because we either think we know or are afraid of admitting that we don't.

So what has killed our questioning? In his book, Warren Berger says several things contribute to us stopping asking questions, such as:

- Our parents got tired of all the questions and may have said, "No more!"
- Our teachers said, "I want answers, not questions!"
- Our boss may have said, "This is the way we do things around here; who are you to ask questions?"
- Our older brain got overloaded with other things and we didn't have the time to ask more questions.

So we stopped. We stopped being curious because we were conditioned to give answers rather than ask questions.

Great questions lie at the heart of being curious.

However, for some of us, we have to relearn how to be curious and how to ask questions again. When we do become good at asking questions, though, we discover that the art of asking can be **transformative.**

Questioning is not about interrupting the other person with too many questions, or asking questions to serve your own ego and show how clever you are. It's asking questions because you really want to know. **The key to questioning is being genuinely curious.**

Types of questions

Closed versus open questions

What are closed questions?

Closed questions can usually be answered with one word. They are mostly used for clarification if you require more information. In mentoring or coaching conversations, many people may be under the impression that they should not ask closed questions. Closed questions are indeed needed! As stated before, they are often used for clarification, especially when you are exploring the issue at hand or what needs to be discussed in the mentoring conversation. By asking clarifying questions, you are ensuring you are understanding what the mentee is saying.

Closed questions often begin with **Where, Who, When** or **Which**. They can be answered with one word and often do not lead to further dialogue. If the conversation feels like an interrogation, or is becoming stilted, ask yourself if you are maybe asking too many closed questions. Can you ask those questions differently to open up the conversation?

It's important that you know why you are asking questions in the first place. You want your mentee to do their own thinking first, so ask questions to help the other person do their own thinking. Even ask questions for which you have no answer.

By asking questions, you are facilitating the thinking of the other person so that they come up with their own solutions, which means they then take ownership! Using more open questions will facilitate further dialogue and get the mentee to open up and go deeper.

Closed questions often elicit the following:
- Answers that provide facts
- Easy-to-answer questions
- Answers that can be given quickly and require little to no thought

What are open questions?

Open questions can't be answered with a simple yes or no. When people feel backed into yes-or-no corners, they sense they're being interrogated. Open questions allow the mentee to answer in many different ways and direct the conversation to what is most important. Open-ended questions can also deliver unexpected insights, which is your ultimate goal as a mentor.

Recognize the characteristics of open-ended questions. Sometimes, people think they have asked open-ended questions when they have not. To successfully ask open-ended questions in conversation, be knowledgeable of the characteristics of an open-ended question. They require a person to pause, think, and reflect.

Often the answers you receive from your mentee when you ask open questions will not be facts, but personal feelings, opinions, or their ideas.

When using open-ended questions, the control of the conversation switches over to the person being asked the question. If the control of the conversation stays with the person asking questions, you are asking closed questions.

Open questions often begin with the following words: **Why, How, What, Describe, Explain, Tell me about,** or **What do you think about...**

Although "Tell me about" or "Describe" do not begin a question, the result is the same as asking an open-ended question.

I love **"What if..."** questions. They tend to open up your mentee's thinking, to allow them to dream and think bigger. When you find that your mentee is getting too narrow in their focus, ask them a "What if" question to broaden their thinking. Such as: "What if you had unlimited budget, what would you do then?" or "What if you had all the time in the world, what would you do differently?"

Queggestions: Be aware of asking "queggestions", which are suggestions disguised as questions. You may ask, "Wouldn't it be a good idea if you had a conversation with your colleague about that?" You are suggesting they should do that rather than letting them come up with their own ideas.

CLOSED VS OPEN QUESTIONS

Why not why?

How do we turn questions beginning with "Why", which may be

considered judgmental, into questions that come from a place of curiosity and open up our mentee's thinking?

Instead of, "Why do you want that?"
Ask: "What is it about that that is important for you?"

Instead of, "Why do you feel that way?"
Ask: "What situations cause you to feel that way?"

Instead of: "Why did you do that?"
Ask: "Help me understand..."

However, "why" questions can also be used effectively if you are really wanting to challenge your mentee. For example: "Why should you get the promotion over your colleague?" This pushes the mentee to think more deeply about their intention and ability. Used well, "why" questions can be very effective if you are confident you can use them without the perception of judgment.

NARROW VS BROAD QUESTIONS

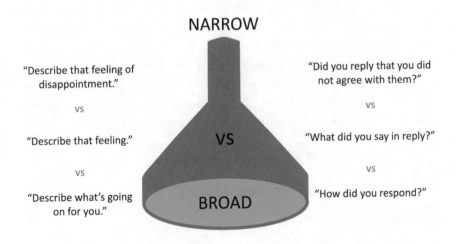

Narrow versus broad questions

Too often we ask questions that may be open questions but are too narrow. A broad question is an open question that can be answered in many ways and lets the mentee take you to what is most significant.

What do broad questions look like?

Asking, "What did you say in reply?" will lead to a response with words that were said – it limits the answer to just what was said. This is a narrow open question.

Asking, "How did you respond?" will lead to a fuller response. The most significant response may not have been just words, but also allows for emotions, feelings, and other reactions.

To make a question broader, redesign it to allow for a wider range of answers.

Another example of asking narrow versus broader questions is the following: we may ask a person to "describe that feeling of disappointment". This will narrow the person's response to only talk about the disappointment and nothing else. If you ask instead, "Describe that feeling," you may get a broader response. However, if you say: "Describe what's going on for you," this now opens up the answer even more, so the person has the opportunity to really give you a lot more detail.

Leading questions

Be aware of asking leading questions. A leading question is one in which the question is framed so that the respondent answers in a specific manner – it leads them to the answer.

An example of a leading question may be, "Did you have a good day today?" This may lead your mentee to think about all the good things that have happened today. It is also a narrow question. This question can be rephrased as, "How has your day been going today?"

Questioning techniques

Probing questions

1. Double clicking

When we want to dig for more information on our search engine on our computer, we use our mouse and double click. The same way, when we want to probe for more information and for our mentee to go deeper, we can double click on what they are saying.

"Can I double click on that?"
"Can you say a little bit more about that?"
"Can you expand on that?"
"Tell me more about…"

This can help clarify things for you as a listener as well as help the mentee go a bit deeper into their thinking.

2. Multiple angles

Looking at a situation from different angles is another probing technique. Sometimes you need to probe a bit more in order get your mentee to do some more thinking. If you look at a situation or a problem from a different angle, it can give you a better perspective on things.

Commit to probing, and listen before examining solutions.

- **The past:** "Give me some background…", "What have you done in the past that is similar to this issue that we are exploring?"
- **The future:** "Where do you see this going?", "What does this issue look like in the future if we do nothing about it?"
- **Patterns:** "How have similar situations affected you and how did you respond?"
- **Other viewpoints:** "How do you think your boss/spouse/colleague would see this?"
- **Values:** "What value do you hold that will influence your response to this?"

MULTIPLE ANGLES

THE PAST: "Give me some background…"

THE FUTURE: "Where do you see this going?"

PATTERNS: "How have similar situations affected you and how did you respond?"

OTHER VIEWPOINTS: "How do you think your boss, spouse, colleague, etc. would see this?"

VALUES: "What value do you hold that will influence your response to this?

Challenging questions

Many people do not like to have their ideas challenged, but this is one of the things that both of you will have discussed upfront – to **positively challenge** each other. Through challenge comes learning and growth.

For the conversation not to be confrontational, it is important to ask questions in the right way. As a mentor, or mentee, you do not want to close the other person down and stop them from thinking. You want to give the right amount of challenge to nudge them to think more openly, or broader, rather than to stop them thinking at all.

Here are some questions that you can use to challenge your mentoring partner:

- "Help me to understand…" rather than, "Why are you doing that?", which can feel judgmental to the other person. By asking them, "Help me to understand…", you are giving them a chance to explain their thinking to you, helping them to work through their own logic, which can lead to an insight into any gaps they may have missed, or a chance to question the way they do something.
- "What are you hoping or intending to achieve?"
- "Please can you explain to me the context of how you are looking at this, so that I can understand…"
- "What assumptions are you making?"

You can also challenge them by reflecting your feelings back to them and thus taking the focus back to yourself, but still challenging them to think deeper:

- "I'm feeling as though there is more to the story…"
- "I'm feeling really confused right now…"

The most important thing is to remember that challenging someone is to help them with their thinking and learning, not to shut them down.

Powerful questions

As mentors, you should be asking your mentee powerful questions to stimulate their thinking.

Here are some attributes of powerful questions:

- They generate curiosity and encourage creativity.
- They stimulate reflective conversation.
- They surface underlying assumptions.
- They explore with genuine curiosity.
- They do not imply intent.
- They use neutral language and tone.

Powerful questions set the tone for the conversation and set the change in motion. They allow us to move beyond "what is" to "what could be".

UK mentoring and coaching expert David Clutterbuck and his team have been looking at what it is that drives the power in a powerful question. He and his team have drawn up a series of powerful questions for mentors to ask mentees.

Powerful questions change your perspective on things or may facilitate an insight for the mentee. They take you to a different place from where you can look at the issue in a different way and you can then see different options for resolving that issue.

In his book *Powerful Questions for Coaches and Mentors*, Clutterbuck categorizes powerful questions with the acronym P.R.A.I.R.I.E.: personal, resonant, acute and incisive, reverberant, innocent, explicit.

Personal: The question is unique to the person – it relates to you. Instead of, "Explain to me how you came to that decision," try, "How would you explain your decision to your adult daughter or your husband?"

Resonant: It hits you emotionally as well as intellectually. It often does give you a shock or feel like a punch in the stomach. "What stories are you telling yourself about this situation?" "How might you be fooling yourself?"

Acute and **incisive: It gets right to the point and focuses on the specific.** "How did you want your boss to respond?"

Reverberant: It may not be something that you can answer right away and keeps coming back to haunt you... and each time you think about the question, your understanding deepens and changes. "How do you celebrate your successes?" In my mentoring relationship, my mentor kept on asking me, "What is your purpose, what are you meant to do?" It took me a long time to reflect on these questions and to realize what my purpose is.

Innocent: It doesn't have the agenda of the person asking it – it has **no ego** – no vested interest, just genuine curiosity. "What are you assuming in this situation?" "What do you want to achieve?"

Explicit: It is just simply expressed. You can ask the question in 10 words (12 words maximum). So often, we ask a question followed by another two questions instead of one at a time. Our mentee can be so confused with what you have asked them that they forget what the first question was.

Examples:

Closed question: "Do you have experience?"

Open question: "What experience do you have?"

Powerful question: "How might your experience impact the project's success?"

Worksheet 15: Powerful questions

Now is the chance to do some reflection by asking yourself some of these powerful questions. You can write the answers down or simply think about them. Most importantly, how did these questions feel to you? How do you think a mentee would feel if you asked them these questions?

- Who are you and who do you want others to think you are?
- Who is the person you aspire to become?
- What has fear (of failure) kept you from doing?
- What's the most courageous decision you've ever made?
- What's a conversation that you really need to have with someone, but haven't had so far?
- What dream have you yet to have the courage to act on?

- What self-limiting beliefs might be getting in the way of your own personal development?
- What mistakes do you find yourself regularly repeating?
- What have you learnt about yourself recently that has surprised you?
- With all that's changing in the world and in our customers' lives, what business are you really in?

Unlocking questions

Many mentees have assumptions that they make about things that cause issues for them. They have beliefs that they find difficult to remove in order to see things from another perspective. It almost feels like their mind is locked and these stories are locked inside their head. As a mentor, your role will be to unlock their mind and remove these limiting assumptions that are preventing them from seeing a way forward.

(In Nancy Kline's book *Time to Think*, she refers to this as incisive questions.)

Here is how it seems to work:

Our thinking, feelings, decision-making, and actions are driven by assumptions. We have some limiting assumptions, which are untrue, and we need someone to help us unlock these. This is where a mentor comes in.

You as a mentor could unlock an insight and ask the following questions if you realize that your mentee may be holding onto an untrue assumption that is limiting their thinking.

- What are you assuming in this situation?
- What assumption could you be making that is limiting your thinking?
- How true is that assumption?
- If you can remove that assumption, that is, if that assumption is not true, what would you believe?
- How could you look at the situation now without that assumption?

On paper this sounds pretty dry. But in practice it is one of the most exhilarating and transformative things you can do as a mentor to help your mentee unlock an insight.

The mind does it for itself in a flash when it can. When it can't, it does it a bit more slowly, but just as powerfully, with the help of those five questions and extraordinary attention from another person.

Worksheet 16: Unlocking questions

Here are some examples of unlocking questions. Grab a pen and paper or your laptop and choose some that resonate with you. Take your time and answer them.

- If you were not to hold back in your life, what would you be doing?
- If you knew you were vital to your organization's success, how would you approach your work?
- If you were to become chief executive, what problem would you solve first, and how would you do it?
- If things could be exactly right for you in a situation you are facing, how would they have had to change?
- If you knew you had all the skills necessary, what would you do?
- If you were not afraid (if you were brave), what would you do?
- If you knew you were good enough, what would change for yourself?
- If you knew your children were taken care of in all aspects, what would you do with the rest of your life?
- If you knew you were worth it, what would you want?
- If you knew something wonderful was going to happen today, how would you feel?

You can now get the feeling of what that feels like. Truly liberating, isn't it?

Role play using unlocking questions

Mentor: You said that you had an issue with your time. Tell me a bit more about that.

Mentee: I feel as though I live in chaos and go from one thing to another. I need to restructure my time. In fact, that is one goal I would like to achieve… restructuring my time.

Mentor: What are you assuming that is stopping you from restructuring your time?

Mentee: I have so many commitments at home, at work and with my family and friends that I can't seem to think clearly any more. I'm also not a very organized person, so everything seems in chaos.

Mentor: What else are you assuming that could be stopping you from restructuring your time?

Mentee: I don't know how to prioritize as I have so many demands from work that are all time pressured.

Mentor: What I'm hearing so far is that you have many commitments at work, home and socially, and that it feels chaotic. You don't see yourself as an organized person and that you struggle to prioritize. Anything else?

Mentee: I feel as though I'm a victim of time pressure as everyone seems to need everything at once.

Mentor: Looking at this list, what are you most assuming that is preventing you from restructuring your time?

Mentee: That I'm a victim of time pressure. Being a victim, I'm not able to restructure my time as I let everyone else dictate to me.

Mentor: Is it true that you are a victim of time pressure?

Mentee: I feel as though it's true, but I suppose that I always take on the victim role.

Mentor: If you remove this assumption, that you are not a victim of time pressure, what would you do?

Mentee: Well, I suppose I would have a choice in restructuring my time.

Mentor: If you knew you had a choice in restructuring your time, what would you do?

You can see how this line of questioning works on removing the mentee's limiting belief of being a victim of time pressure, moving towards having a choice. They can now think freely of what they want to do about it, without having that limiting belief preventing them from doing their own creative thinking.

Pause questions

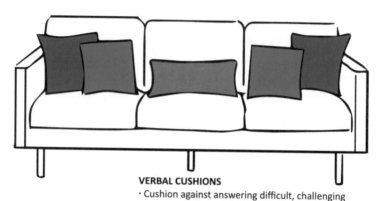

VERBAL CUSHIONS
· Cushion against answering difficult, challenging or complex questions.
· Buy us time to craft our answer.

CUSHIONS

QUESTIONS WITH CUSHIONS
· "Do you mind if I ask..."
· "Would you like to tell me..."

Cushions

A cushion is something you'd say (or do) to show respect for the question you've been asked, buy some time to think of an answer, while also helping to drop everyone's defences. A cushion can be used by a mentor or mentee to put a pause between being asked the question and answering it.

We use cushions when asked difficult, challenging, or complex questions, whether it's during an interview or in everyday conversation.

Showing respect for the question means your cushion must create the impression that you've heard the question and are considering your answer. It means not answering a question with a question of your own.

Sometimes you need to insert a cushion before firing off your answer.

Examples of your response (your cushion) could be:

"I understand why you'd ask about that. Let me explain..."

"I get that question from time to time..."

"If I were in your shoes, I'd wonder about that as well..."

"I've not been asked that before. Let me think about that..."
"That's an important question and something I take very seriously..."
"Help me to understand..."
"Well, ..."
Cushions fill precious seconds to allow us time to craft our answer.

Never-fail questions

Sometimes it's good to have some questions up your sleeve that you feel comfortable asking in many different situations and can use if you are not sure what to ask next. These are some below, but you may have others that you feel comfortable with.

"What would be most useful for you right now?"
"Say more about that..."
"Keep going."
"Tell me more."
"What else?"
"And?"

NEVER-FAIL QUESTIONS

Tone

Always try to frame questions in an **appropriate tone.** People are more forthcoming when asked in a casual rather than confrontational manner. They're more willing to respond. Phrase questions in a conversational, friendly tone and listen eagerly as to a friend.

Key takeaways:

✓ Great questions lie at the heart of being curious.
✓ Open, broad questions elicit more thinking and longer answers.
✓ Use powerful and unlocking questions to facilitate insights for your mentee.
✓ Always try to frame questions in an appropriate tone.

24

GIVING AND RECEIVING FEEDBACK

Receiving feedback can be stressful

How do you feel about feedback? Do you like giving it? How do you feel about receiving it? Most people do not enjoy feedback. When people hear the word "feedback" they immediately think it's going to be negative. In fact, if you said to your employees that they were all shortly going to receive feedback from their managers, the cortisol levels in the office would shoot through the roof! It's just how our brain is wired, to detect threats. There are a few better ways that we can tackle feedback, which will lead to more positive outcomes.

Like most people I know, I've always had an aversion to feedback. It probably started when I was in my first job, and we had our annual performance reviews at which we received feedback from our boss. For me, it was one of my worst days of the year. A specific feedback session stood out for me when my boss said that I was not being a team player and needed to be like everyone else. I think that was the day that I decided that I could not work for anyone again… the seed to being my own boss was planted.

My staff have told me they also dread annual reviews, so we

stopped making them a once-a-year formal meeting. We continually give feedback throughout the year, so that by the time the end of the year comes around, everyone knows exactly how they performed. I was trying to do away with the end-of-year review, but the employees still wanted a meeting. However, I keep it short and informal. That dreaded formal end-of-year "performance review" is now a less formal meeting discussing the year and reflecting on their performance.

Giving feedback is as stressful as receiving feedback, so I also dread it!

So why do we dread feedback and always think it's going to be "bad news"? Why does our head go to the negative? Why does the word "feedback" trigger a threat response in us?

The neuroscience behind feedback

Our brains are still exquisitely attuned to threats, though most of us are not fighting off sabre-toothed tigers any more. MRI scans by neuroscientists show that the brain lights up in exactly the same area whether we are exposed to social threats or physical threats. Someone saying to us, as we have just come out of a presentation, "I would like to give you some feedback on the presentation you have just done" is as threatening as being in physical danger and activates a rush of cortisol and adrenaline in our body. Our face may flush, our heart rate may increase, we may sweat more excessively, our hands may become clammy, and our brains shut down. This means that even if we are being given feedback that could be useful for us, we have shut down and stopped listening.

A study by Katherine Thorson and New York University psychologist Tessa West found that receivers' heart rates jumped enough to indicate moderate or extreme duress in unprompted feedback situations.

Triggering

David Rock, the co-founder and CEO of the NeuroLeadership Institute, says in his book *Your Brain at Work* that if we trigger someone by asking for feedback, or maybe even giving too much advice, we go into an "away" or threat state that triggers our reptilian or survival brain to go into an "amygdala hijack", when we literally feel as though we cannot even think. Cortisol and adrenaline start to course through our body. It's like our brain fogs over. Our heart races, we can get sweaty palms, our face may flush, and we cannot answer. This is because we are going into a state of fight, flight, freeze, or appease.

Have you ever felt this? I'm sure you have. Remember being asked something in school or college by the teacher or professor when you weren't expecting it? Remember deciding if you should put up your hand to ask a question and feeling your heart pumping in your chest? Remember going into your annual review? Remember walking out of a meeting and your boss saying he wanted to give you some feedback? What is your default state you usually go into? Do you want to fight? Do you want to run away? Do you freeze and want to go inside your shell? Or do you just agree to appease someone?

TRIGGERING

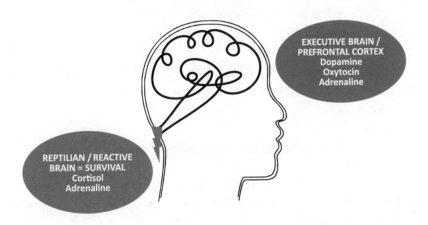

I was sitting on a global committee when, during one of our meetings, a colleague started to question everything that I was doing and giving me feedback that I had not asked for. Before I could answer, he would interrupt and ask the next question. The more he did it, the quieter I got and the louder and more confident he got (he was getting a dopamine kick by doing that!) I started to shut down to the point at which I was unable to think, and this on a subject about which I knew a lot. My brain fogged over. My heart was racing. I went into my shell and closed down.

This can happen if the feedback we are given/giving is not done correctly or we give/receive too much advice. If we are aware of what can happen to the other person, as well as what the signs are when we are triggered, then we can control it. To do this we need to notice the following:

> What are the signs that we are being triggered? Are we starting to sweat? Close down? Is our heart pumping? Are our hands getting clammy?
>
> Acknowledge that you are being triggered and say to yourself, "I'm being triggered."
>
> Are there certain people who trigger you? If you have had one experience of being triggered by someone, then just meeting that person again can activate the triggering signals again. However, the good news is that if you are aware of it and understand the signs that you are being triggered, then you can stop it before it becomes an issue and closes down your thinking.

If your mentor or mentee has triggered you in your session, try to have a discussion with them to discuss what triggered you and how you can stop it happening again.

Making feedback a pleasant experience

How can we turn this response on its head and make feedback a more pleasant experience for everyone? How can you give compassionate feedback?

1. **Intentions:** Start with examining your intentions. What do you want to get out of a conversation about feedback? What results would you like to see? Why am I giving feedback to my mentee or mentor, or asking for feedback?

2. **Regular:** Make giving positive and critical feedback a frequent event in your mentoring relationship. Giving feedback regularly, rather than waiting for the end of your mentoring journey, will start a habit of feedback where it is something that you both do regularly. Regular

feedback means that we get used to it and it becomes less of a threat.

We need to make feedback a **habit**. It's important that it is a habit for both parties. Sometimes there will be moments when mentors may give unsolicited feedback. However, if you have already created a habit of giving each other feedback regularly then you both become emotionally well-equipped to give and receive feedback in these situations too.

3. Ask permission: Ask for permission to give feedback before rushing into just giving it. This will mean that your mentoring partner will be more open to receiving it. For example, "Would this be a good time for me to give you some feedback?" or "Would you be open to receiving some feedback now?" Asking permission to give someone feedback will lessen the threat of getting feedback that is **unsolicited**. When we ask permission, the threat response goes from a level 10 to maybe a level six.

4. Positive: Start with feedback that is positive. Everyone expects feedback to be bad, so if you start with something positive, the other person becomes less defensive and is in a more receptive state of mind to receive feedback that could otherwise be difficult to digest.

5. Ask for feedback: Ask for feedback yourself. By asking for feedback the likelihood of your mentoring partner also asking for feedback increases.

Research is suggesting that we need to switch from giving feedback to asking for it. West and Thorson's study found that participants' heart rates jumped as much as 50% during feedback conversations, leading to shutting down and people not being able to listen any more. They found that asking for feedback led to minimal threat response. It appears to offer the receiver and giver much more psychological safety than a giver-led approach.

By asking for feedback from the other person, you are encouraging them to ask you for feedback in return. This quickly dampens the threat response as it is not unsolicited feedback.

6. Specific and explicit: Be specific and state what you have observed. Focus on a specific behaviour, not the person. In a mentoring relationship, this will be confined to what you have observed in your meeting and your experience of the engagement. For example, "I've noticed that you keep cancelling meetings or arriving late."

Let them know the impact of the behaviour on you or on others and be specific about it. Do not be judgmental, but rather focus on your perspective. For example, "I feel like you are not committed to the journey."

If we ask for specific feedback rather than general feedback, it focuses the feedback on what you are wanting to receive, such as: "Can you give me feedback on my presentation skills so that I can improve going forward?" This is asking specifically for feedback on a certain topic as well as asking for positive feedback to help you improve. Feedback that is specific tends to be richer and has more useful information.

7. Learning opportunity: If we reframe feedback as an opportunity to learn, rather than criticism, we will be more open to receiving it. Honest feedback may not always be what we want to hear, but if it is given respectfully then it will be received more easily.

8. Ask for feedback on your feedback: Ask for their comments on the feedback that you have given. This will give you feedback on how you are giving it.

9. Move forward: Find a way to move forward. Both of you can think of some new actions that can now take place.

Feedforward versus feedback

There are some ways feedback can be given so as to reap benefits from it.

You may have heard about **feedforward**.

"When a person receives feedback, they get information about how they're presently performing. **Feedforward is the reverse exercise of feedback**. It's the process of replacing positive or negative feedback with future-oriented solutions. In simple terms, it means focusing on the future instead of the past."

Dr Marshall Goldsmith, a global leadership thinker, came up with the Feedforward Tool to help organizations and leaders look at future behaviour rather than focusing on the past. I often put this into practice with my team at work; however, I often don't follow it myself in my day-to-day life.

Dr Goldsmith's seven steps of feedforward are as follows:

1. Ask
2. Listen
3. Thank
4. Think
5. Respond
6. Change
7. Follow up

A practical example of feedforward with a mentee

A mentee brought home to me the power of feedforward. He was a newly appointed manager who had been assigned to a mentor within his organization.

The mentor was having a monthly session him and challenged her mentee a bit more than she normally had before. She also went into telling him what he should be doing. The mentee started closing down, and they ended the session early with the mentee feeling deflated, a bit angry, and not sure that he wanted to continue with the mentoring sessions.

During the next two weeks, he had time to reflect on what had happened in the session. Instead of walking away from mentoring, he decided to speak to his mentor at the next session and give some feedback from the last session and how he was feeling. At the beginning of the session, he asked his mentor if he would be able to give her some feedback on the last session. With her permission, he said, "I felt during the last session that I was pushed into a corner by being challenged a bit harder than I was able to handle. This made me feel defensive and caused me to shut down. I also felt as though I was being told what to do, rather than helping me explore my own ideas. I appreciate that you probably know what I should do, but what would help me is if we go through lots of possibilities first and then I ask you to share your experience with me."

Now, there are several ways the mentor could have reacted to this.

Reaction # 1: Deny it

The mentor could reject the feedback and say, "What are you talking about? I spoke to you as I would to anyone else. Of course I wasn't telling you what to do. Don't make baseless accusations."

What would this response have done to the mentee? Possibly it would have led to an argument with both disagreeing with each other and finding no resolution at all.

Or it may have led to the mentee walking away, saying that he did not want to continue with the mentoring relationship at all.

Lesson 1: Don't deny or reject feedback. You cannot stop a person thinking or feeling what they do.

Reaction #2: Reason with it

The mentor could try to reason with her mentee and say, "I needed to speak to you like that as I have been in that situation before, and I know what you should do. I didn't want you to waste time thinking about it as I could see the solution so clearly."

Would this help her mentee feel any better or lead to a constructive conversation?

Lesson 2: Reasoning with feedback does not change people's perceptions of what they think and feel.

Reaction #3: Accept and acknowledge feedback and ask for feedforward

The mentor could accept the feedback and acknowledge her mentee's feelings. She could have said, "I'm sorry that you felt that I told you what to do and challenged you to the point of shutting you down. I didn't mean to, as I acknowledge that you probably have so many good ideas and solutions that I should have asked you about first. What can I do in the future to make you feel that I talk to you in the right way?"

This would probably lead to reconciliation, defusing of the situation and a way to move forward. It would lead to a conversation that could help both move forward, and improve future conversations.

Lesson 3: Acknowledging feedback and the person's feelings using feedforward is the best way to handle feedback.

Feedforward is future-oriented. It is not looking at the past, but for suggestions for the future.

Feedback is a gift, and if we start to look at it this way, our response may change for the positive. Feedforward allows us to improve our performance. It allows us to get better. There cannot be any improvement without feedback and feedforward. We just need to try to reframe it and embrace it.

When to give feedback and feedforward using the Catherine Wheel

Feedback should be done regularly and when you think it's a good time to do it instinctively. However, there are also certain times along your mentoring journey when you have to give feedback.

At the beginning of each mentoring meeting, during the update, the mentee should be giving feedback to their mentor on what happened since they last met and what action points they implemented.

At the end of the mentoring meeting, during the wrap up, both the mentor and mentee should give feedback on how the meeting went for them and whether they received value from it.

During your mentoring journey, you should both be giving feedback as well as feedforward on your relationship and how you are feeling about it.

Finally, at the end of your journey, you should both give feedback and feedforward on your mentoring journey, what value you received and what positive improvements you could both make for the future.

At the end of my mentoring journey with my mentor, we spent a large portion of our time giving feedback to each other. It felt non-threatening and was an opportunity to learn and take that knowledge forward with us.

Seven tips on feedback

7 TIPS ON FEEDBACK

1. REGULAR
Give feedback regularly.
Create a culture of giving and receiving feedback. Make it a habit.

2. ASK PERMISSION
Ask for permission before giving feedback.
"Is this a good time to give you some feedback?"
Unsolicited feedback can be seen as a threat and may not be received well.

3. POSITIVE
Start with feedback that is positive before moving on to more difficult feedback.

4. LEARNING OPPORTUNITY
Feedback should be seen as an opportunity to learn.
It is not criticism.

5. SPECIFIC
Be explicit with your feedback rather than giving general feedback.
This ensures it is richer and has more useful information.

6. ASK FOR FEEDBACK
Don't wait to receive feedback — **ask** for it. By asking for feedback you dampen the threat response of receiving feedback.
Asking for feedback also encourages the other person to reciprocate and ask for feedback themselves.

7. FEEDFORWARD
Feedforward is the reverse exercise of feedback. It replaces positive or negative feedback with future-oriented solutions. It means focusing on the future instead of the past.

Worksheet 17: Feedback

Take some time right now to answer the following questions about feedback:

- How do I feel about receiving feedback?
- What would make me more open to receiving feedback?
- How can I express this to my mentoring partner?
- How do I feel about giving feedback?
- How can I make my mentoring partner be more open to receiving feedback from me?
- Do I use feedforward?
- How can I use feedforward in my mentoring relationship?

Key takeaways:

- ✓ Make feedback a habit.
- ✓ Ask for feedback or ask permission to give feedback.
- ✓ Be respectful and compassionate when giving feedback.

25

ADVICE

One of the most common answers I get in my Mentoring Masterclass when I ask the participants "What is your role as a mentor?" is "It is to be an advisor". Yes, I do agree that advising plays a crucial role in sponsorship mentoring, but it plays a lesser role in developmental mentoring.

Are you judging your mentee when you think they need your advice?

As a mentor, you will most probably be asked for your advice by your mentee. They chose you as a mentor because of your experience and wisdom, so they want to learn from you. However, if you are asked for advice, you need to understand how to give advice so that it is given in the correct way and does not trigger the mentee.

Instead of thinking of yourself as an advisor, think of yourself as their **guide or sherpa**. This will change the way you think about giving advice.

The most important thing to ask yourself is, "Am I sharing this because it's making me feel good?" In neuroscience, it's been shown that when we give advice, we release a chemical called dopamine, which is a "feel-good" hormone. Giving advice to someone literally makes us feel good and we want to give more advice because then we get more of a dopamine kick. Great for us, but a nightmare for the person receiving all this advice!

We need to focus less on the advice itself and more on creating a conversation that helps your mentee see the issue from a new perspective.

Giving advice

If you remember these points about giving advice, then it should help you to give advice that would be useful to your mentee.

1. **Last resort**: Explore the mentee's own thinking first. Listen to what they have to say. Ask them questions to stimulate further thinking and options. If they come into a meeting and ask you for advice near the beginning of the session, say, "Let's explore your own thinking first and then I'm happy to share my thinking with you."

2. **Hazardous and serious mistake**: If your mentee is about to make a grave mistake, then you as a mentor have a duty to warn them of the outcomes of this and may have to offer advice. Ask yourself if your mentee's physical, mental, or financial well-being will be in danger if you do not give advice.

3. **Ask permission**: In general, do not give advice unless you have asked permission to do so. Say to them, "Is now a good time to share my thinking with you?" If you do not ask permission and you give advice that is unsolicited, it could trigger your mentee.

4. **Be precise and concise**: Ask yourself if the advice could help the mentee with their thinking or decision making. Don't waffle on about your own story for too long – what part would your mentee find most useful?

5. **Specific use**: Is this for your own ego? Get to the point and ensure it is relevant to what you are discussing.

6. **Facts:** Stick to facts rather than opinions.

7. **Right words**: Pay attention to the language you use. Instead of, "You should be doing this..." try an approach in which your mentee will not feel as though they are being told what to do. Instead you could say, "Let's go through all the options together. What other options can you think of? Let's go through the pros and cons of each. What do you think is a better solution now? Would you like to hear of some options that

I have thought of?" Instead of, "This is what you should do with your business," say, "If this were my business or my money, I would…"

8. Put your own ego and emotional needs aside: Ensure that your mentee feels that the solution was their idea or their decision, so that they take ownership of it.

9. Emotional intelligence: Advice offered with emotional intelligence is likely to be better advice. The number one sign of emotional intelligence is more question marks at the end of your sentences!

10. Engage with other experts: Encourage your mentee to check out their question on which they'd like advice with other experts. You do not need to take responsibility for what you share.

11. Understand your mentee: You will get a feel for what your mentee is wanting from you after a time. Have a conversation to discuss how they would like to receive advice if they keep on asking for it.

The reason advice needs to be given with caution is:
- Old ways may be obsolete. What you did in the past may not be relevant now.
- Too much advice can weaken relationships and your mentee may lose trust. Your mentee may take your advice and use it; then if it does not work out, they may hold you accountable for giving them the advice.
- It stops the mentee doing their own thinking if they have not been given the chance to explore their thinking first.
- Your mentee may become overly reliant and dependent on you for decisions they need to make themselves.

What happens if you give what you think is good advice, and your mentee does not follow through with it or act on it? Don't let your ego get in the way! If your mentee does not take your advice, that's okay. It's completely up to your mentee whether they wish to act on your advice or not.

Hold your advice lightly, offer it, and then step back and let it go.

Being an advisor your mentee can trust

In his book *The Trusted Advisor*, David Maister says that a trusted advisor is a label you have to earn. Therefore, as a mentor, to be a mentee's trusted advisor, you have to earn it by building trust. Maister and his co-authors came up with a **Trust Equation** that looks like this:

$$\frac{\text{Credibility + Reliability + Intimacy (Vulnerability)}}{\text{Self-orientation (Ego)}}$$

Credibility is about the words.
What does that mean? It means that you need to know what you say you know, that you're honest, and that you're present. Your mentee will come to a conclusion quite quickly about whether you are credible or not, based on what you say, how you say it, and how you come across.

Reliability is about actions.
Do what you say you are going to do. If you promise your mentee that you will do something, either send them something or introduce them to someone, then do it. They want to know that they can count on you to keep your commitment. If not, you will come across as unreliable.

Also be consistent, as inconsistency can lead to unreliability. So, it's no good if you follow up on your commitment once, but the next time you don't. You need to be reliable all the time.

Intimacy is about emotions.
I also like to call this **vulnerability**. How in tune are you with your feelings? How open are you to expressing your feelings? If you are open about your feelings, it means that your mentee will be open about their feelings too. If you show vulnerability, the chances are that your mentee will feel open to sharing their vulnerability too. For example, how did you feel about selling or exiting your business? Chances are that your mentee is feeling the same way too. You have to create the space to allow them to express their feelings.

We have now covered the top three ingredients above the equation line for you to be a trusted advisor. However, remember that these three are now to be divided by self-orientation.

Self-orientation is about motive.

Self-orientation is all about your **ego**. It's about your selfishness or greed. It is often connected to arrogance and cockiness. Self-orientation can also be your need to be right, such as the need to look right to others, having to be at the top, name-dropping, jumping to a solution right away, wanting to have the last word or worrying about your reputation.

For example, if you are with your mentee and you start to interrupt them, finish their sentences, or start talking about yourself without listening to them, then they will see you as being self-oriented. This will then affect how much they will consider you as a trusted advisor.

A fun exercise is to put this formula into practice to see how you fare as an advisor whom your mentee can trust. Try it now...

Worksheet 18: Are you an advisor your mentee can trust?

- Credibility: Put down a number from 1 (not at all credible) to 10 (highly credible) rating how credible you are. How honest are you? If you say that you know something, how much do you know about it?
- Reliability: Put down a number from 1 (not at all reliable) to 10 (highly reliable) on how reliable you are. Do you follow through with your commitments all the time, or only some of the time? Can others rely on you all the time?
- Intimacy/vulnerability: Put down a number from 1 (not at all in tune with my feelings and emotions or unwilling to be vulnerable) to 10 (highly in tune with my feelings and emotions and willing to be vulnerable) on how vulnerable you are and ready to share your feelings with others.
- Self-orientation/ego: Put down a number from 1 (not

---

at all self-oriented) to 10 (highly self-oriented) on how self-oriented you are. How important is it for you to be liked by others? How important is it for you to be right? Do you let your ego get in the way? Do you interrupt others, finish their sentences, or not listen to them?

- Now add up the first three numbers you put down for credibility, reliability, and intimacy. Divide that number by your self-orientation number and you will get your trusted advisor number. The higher the number, the more you are regarded as a trusted advisor. If you scored 9 + 10 + 8 = 27 / 3 = 9, then you are highly regarded as a trusted advisor. If you scored 6 + 5 + 3 = 14/7 = 2, then you have a bit of work to do to be regarded as a trusted advisor.

Catherine Johns, in her article "Are you a trusted advisor or just giving advice?", says that **credibility, reliability, and intimacy can be *multiplied* by other-orientation.**

We manifest other-orientation when we:
- Ask open-ended questions.
- Invite our mentee to talk about what's behind an issue.
- Listen closely and check to make sure we really understand our mentoring partner.
- Acknowledge their feelings.
- Hold off on offering a solution until we deeply understand the issue.
- Trust our ability to give them something of value after we've really heard them.
- Give them the gift of our full attention.

In your conversations notice how much of the time your focus is on your mentoring partner, and how often you're really focused on yourself:

how you look, how you sound, the impression you think you're making.

Pay particular attention to the way you ask questions – and especially to the way you listen to the answers.

Shine a spotlight on those interactions for the next few weeks. Keep the trusted advisor formula in mind, and you're likely to spot opportunities to shift out of self-orientation into other-orientation.

When you do that, you'll increase the level of trust people put in you. You'll have a chance to deepen your relationships. Who knows what other rewards will come your way?

Key takeaways:

- ✓ Instead of thinking of yourself as an advisor, think of yourself as their guide.
- ✓ Explore your mentee's own thinking first before giving advice.
- ✓ Rather share your experience and own stories than give advice.
- ✓ If you do give advice, ask permission first. Is the advice relevant, concise, and precise?

26

SHARING EXPERIENCE AND STORYTELLING

Instead of giving advice, we can learn how to share our experience in the form of telling stories. Storytelling has been around for so long and we have used it to pass on important lessons and experiences to others, as well as to define our values, desires, and dreams. It is a powerful tool in a mentor's toolbox.

Telling stories is so useful to help us explain ideas and paint a picture for our mentee. Stories link with our collective knowledge, emotions, and values, so they can strengthen the mentee's understanding and identification with the issue or topic under discussion.

Why should we share our experience and stories with our mentee? Stories are a wonderful way:

- To generate new thinking for your mentee and open them up to new ideas and ways of looking at things.
- To help your mentee see what you or someone else experienced, so they can compare it to their situation.
- To show that you understand their issue and are showing empathy.

Rules of thumb for storytelling

Ask yourself the following:

- Is the story relevant to what is being discussed here?
- Is this the right time to tell the story, or is it best to keep it for later?
- Is the story going to help my mentee with their learning and thinking?
- If I were the mentee, would it help me with my thinking?
- Am I telling the story for my own use/ego, or for my mentee's use?

Ground rules for storytelling

Here are some ground rules for storytelling:
- Remember to keep your story **short, to the point, and relevant.**
- Make sure that you tell your mentee the **purpose** of sharing your story before launching into it. For example, "I would like to share a story with you about a significant lesson I learnt when I set up a board in my family business, as I believe you will find it relevant to what you are facing right now."
- **Ask for permission.** For example, "Would you be open for me to share a story with you now?" The mentee may not be ready to hear a story from you at this point and prefer it to be shared later. Instead of causing frustration and them not fully listening to your story, ensure they are ready to hear your story by asking permission first.
- **Ask for feedback** when you have finished your story. "Was that story useful in helping you understand what challenges you may be facing?"

Some people are born storytellers and can go into minute detail to make you feel as though you are there. Others just get to the point and leave out the details. Think of someone you know who goes into great detail when telling a story. In the right situation, it is fascinating as you listen to the story and feel yourself transported to another place. In another situation, it can be mind-numbing as you itch to get away, wanting to put them on fast forward. Now think of a person who tends to most often be brief, concise, and to the point. In the right situation this is wonderful, in another, they may be seen to be closed and uninteresting.

It's important to understand your mentee to gauge if they are interested in the details or just want the crux of the story. There is nothing worse than a mentor spending valuable time telling a story in 20 minutes when it could have been told in five. Keep your long, detailed stories for friends and dinner parties, rather than your mentoring meetings. Unless of course your mentee asks you lots of questions to get more details!

I am not going to go into how to tell your story, as there are a lot of books on how to become a good storyteller. However, if you are authentic and share your experience or story from your heart... then everything else usually falls into place.

Key takeaways:

✓ Instead of giving advice, share your experiences and tell stories.
✓ Keep your story short, to the point, and relevant.
✓ Make sure that you tell your mentee the purpose of you sharing your story before launching into it.

PART 4: IT'S A WRAP – ENDING YOUR MENTORING JOURNEY

Every mentoring journey must come to an end, as you will remember from the Catherine Wheel, step 5 on the outer green wheel. How we conclude our conversation and journey will influence the lasting impression we have of our mentoring relationship. So wrap it up and end it well!

THE CATHERINE WHEEL

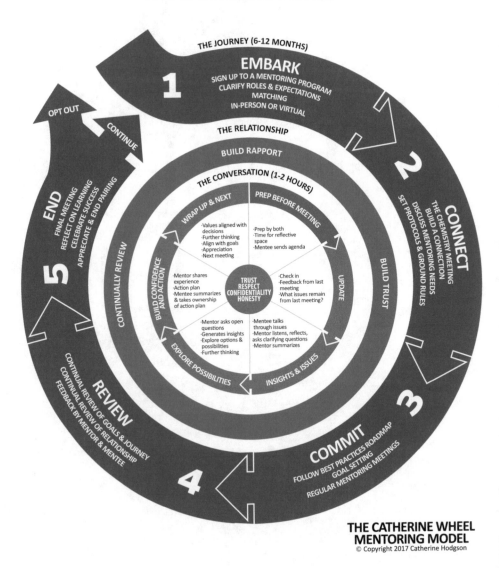

THE CATHERINE WHEEL
MENTORING MODEL
© Copyright 2017 Catherine Hodgson

27

REVIEWING – LOOKING BACK TO LOOK FORWARD

Reviewing your relationship

Your relationship requires **constant care and reviewing**, ensuring that it does not get ignored. You have spent so much time building rapport and trust, you now want to nurture that relationship. As you can see in the relationship wheel of the Catherine Wheel, the relationship needs to be continually reviewed.

Therefore, it's important to review your relationship regularly, even if **you** think it is going well. Do so after the third meeting to check if you are both on track for a successful relationship.

Beat the droop

When I first started mentoring training, I was often asked if the relationship should just be reviewed in the beginning or throughout the mentoring journey. At first, I thought it should only be reviewed within the first three months of a 12-month journey. However, after witnessing hundreds of mentoring partnerships, as well as being part of some myself, I realized that it needs to be reviewed throughout the journey. The reason is that your mentoring relationship is core to your mentoring experience. **Relationship droop** is a reality, where it just feels stale or maybe neglected, and needs a boost. To keep your relationship healthy, it's a good idea to continually review it **throughout** your mentoring journey.

THE CATHERINE WHEEL

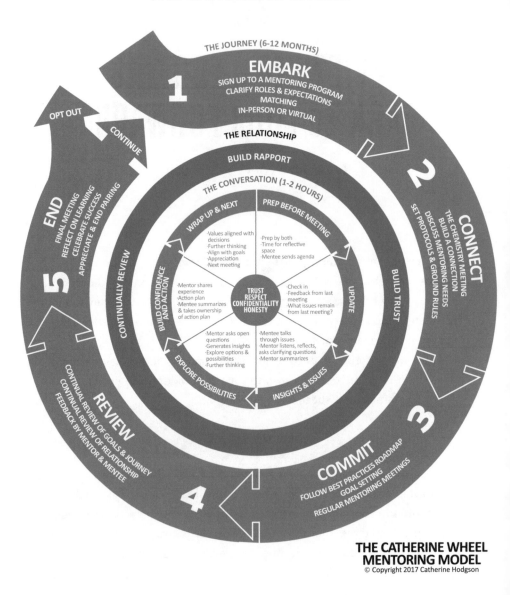

**THE CATHERINE WHEEL
MENTORING MODEL**
© Copyright 2017 Catherine Hodgson

Although your relationship may seem good to you, perhaps it is not going so well for your mentoring partner. Best practice is to have an open and honest conversation with each other every third or so meeting. However, if it really is not going well for you, then have that conversation sooner.

Reinvigorating your relationship

If you have spent the time building rapport and trust with your mentoring partner, then having that open and honest conversation is a whole lot easier.

To start the conversation, you may want to add it to your agenda, right at the beginning of the meeting.

You can even send a few questions for both of you to reflect on before your meeting, such as:

- What is going well in our relationship?
- Am I satisfied with the frequency of our meetings?
- Are we ensuring that our agreement for engagement is adhered to?
- Have we spent enough time building rapport and trust?
- Do I think that I am meeting the expectations of my mentor/mentee as discussed in our first meeting?
- Is my mentor/mentee meeting my expectations?
- What would I like more of and less of from my mentor/mentee?
- Are we able to have an open and honest dialogue?

Here is an exercise you can do to help you with having the dialogue. You can do this exercise outside of your mentoring meeting, write down the answers, and then exchange your answers with each other – this is sometimes a bit easier than saying it out loud.

Worksheet 19: Can we score our relationship 100%?

Ask each other to write down on a scale of 1 to 100% how you would rate the relationship. Remember that not every relationship needs to be 100%. An 80% may be enough for some people.

Next, write down on a scale of 1 to 100% where you would like the relationship to be.

Now ask yourself:
• What can I do to get it there?
• What can my mentor/mentee do to get it there?

Share the information with each other. Now have the conversation and share what you have reflected on.

Feedback on your relationship

In the meeting, you could start by saying to your mentoring partner, "Is now a good time to review our relationship to check if we are meeting each other's expectations?" Asking permission first or putting it onto the agenda will ensure the other person is more open to receiving feedback.

Start with the positive

It is always best to start with **positive feedback first**. Ask the other person what they think is going well in the relationship. Let them know what you think is going well. Share what you are getting out of the mentoring journey, what you are learning and what you enjoy about it. Then look at what needs to be improved or worked on. Take turns to be open, honest, and vulnerable. Talk about all the ways certain issues could be improved – brainstorm some ideas. Come up with a list and write them down. Commit to making the changes that need to be made. Discuss how you can both check in again in two meetings' time to see if things have changed and how you both feel about the relationship.

At the end of each meeting

You can also build in a relationship review at the end of each meeting. Questions that you can ask each other at the end are:

- Who did most of the talking? (Remember that the mentor should do 20% talking and 80% listening – not the other way around.)
- Were enough questions asked to stimulate thinking?
- Was one person dominating the meeting? Was there uneven power? (Remember that in a mentoring relationship, both of you are equal.)
- Is there anything that we should change going forward to improve the relationship?

Review regularly

If you do not deal with something that may be bothering you in the relationship early on, it could fester, and the relationship will eventually break down.

For a relationship to grow strong, it needs to be reviewed regularly. Build it into your mentoring journey.

You will feel that your relationship is on the right track if you:

- are looking forward to your meetings,
- feel comfortable in the meeting,
- feel challenged and that you are learning,
- leave the meeting feeling as though it was valuable and worthwhile, and
- are looking forward to the next meeting.

Be brave to have those honest conversations and you will be rewarded with a positive mentoring experience.

Here is a short feedback worksheet that you could use with each other if your mentoring program does not have one. You can both fill it out and share it with each other at your next meeting. I would do this evaluation after your third meeting if you both feel comfortable being completely open and honest with each other.

Worksheet 20: Feedback Survey

1. Are the mentoring sessions meeting your expectations?

1 Not what I expected	2	3	4	5 Exceeding my expectations
○	○	○	○	○

2. How is your relationship with your mentor/mentee?

1 Not good at all	2	3	4	5 Very good
○	○	○	○	○

3. Can you share two to three takeaways or learnings so far? What is going well? What are you struggling with?

ROADMAP FOR YOUR MENTORING JOURNEY

1. YOU'RE MATCHED!
Mentees set up the first meeting – date, time and place.
Reflect on what you would like to discuss and what you
want to get out of your journey.

2. THE CHEMISTRY MEETING
Usually one hour in length.
Ensure meeting is held in a confidential place.
Set ground rules for your mentoring journey.

3. BUILDING RAPPORT AND TRUST
Spend time getting to know each other.
Ask: What are your values? What are you
passionate about? What successes have you
had? What have you learnt from your failures?

4. GOAL-SETTING
Mentees to reflect on aspirations and goals.
Mentors can help to establish goals for the
mentoring journey.
Goals should be achievable with some stretch.
Goals should align with your values.

5. PREPARING FOR MEETINGS
Mentees spend time reflecting on what they
would like to bring to the next mentoring
meeting. The more prep you put into your meeting,
the more you will get out of it.
Mentees send the agenda a few days before the session.

6. REGULAR MEETINGS
Set up your meetings in advance. Ensure
meetings are regular, at least every 4 – 6 weeks
apart to ensure you do not lose momentum.

7. ACTION FOR NEXT MEETINGS
Have a written action plan at the end of each
meeting which mentees can work on before
the next meeting.

8. REVIEWING THE RELATIONSHIP
Review your relationship regularly – be open and
honest. The deeper the trust, the deeper the
conversation.
Reflect on and discuss:
What can I do differently?
What can my mentor/mentee do differently?

9. REVIEWING GOALS
Review the goals regularly and check that
they align to the mentee's values.
Goals do not need to be static and can change
along the way as you get more clarity from
your journey – be open to the changes that
need to be made.

10. ENDING OR TRANSITIONING THE JOURNEY
Prepare for your final meeting. Reflect on what
you have achieved.
Celebrate your successes.
Appreciate and thank each other.

**ROADMAP FOR YOUR
MENTORING JOURNEY**
© Copyright 2023 Catherine Hodgson

Reviewing your goals

Goals are set during your first or second mentoring session and do need to be reviewed regularly. Over time, goals may need to change. They do not need to be fixed or static. Don't be afraid to amend or change goals as you go along.

Here are three key tips for reviewing goals:

1. **Keep it regular.** Review your mentee's goals every few meetings. Ensure that this is part of the meeting agenda and that your mentee writes down their goals.

2. **Be flexible.** Your mentee's goals may change along the way as your mentee gains more clarity along their mentoring journey. Check in with them and change or alter their goals if it's necessary to do so.

3. **Celebrate!** Celebrate their successes along the way. If your mentee has achieved a milestone, take the time to celebrate with them.

If you review goals regularly, you will have the discussion on whether you are on track with the goals or whether they need to change. How do you do that?

- At the end of each meeting, go through your goals again and check that the action plan aligns to the goals.
- Check where you are in reaching your goals – what milestones have been met so far? If milestones are not being met, you need to check what could be getting in the way. It may mean that the goal needs to be changed.
- Regularly ask if the goal still feels right? Does the goal still feel achievable?

If a goal needs to be changed, then ensure that you still set milestones and a timeline to achieve the new or amended goal. Best practice is to review your journey at the three-month, six-month, and nine-month mark if you are in a 12-month mentoring journey. This should be done with each other in a session, or it can be done by email and then discussed in the session together. You may find that if you are in a mentoring program in an organization, they will send you an evaluation to check in to see how your journey is going. These are usually confidential although they may ask if you would like the evaluation shared with your mentoring partner.

What should you discuss when reviewing your journey?

First and foremost, it should be agreed that both of you will be completely honest. This is all about feedback, so you need to be open, honest, start with the positive, and look at it as a learning experience and a chance to improve it.

Some questions you could ask each other are:

- Have we spent time building rapport and trust so that we both can be completely open and honest with each other?
- Do we both feel that the place we meet is safe and confidential to share information with each other?
- Have we set goals that are aspirational, achievable, and a bit of a stretch for the mentee?
- Are we working towards our goals?
- Are we on track? Has there been progress?
- Are we both learning, and do we look forward to the meetings?
- Do we leave the meetings feeling encouraged and energized?
- What is lacking? What should we do more of? What should we do less of?
- What can I do better? What can you do better?
- Is the mentoring program meeting my expectations?
- Are we still on track to end our mentoring journey in x meetings' time?

Be specific in giving feedback, give examples if necessary, and be generous.

I've put together evaluations for mentoring programs and online platforms for the mentors and mentees to complete at intervals during their journey. What I have found over my years of experience with this is that very few are willing to fill them out. This is terribly frustrating for the program manager, who is trying to improve the program and relying on your feedback. So, if you do join a program and get sent an evaluation, then please do fill it in, for your sake and the health of the program. Of course, you don't need to wait for evaluations to be sent to you! You and your mentoring partner can do your own feedback with each other using the questions above.

Key takeaways:

✓ Review your relationship continuously throughout your journey to keep it healthy and beat relationship droop.

✓ Have open and honest conversations if the relationship is not going well.

✓ Review your goals as well as your journey to ensure you and your mentoring partner are both aligned and getting value from your mentoring journey.

28

WHAT CAN GO WRONG?

In all my years of being involved in mentoring programs, I have seen a lot of things go wrong in mentoring relationships. If you are aware of them upfront, then hopefully you will be on the lookout for them and be able to deal with the issue before it becomes a problem.

Nine most common things that can go wrong

In my experience with mentoring, here are the most common things that can go wrong in a relationship.

1. Confidentiality is not upheld

It's important to set ground rules right at the beginning of the relationship when confidentiality is discussed. Confidentiality is crucial for trust to be built and a safe place created for sharing. What do we mean by confidentiality in a mentoring relationship? Can I discuss anything from my mentoring meeting with my spouse? Friend? Business colleague? The answer is a simple **no! Absolutely nothing** can be discussed outside of your mentoring session unless it is agreed that something can be shared with someone. If confidentiality is broken, an open conversation needs to take place to see whether the relationship can continue or not.

Ensure that you reiterate the importance of confidentiality at the beginning and end of each session. I cannot reiterate how important confidentiality is – it really is the core of your relationship!

2. Lack of time and commitment

Sometimes things come up where one party may no longer be able to continue with the relationship. There may be new time constraints, and one person may begin cancelling meetings, arriving late, or leaving early. A conversation to discuss whether you can make changes to your meeting schedule or whether to terminate the relationship needs to take place. Try not to hold a grudge against the person who cannot carry on with the mentoring journey because something has come up for them. You could ask if you can still email them or give them a call if you need to discuss an issue with them. They may be open to that.

3. Mentee does not drive the relationship or take ownership

It is up to the mentee to take ownership of the journey and drive the relationship. If a mentor is setting up the meetings, sending agendas, and chasing the mentee, discuss how this can be switched around so the mentee takes ownership.

If you set ground rules right in the beginning of your relationship and discuss your roles and expectations, then this will not be an issue.

This is perhaps one of the most frequent things that I deal with in mentoring relationships. Often a mentee feels intimidated or is concerned they may come across as pushy if they reach out to set up meetings or send agendas. It is up to the mentor to discuss with them the necessity to do this and "give permission" so the mentee feels comfortable doing so.

4. Expectations are not met

In your first meeting, discuss the role of the mentor and what the mentee expects of them, as well as the role of the mentee and what the mentor expects of them. This will help avoid unfulfilled or unrealistic expectations.

Check with each other to discuss if your expectations are realistic or not. In the first or second meeting, you can discuss what your mentor or mentee expects from you and then discuss whether these are unrealistic expectations or not. Refer to the **Seven Strengths of Highly Effective Mentors and Mentees** models to review your roles.

5. Mentor lacks confidence

Training is required, however experienced you feel as a mentor. This will give you the confidence, knowing you are following a structure and ensuring both of you get the most out of your mentoring relationship.

If it is your first time being a mentor, discuss this with your mentee and let them know how you feel about it. Tell them your hopes and fears. Ask for feedback from them. They will respect you for this, and it will help with your own learning so you can become a better mentor.

It's very common for someone not to feel "qualified" or ready to be a mentor. The task and responsibility can feel daunting. Be open about it and open to learning. If you have experience in an area in which the mentee is seeking mentoring, then you do have something valuable to offer your mentee. Just being there for them, being a sounding board, an ear to listen, or a person to challenge them positively may be all that the mentee seeks. So often, a mentor comes to me after a mentoring relationship and tells me that they think they learnt as much as, if not more than, the mentee. It really is a mutually beneficial relationship! Your confidence will grow as you experience more mentoring relationships.

6. Too much advice-giving

Although a mentee is usually going into a mentoring relationship to seek learning from the mentor and to receive advice, one of the biggest downfalls that I have come across is the mentor talking too much and giving too much advice.

Be cautious of giving advice too early, too quickly, without knowing the full details, or if it is not asked of you. Give advice cautiously, when appropriate, if it is relevant, and with permission. Share your stories and experience instead. Be their guide.

7. Different values

If values are aligned, research shows that the chances are greatly increased for both of you to create a deeper relationship.

You may wonder why this is the case. Surely if people's values are different, it can bring different perspectives to a situation?

It is acceptable for values not to be completely aligned and for both of you to respect each other's values. However, if someone else's values are in deep conflict with your own, then it will be very hard to have a relationship that is trusting and deep. Values need to be discussed at the beginning of your relationship. Ensure you do the exercise on values at the beginning of your journey to open up the conversation about them. (Values list on page 298)

8. Dependency

It can be easy to create dependency on each other. Be aware if this starts to develop. The mentee may seek "approval" or input from their mentor every time they need to make a decision, questioning their own decision-making ability. This makes the mentee over-reliant on the mentor and afraid to make a decision without them. A mentor will start to see this and should stop it before it continues into a relationship of dependency.

A mentor may also become dependent on their mentee. For example, the mentee may be a similar age to their son or daughter, and they start to treat them as one, seeking their input on things that they should normally ask their own son or daughter.

If a relationship of dependency starts to develop, discuss this and how you can end it so you can both move forward without relying on each other.

9. Offers of investment or employment

A mentor I had recently matched to a mentee phoned me one morning at my office. "Catherine," he said, "I'm just loving my mentoring relationship and my mentee is so enthusiastic. I can also see so much potential in his business. However, he just needs help with some marketing and doesn't have funds to do it." I immediately saw a red flag but listened and let him continue. "His food business in the shopping mall offers great food and is in a good position. However, he cannot afford a sign to put above the shop. I would love to give him some money to do this. What do you think?"

I would have loved to have told him that I thought this was a good idea, for the sake of the mentee. However, investing in your mentee's business is a huge **no**. The reason is that it starts to blur the lines between mentor and mentee. Now the mentor feels invested in the business and cannot remain objective. The mentee also feels obliged to go ahead with what you as a mentor decides, as you are an investor. If this situation does happen and you decide to invest in your mentee's business, then end the mentoring relationship. Or rather, wait before investing, complete the relationship, and then invest. Either way, you cannot be a mentor and an investor at the same time.

The same goes for hiring someone you are mentoring or using their business to supply your business with something. I had a mentor ask how I felt about him hiring his mentee. My answer was to end the mentoring relationship and hire her if that was the right thing for both people. It may also feel tempting to use the services of your mentee's business. Rather wait until you have completed your mentoring relationship before doing so. You really don't want the lines to be blurred. I had a mentor who told me that they loved their mentee's business so much that after their mentoring relationship (thank goodness!) the mentee started supplying the mentor's business with their products. It has been a very successful business relationship since then.

Don't feel bad if some things do start to go wrong. It can happen. An honest open conversation can often sort it out. If it cannot be resolved, then a conversation with the program manager is needed.

Key takeaways:

✓ Confidentiality and commitment are key to a successful mentoring relationship.
✓ Setting ground rules at the beginning of your mentoring journey can iron out potential problems.
✓ If things do start to go wrong, have an open and honest conversation with each other.

29

ENDING THE JOURNEY

Step 5: End

It is important for both of you to know that every mentoring journey comes to an end. It may be a relief for some that there is an ending – after all, it would be difficult to commit to a program where you were a mentor for life! This is why it's crucial that from the beginning, you both know that the journey has a definite end.

A significant amount of time has gone into the journey, so it is important that you celebrate the end, reflect on your learning, and appreciate each other. Then decide on what you would like to do next.

Hopefully as you prepare for your final mentoring meeting you will be thinking… "All good things come to an end."

That is how I felt when I was heading for my final meeting with my mentor. It had been a long journey, we had achieved so much, but it had a definite end date and we needed to celebrate the successes we had achieved.

In my experience with running mentoring programs, if a mentoring relationship is not ended properly, then both parties feel slightly dissatisfied, even if the relationship was successful. Step 5 on the outer wheel of the Catherine Wheel shows that the mentoring journey does indeed come to an end.

THE CATHERINE WHEEL

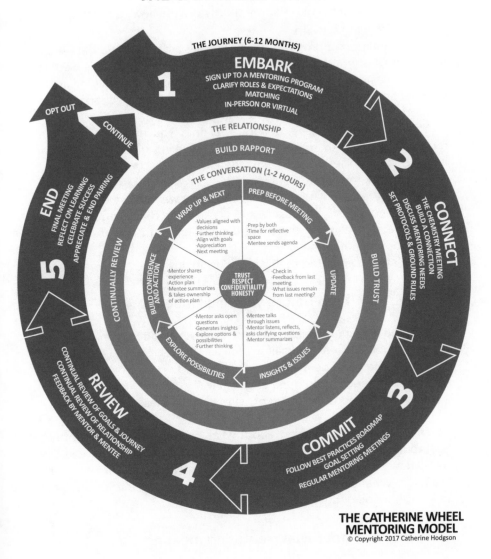

THE JOURNEY (6-12 MONTHS)

EMBARK
1
SIGN UP TO A MENTORING PROGRAM
CLARIFY ROLES & EXPECTATIONS
MATCHING
IN-PERSON OR VIRTUAL

OPT OUT

CONTINUE

THE RELATIONSHIP

BUILD RAPPORT

CONNECT
2
THE CHEMISTRY MEETING
BUILD A CONNECTION
DISCUSS MENTORING NEEDS
SET PROTOCOLS & GROUND RULES

THE CONVERSATION (1-2 HOURS)

WRAP UP & NEXT

PREP BEFORE MEETING

·Values aligned with decisions
·Further thinking
·Align with goals
·Appreciation
·Next meeting

·Prep by both
·Time for reflective space
·Mentee sends agenda

BUILD TRUST

END
5
FINAL MEETING
REFLECT ON LEARNING
CELEBRATE SUCCESS
APPRECIATE & END PAIRING

CONTINUALLY REVIEW

BUILD CONFIDENCE AND ACTION

·Mentor shares experience
·Action plan
·Mentee summarizes & takes ownership of action plan

TRUST
RESPECT
CONFIDENTIALITY
HONESTY

·Check in
·Feedback from last meeting
·What issues remain from last meeting?

UPDATE

·Mentor asks open questions
·Generates insights
·Explore options & possibilities
·Further thinking

·Mentee talks through issues
·Mentor listens, reflects, asks clarifying questions
·Mentor summarizes

EXPLORE POSSIBILITIES

INSIGHTS & ISSUES

REVIEW
4
CONTINUAL REVIEW OF GOALS & JOURNEY
CONTINUAL REVIEW OF RELATIONSHIP
FEEDBACK BY MENTOR & MENTEE

COMMIT
3
FOLLOW BEST PRACTICES ROADMAP
GOAL SETTING
REGULAR MENTORING MEETINGS

**THE CATHERINE WHEEL
MENTORING MODEL**
© Copyright 2017 Catherine Hodgson

Don't let it fizzle out. Celebrate it!

Most mentoring programs have a defined start date and end date. This is best practice as we then make the most use of the time allocated for our mentoring journey, and it allows both parties to have an ending to the relationship and move on to new things. It's also a good thing to leave on a high note, wanting to see each other again, rather than leaving the relationship until it's dysfunctional or there is resentment.

Saying goodbye at your final meeting does not necessarily mean that you can never meet again. We will shortly discuss how to redefine your relationship going forward.

If your mentoring program does not have a defined end date, then have a conversation with your mentoring partner to discuss this. Setting ground rules and discussing expectations right at the beginning of your relationship is a good idea and can prevent misconceptions that a mentoring relationship will last forever.

You may, before the end date, feel that you need to end your relationship sooner than expected. If you are feeling any of the following, it may be time to set up your final meeting:

- I don't look forward to our meetings.
- I've achieved all my goals we set and don't want to set any more.
- We are not meeting regularly, and we keep on cancelling meetings.
- I've learnt everything that I set out to learn and now want a new mentor for another need.
- I don't feel committed to this relationship any more.

Prep before your final meeting

Spend time reflecting on the goals you both set at the beginning of your mentoring journey. Ask yourself the following:

- Have these goals been achieved?
- What still needs to be done to get there?
- What may need to be put in place to achieve these goals?

Then spend time thinking about what your mentoring partner has contributed to your learning and journey so far. What would you like to acknowledge and tell them about? What would you like to thank them for? What do you still want to say to them? How do you see your relationship going forward?

Your final mentoring meeting

Your last meeting does not need to be as formal. You can plan a lunch or book a special venue. This is the time to celebrate your mentoring journey and the successes you have had along the way.

My mentor, Rob, and I had been meeting for 18 months and now it was approaching the end of our journey. We both acknowledged that the next meeting would be our last and I asked Rob if I could take him out to lunch for our final meeting, at a restaurant of his choice. We had had such a successful mentoring journey together and I wanted to celebrate it.

250

We met at a lovely restaurant, and I brought a small gift for him with a card to thank him for so generously giving of his time. We spent the afternoon together reflecting on our journey, what I had achieved, what he had remembered about the journey and what I had remembered about it. There were many little things that I had forgotten, so it was wonderful to be reminded of them and it felt satisfying that we had achieved so much. We also discussed what we wanted from our relationship going forward. We had become friends and decided to meet for a coffee every few months to have a catch up and check in. Having this final meeting was a true celebration of the success we had achieved, of our relationship and the journey we had walked, side by side.

Preparing for your final meeting and taking time to celebrate each other means that your mentoring journey will end on a much higher note than allowing it to fizzle out. All good things do come to an end, but it also means that you have both achieved so much and now it's time to move on to something new.

In your final meeting you may want to talk about the following:

1. Goals

Discuss the goals that were set and discuss what was achieved. Each of you needs to share with the other. I found that I had forgotten a lot that had happened along our mentoring journey and my mentor reminded me of certain milestones achieved and vice versa. It felt so satisfying that we had achieved so much together!

Are there things that still need to be achieved to reach some unmet goals? Discuss how these can be achieved. Are there new goals that you want to discuss with each other?

2. Feedback and feedforward

Ask for feedback and give feedforward to each other. What did you enjoy about your mentoring journey? What did you learn? What could be improved on for a future relationship?

3. Future

How do you want to redefine your relationship going forward? Do you still want to see each other for an informal chat and coffee? Do you want to keep in email contact? Do you want to check in with each other every now and then? Or is this the end and you do not care for any more contact? Have the conversation about your relationship going forward. In my mentoring relationship, we agreed to meet every few months for a coffee or a catch-up call as we both wanted to keep in touch.

4. Appreciation

Don't forget to thank your mentor or mentee for their commitment, time, and contribution to your journey. Do so sincerely and thoughtfully.

Key takeaways:

✓ End your mentoring journey by celebrating it rather than letting it fizzle out.

✓ A mentoring journey ended well will leave both parties feeling that it was a good experience.

✓ Spend time reflecting on what you achieved during your mentoring journey as well as what is next for both of you. Then appreciate each other sincerely and thoughtfully.

30

BEST PRACTICES FOR YOUR MENTORING JOURNEY

Here are some best practices that I have learnt over the years of running mentoring programs, as well as having been a mentor and mentee myself.

Seven best practices

1. Length of your mentoring journey

Formal mentoring relationships in a structured program usually last anywhere between three to 12 months or six to 10 meetings. Three months is a little on the short side, as it usually takes a couple of sessions to get to know each other, start to build some rapport and trust, set goals, and build momentum, unless of course you meet more frequently. However, this may also depend on the program that is designed for you by your organization or what is offered on a mentoring platform. Many people tend to opt for a shorter duration to start with, so that if it is not working, it is not too long until it ends. They can then lengthen the relationship if it is working. I usually do not recommend a proper developmental mentoring relationship that is shorter than six months, although I know organizations are opting for shorter durations. If you are dealing with and seeking some mentoring on just a certain issue, then a shorter relationship is perfect for you, as it will be more transactional. Sometimes, one session, which I call **flash mentoring**, is sufficient for some people dealing with a specific issue.

2. Frequency and length of sessions

Best practice is to meet every four to six weeks to maintain momentum and build the relationship. I find that meeting more often in the beginning is great because you are wanting to build the relationship and it's easier to do so if you are meeting more frequently. So, you can even meet every two to three weeks in the beginning and then you can stretch it out to five to six weeks after that. Meetings that happen more than eight weeks apart mean you can start to lose momentum and forget what happened in the last meeting. You then stand the chance of your relationship fizzling out.

The meeting should be approximately one hour if virtual, but can be up to two hours if in-person and both parties agree. Why do I say only one hour virtually? I have found that people get more tired when on a virtual call due to the intensity of looking at a screen and staying concentrated on a person's face and voice. However, if you find you can both manage longer, then discuss it and extend it to 90 minutes. Two hours in-person is really a gift; however, I know many organizations only allocate 30 minutes to one hour for face-to-face sessions. Just ensure you are fully prepared so that you get the most out of this shorter period.

3. Set ground rules

Ground rules should be established in your first meeting. Discuss the following:
- How often will we meet and for how long?
- Where will we meet – virtually (using what platform) or in person?
  - Virtual: Ensure that both parties are familiar with the platform. If one person is not used to the platform, give them a tour around the platform during your first session so they feel comfortable using it.
  - In-person: Ensure that you choose a place that is private and confidential, where both of you feel comfortable to share and be vulnerable. If your mentor chooses to have the meeting in their office, try not to sit at the mentor's desk, but rather next to each other or in chairs away from the desk. Remove all feeling of hierarchy.
- **Agreement on confidentiality, honesty, and openness.** This

is core to your mentoring relationship and it's important you discuss this upfront as well as at the beginning of each session, reiterating that confidentiality is key.

- **Commitment to the time it will take.** Discuss what to do if you have to cancel or change sessions. Discuss if you are both committed to this relationship. What could get in the way? How will you deal with it?
- **How to contact each other and how often.** We cannot presume that we can just pick up the phone at any time to contact our mentoring partner or send them a message. Boundaries need to be put in place. What are appropriate times and days to contact each other? Are evenings and weekends out of bounds except for emergencies? Discuss this upfront to avoid any awkward situations.

4. Set goals

Start with the bigger picture. Explore your mentee's purpose and aspirations. Then set goals that align to their values and purpose. Goals should be achievable but also a bit of a stretch for the mentee. If you do not have something to work towards then you do not have anything by which to measure the success of your journey.

Also remember that goals may change along the way, so remain flexible to doing so. Review your goals regularly to assess if you are on the path to achieving them.

5. The mentee drives the relationship

The mentee is the one who drives the relationship and takes ownership. They set up the meeting, send the agenda to their mentor a few days before their mentoring session, prepare for each session, give an update to their mentor, and ensure they expedite their action plans.

If the mentor is chasing the mentee for meetings and an agenda, then something is wrong!

6. Training

Both the mentor and mentee need training so you both get significant learning from your relationship. We only retain information if it is "sticky". So, even if you are reading this book and receiving learning from it, you will need to ensure it sticks with you. Tell someone about what you have just learnt. Watch a mentoring video. Read some one-pagers in a few weeks' time. Come back to this book and do some more exercises in a few months' time. Continue your journey of lifelong learning.

7. Closure

Ensure that you end the relationship formally, don't let it fizzle out! Set up a final meeting and reflect on your journey together. Ask each other questions such as: What did you learn? What will you take away from this relationship? What new ideas will help you going forward? Are there still goals that were not achieved and how will you go forward to achieve them? What was most useful in this relationship? What would you do differently? What did you enjoy the most? Do we want to keep in contact and how will we do that? Then appreciate each other sincerely.

31
REFLECTIONS AND "MY ASK"

Looking back over the past years and reflecting on my journey with mentoring, I can now appreciate and see what an exhilarating ride it has been.

Building and developing a global mentoring program has been one of the steepest learning curves of my life. It brought with it challenges that I had to navigate personally, in my marriage, and with fellow colleagues. It taught me that hard work, drive, and perseverance are not the only things that are needed to build something in a corporate culture. One needs teamwork as well as support and "buy-in" from the top.

However, it also revealed that having an entrepreneurial approach within a corporate environment can achieve things a lot quicker than doing things the traditional corporate way. I approached building the global mentoring program like building my own business. As an entrepreneur you start small, get your hands dirty, get things done, and you are involved in everything.

However, just as one person cannot run a big company, I could not run the mentoring program alone. It needed a passionate team. I was lucky enough to have the support around me when I needed it and I appreciate all those members and managers who believed in the program.

Through mentoring I was also able to find a passion that I never knew I had. I found my heart in mentoring. My purpose. My ikigai. I continue to meet the most amazing people through the workshops that I run and find myself drawn to furthering my studies of understanding the human mind, psychology, human behaviour, and communication. I've always been a lifelong learner and know that through mentoring and coaching, I will be able to continue to grow and give.

Pay it forward

When we receive mentoring, we are often forever grateful to the mentor who gave so generously of their time. "How can we repay them?", we may ask. I am hoping that the repayment will be that **you can pay it forward to someone else.**

I am not sure how many of you remember the movie *Pay it Forward* released in 2000? It is a story of a social studies teacher who gives an assignment to his junior high school class to think of an idea to change the world for the better, then put it into action. When one young student creates a plan for "paying forward" favours, he not only affects the life of his struggling single mother, but he sets in motion an unprecedented wave of human kindness which, unbeknown to him, has blossomed into a profound national phenomenon.

Although some may view the movie as a bit "cheesy", the notion of paying it forward is powerful and can have a ripple effect in society. The idea of traditional mentoring, taking someone under your wing and looking out for their career, lost for many years, seems to have suddenly returned in a new form of developmental mentoring as well as sponsorship mentoring. The need to ensure the wellbeing of employees as well as retention of our good employees has accelerated mentoring programs post-Covid.

If you have received mentoring and benefited from the experience, my wish is that you now pay it forward, just like the elders did in the past. Imagine the positive effect if everyone could pay it forward to one or two people? Even if you have never formally mentored anyone before, if you have some knowledge, you can impart it to others and be their support and guide. If you have the skills for the conversation, just being a sounding board and someone who can listen is perhaps all that is needed.

Ravishankar Gundlapalli, the founder and CEO of Mentorcloud, an online mentoring platform, is on a mission to impact 100 million people with the transformative power of mentorship. Let's all be on a mission to help with this and increase the number to one billion!

Don't be complacent. Don't sit on the sidelines. Do something now. Make a difference by being a mentor at some time in your life. Make a positive impact on someone else's life. Let's ignite, inspire, support, and start a global mentoring culture in our workplaces and our homes.

The world will surely be a better place as a result of it.

PART 5:
RESOURCES, WORKSHEETS, AND MEETING AGENDAS

FREQUENTLY ASKED QUESTIONS

Mentee FAQs

Do I need a mentor?

- You may need a mentor if you are about to experience or are currently experiencing a transition in your career, your work, or your life.
- You may be facing issues and challenges that will be better supported with a mentor.
- You may want to develop certain skills that will be more easily acquired if you had a mentor.
- You may want to develop and advance your career and have a mentor to help you do this.

What is the benefit of having a mentor?

Mentors usually have experience in what you are wanting to achieve and are able to help, guide, and support you on your journey. By encouraging you, guiding you, and sharing their wisdom and experience, they can help you with new insights and broaden your outlook. They can also be someone to hold you accountable to achieve the goals that you have set.

What can I expect from a mentor?

A mentor encourages, guides, and supports you. They are a sounding board and can help you develop your thinking around issues that are important to you so that your goals are achieved. They will share their wisdom, learning, and experience with you when appropriate. They can also make introductions to their network for you if they feel comfortable to do so.

How many mentors can I have?

You can have several mentors at the same time, for different areas of your life. However, ensure that you will be able to fulfil the needs of being a mentee and do not take on more than two if you cannot agree to commit to the process. A formal mentoring relationship requires time and commitment from the mentee, so be cautious if you take on more than one formal mentoring relationship at the same time.

How do I know if the mentor is a good match for me?

You will leave the meeting energized and look forward to the next meeting. You will feel positively challenged and be making progress towards your goals. You will usually feel that you have rapport and trust with the person, or that you are able to build it. You will feel that the mentor is making a valuable contribution to your life.

How do I contact the mentor once we are matched on a platform or by a program manager?

You can follow the process recommended on the platform, whether this is by email or a phone call. When contacting them, introduce yourself and ask for a first meeting.

How do I ask someone to be my mentor if I am not in a mentoring program where I will be matched?

If you have identified someone within or outside of your organization whom you think would be a great mentor for you, then you could contact them and ask if you could meet with them to ask a few questions or to get some advice. Most often, people are only too willing to help. Ensure you only book them for about 30 minutes, so they can commit to it. During your meeting you can mention some issues that you are facing and ask if they have faced a similar issue and if you could talk it through with them. If the meeting went well, you can ask if they would be prepared to meet with you again to discuss the issue with you. If the next meeting goes as well, and you think that both of you are getting value from it, then maybe you could ask if you could have regular meetings. With this soft approach, the person becomes your mentor without it formally being called mentoring.

I often find that if you approach someone and say, "Would you be my mentor?" they may feel they don't have time, or they are not sure what this would involve, or they are perhaps cautious of accepting such a big title. Going about it using a softer approach usually works very well.

How should I prepare for my meetings?

As a mentee, you should spend at least one hour preparing for your mentoring meetings. Send a calendar invitation to your mentor, a link if it's a virtual call, and an agenda at least a few days before your meetings. Spend some time in reflection asking questions such as:

- What has happened in the last weeks/month since our previous meeting?
- What has been challenging for me since we last met?
- What do I want to bring to the next meeting?
- What issues or challenges am I facing right now?
- What do I want to work on so that I move closer to my goals?
- How can my mentor help me with any of these issues or challenges?

Go through the action points you made from your last meeting and make notes on the progress made on each action point.

If you have kept a journal, go through your journal reflecting on what has happened in your life since your last meeting.

Mentor FAQs

How do I know if I will be a good mentor?

If you have some life experience or experience in your career, then you have wisdom and learning to share with others. Ask yourself the following questions:

- Do I enjoy developing other people?
- Do I understand myself and have I done self-reflection?
- Do I want to share my knowledge and learning with others?
- Am I open, honest, and prepared to build rapport and trust with other people?
- Have I got good communication skills? Am I a good listener?
- Can I ask questions and challenge other people when appropriate to help them with their thinking?
- Do I want to give back and make a difference in people's lives?
- Do I get fulfilment from helping and supporting other people?

What benefit will I get from being a mentor?

Mentoring is mutually beneficial so you will get great learning from this experience. You will learn as a mentor, not just from your mentee (seeing the world through their perspective or perhaps learning new skills through them), but also about yourself. You will be able to reflect on your own career and journey. You will also practise and develop your communication skills, which will benefit your career.

How much time will it take?

Your mentoring meeting is usually approximately one hour every four to six weeks. A gap longer than that usually decreases the momentum of the relationship and ability to achieve goals. Prep before a meeting will take approximately 30 minutes.

How many mentees can I mentor?

It depends on how experienced you are in being a mentor and how much time you have available, then you can have up to five mentees at a time. If you are not confident at mentoring, then start with one mentee. Most people find that one or two is sufficient at any one time.

Does a mentor always need to be someone senior or older than the mentee?

No. Mentoring can be with anyone who has experience in the area in which the mentee is seeking mentoring. Mentoring can be peer-to-peer, where there is an equal sharing of experience, or it can be senior to junior, or even junior to senior (this is often referred to as reverse mentoring).

Do I need to prepare anything before my meetings?

As a mentor you need to prepare for your meetings in the following ways:
- Ensure that you have enough time before your meeting to be in the correct headspace for your meeting – don't rush in from another meeting without having a gap to do some reflection first. This will ensure you are calm and present for your mentoring meeting.
- Read over your notes from the previous meeting to familiarize yourself with the conversation.
- Are there any actions that you committed to do before the next meeting?

General mentoring FAQs

How long should the mentoring relationship last?

Formal mentoring relationships in a structured program usually last between six and 12 months. If you sign up for six months, then you can usually renew for another six months if both parties agree to do so. It is important that the mentoring relationship has a definite beginning and an end so that there are no false expectations.

How often should we meet and for how long?

Best practice is to meet every four to six weeks to maintain momentum and build the relationship. The meeting should be approximately one hour if it's held virtually but can be up to two hours if in-person and both parties agree. Meetings that last less than one hour mean you don't usually get into the depth of conversation that you should be having.

How do I know if it's working or not?

Ask yourself the following:
- Do I feel energized when I leave the meeting?
- Do I look forward to the next meeting?
- Do I feel positively challenged and have I experienced new insights?
- Are we moving forward towards the goals set?
- Have people around me noticed any positive changes?

How can I improve the relationship?

Focus on building rapport and trust with each other.
- Have we spent enough time getting to know each other?
- Are our values aligned? What values do we have in common?
- What are we both passionate about?
- Have we shared something with each other that they may not know about us?
- Are we open, transparent, and honest in our conversations?
- Have an open conversation about how to improve your relationship and build rapport and trust.

What should we do if we just don't connect?

If you have tried everything and you are still not connecting or not getting anything out of the relationship, then have an open and honest conversation about what you both want to do about it. Don't just let the relationship fizzle out. Rather end it formally with mutual agreement. Then start again with someone else.

Can we extend our mentoring relationship after the end date?

Yes, if both parties agree to do so and if your mentoring program allows it. Ensure that you sign another mentoring agreement with a specific beginning and end date.

How do I deal with someone from a different culture to me?

Mentoring across cultures can work very well as people develop cultural awareness and increase their learning of another culture. However, both parties should be sensitive to each other's needs and respect their boundaries. It is important that you spend time at the beginning of the relationship to understand each other's cultural preferences before embarking on your mentoring journey.

Talk about your culture and what is appropriate and comfortable for you during your meetings such as eye contact, how to address one another, how to contact one another, if the meeting is virtual do you prefer the camera off or on, how you both feel about the use of jokes and slang, and so on.

Agree to talk openly to each other if one person offends the other unknowingly.

What should I do if my mentee/mentor is not committed to the program?

Have an open discussion with each other to find out what may be causing the one person to be less committed to the program. Look out for signs of low commitment, such as:

- Cancelling meetings;
- Being late for meetings;
- Ending meetings early;
- Not being present during meetings;

- Not sending through agendas for preparing for meetings;
- Regularly not working on any actions that were committed to at the end of each meeting; and
- Does the person showing a lack of commitment want to continue with the mentoring relationship? If they do, what will they commit to doing to improve their commitment? If not, should we end the relationship?

WORKSHEETS

Worksheets and exercises to assist you on your mentoring journey:

Worksheet 1: Reflection exercise for mentees

Reflect on the following questions to find out if you are ready to be a mentee:

1. Would you like to spend time exploring your personal growth, career development, and purpose in life with someone who is objective?
2. Would you like to have a safe place to discuss your vision, dreams, and aspirations with a mentor?
3. Are you going through a transition in your life that you require support with?
4. Are there skills you would like to develop in your current role or require for a new role?
5. Are you struggling with a particular issue at the moment?
6. Would you like to learn from someone who has experience and wisdom in the area in which you are seeking mentoring?
7. Do you have goals that you would like to achieve, and would you like someone to guide you on your journey?
8. Do you want someone to hold you accountable?
9. Are you ready to be positively challenged?
10. Are you looking for someone to be a sounding board off which you can bounce your ideas and thinking?
11. Is lifelong learning important to you?
12. Are you willing to commit the necessary time to the process?

Worksheet 2: The Seven Strengths of Highly Effective Mentors exercise

Look at the Seven Strengths of Highly Effective Mentors model below. As a mentor, write down or circle what you are good at. What are your strengths? What are your "superpowers"? Now, write down or circle in a different colour those things that you know you are not so good at. What can you do to improve them?

If you are a mentee, write down or circle those things that are important for you in a mentor.

THE 7 STRENGTHS OF HIGHLY EFFECTIVE MENTORS
P.R.E.S.E.N.T.

THE 7 STRENGTHS OF HIGHLY EFFECTIVE MENTORS MODEL
© Copyright 2020 Catherine Hodgson

As a mentor my strengths are:

_____

_____

_____

As a mentor my weak points are:

_____

_____

_____

What can I do to improve them?

_____

_____

_____

Worksheet 3: The Seven Strengths of Highly Effective Mentees exercise:

Look at the Seven Strengths of Highly Effective Mentees Model. As a mentee, write down or circle what you are good at – what are your strengths? Now, write down or circle in a different colour those things that you know you are not so good at. What can you do to improve them?

If you are a mentor doing this exercise, write down or circle those things that are important for you in a mentee – what would you like to see in your mentee?

THE 7 STRENGTHS OF HIGHLY EFFECTIVE MENTEES

P.R.E.P.A.R.E.

THE 7 STRENGTHS OF HIGHLY EFFECTIVE MENTEES MODEL
© Copyright 2020 Catherine Hodgson

As a mentee my strengths are:

_____
_____
_____

As a mentee my weak points are:

_____
_____
_____

What can I do to improve them?

_____
_____
_____

Worksheet 4: Prepare for your chemistry meeting

Reflect on the following questions and make some notes. In brackets is who should do this exercise.

- What are five things that I value most? (Both mentor and mentee) (Go to the exercise on identifying your values on page 294.)

_____

_____

_____

- What are my strengths? My superpowers? What am I good at? (Both mentor and mentee.) There are many tools that can be used for this such as online "strengths finder" tests, or this free one from High 5: https://high5test.com.

_____

_____

_____

- What energizes me? What do I love to do? (Both mentor and mentee)

_____

_____

_____

- What am I prepared to share with my mentoring partner that opens me up to being vulnerable? (Both mentor and mentee)

_____

_____

_____

- What difficulty have I experienced in my life/career that has taught me a meaningful lesson? (Mentor)

_____
_____
_____

- What are my aspirations? In my personal life? In my career/business? (Mentee)

_____
_____
_____

- What do I want to improve on in my life/career? (Mentee)

_____
_____
_____

Worksheet 5: Key questions to ask my mentor

Once you have reflected on these questions and made notes, write down three key questions you would like to ask your mentoring partner in the first meeting.

Three key questions I would like to ask my mentor:
1. _____
2. _____
3. _____

Worksheet 6: Your mentoring needs

Reflect on the following questions and make some notes:

- What do I want to get out of this mentoring process? (Both mentor and mentee)

_____

_____

- What do I want to learn? (Both mentor and mentee)

_____

_____

- What is my role as a mentee? (Mentee)

_____

_____

- What do I expect from my mentor? (Mentee)

_____

_____

- What do I want to learn from my mentor? (Mentee)

_____

_____

- What can I offer my mentee? (Mentor)

_____

_____

- What is my role as a mentor? (Mentor)

_____

_____

Worksheet 7: Goal-setting

GOAL-SETTING WORKSHEET

	Explore different areas that you are dealing with in your work and personal life.		
STEP 1 DISCOVER			

	Filter the list and reduce it to three areas that would be relevant to mentoring.		
	Area 1	Area 2	Area 3
STEP 2 FILTER			

	Define and clarify three primary goals.		
	Goal 1	Goal 2	Goal 3
STEP 3 DEFINE			

	What is needed to achieve these goals?		
STEP 4 NEEDS ANALYSIS			

STEP 5 BLOCKAGES	What can get in the way of you achieving your goal?		
	Goal 1	Goal 2	Goal 3

Write down milestones with a timeline and then an action plan for each milestone.

STEP 6 MILESTONES	Milestone & Action	Milestone & Action	Milestone & Action

STEP 6 ACTION PLAN	Milestone & Action	Milestone & Action	Milestone & Action

	Milestone & Action	Milestone & Action	Milestone & Action

Once you have completed setting up your goals, you are ready for your regular mentoring conversations so you can work towards achieving these goals.

Worksheet 8: Your top five pressing issues

Write down your top five most pressing issues. What is keeping you awake at night? What can you not stop thinking about? What comes to mind first, without thinking too hard about it? It could be business related, family, or personal.

1. Write down what comes to you first – up to five issues.
2. Look at your list and rate these issues according to urgency on a scale of 1 to 5 (1 = least urgent, 5 = most urgent). Put a number next to the issue.
3. Rate according to the importance of the issue to you in achieving your overall goals or purpose (1 = least important, 5 = most important). Put that number next to your urgency number. For instance, you may have a goal of running the next London marathon. Then getting fit would rank as 5 in order of importance for you to achieve this goal.
4. Now add up the urgent and important numbers, and then rank your list from highest to lowest. Circle the highest number – that is your most urgent and important issue.
5. Out of these issues, what is causing you the most stress? Are there any that you would like to bring to the next mentoring session?

You can give this exercise to your mentee to do before their session with you, so that they then have time to think about the issue and what they would like to get out of their next mentoring meeting with you.

Worksheet 9: Visualization exercise

1. Sit in a chair to remain alert, feet firmly placed on the ground. Close your eyes or shift your gaze downward.

2. How does your body feel? Do you need to shift your position to feel more comfortable?

3. Be aware of the chair you are sitting on and your contact with it. Be aware of your feet on the floor.

4. How are you feeling emotionally? Do you feel calm? Relaxed? Stressed? Tired? Impatient? Accept that emotion.

5. Relax and take a deep breath in through your nose to the count of four, hold and release slowly to the count of four. Repeat three times, focusing on your breath.

6. Feel your body relaxing. Notice any spots of tension in your body. Breathe in again and focus on those spots, releasing the tension from your body.

7. Resume normal breathing in and out.

8. Picture a ray of light, bright and warm above your head. It is shining down, the rays moving into your head. You can feel it now shining in your brain. Your brain is open is receive this warmth. Any thoughts you have, judgments and opinions are now being dissolved by this warm light. Bask in this warmth.

9. Your mind is now free of thoughts. You have a completely open mind, ready to learn. You are infinitely curious.

10. Take a deep breath in and as you breathe out, say the word "curious" to yourself.

11. The light is passing through your head, down your neck and into your chest. The light is now shining its warmth on your heart. Place a hand on your heart.

12. You are thinking about someone you love, a person, pet, physical or spiritual being or a place that you love

to be, a place that makes you feel happy and where you feel safe. You feel love. You are grateful. You are joyful. You are generous. You are safe. Your heart is so big you feel it could burst. You are feeling the light warming it and making that love expand. Bask in that warmth and love.

13. Take a deep breath in and as you breathe out, say the word "love" to yourself.

14. The light now travels downwards towards your belly. Your belly starts to feel warm from the light. Place a hand on your belly.

15. Think of a time when you were not afraid, when you did something that was brave, when you were courageous and proud of yourself. Your belly is warm as you think about this. If you were feeling any anxiety or fear beforehand, it has now disappeared. Bask in the warmth in your belly.

16. Take a deep breath in and as you breathe out, say the word "courage" to yourself.

17. The light now travels down your legs, to your feet and out through your toes. You are left feeling full and satisfied.

18. Revisit your head and say the word "curious". Revisit your heart and say the word "love". Revisit your belly and say the word "courage".

19. Take another deep breath in and slowly out.

20. Open your eyes and come back to the room.

Did you have any difficulty with this visualization? Did one area feel uncomfortable to focus on? Were you able to access the other areas more easily? Sometimes, people find that they have difficulty with one area, which is an area that they do not give enough attention to or that they find it more difficult to access. If, for instance, you can do the head or gut but find the heart more difficult, then you know that listening to your heart is probably not what you do very often.

Marcia Reynolds says that people who tend to be helpers listen more easily from their heart than their gut. Risk-takers, who move quickly on instinct, find it easier to listen from their gut than their heart.

In your everyday conversations, try to practise receiving from your most vulnerable place and to listen from your head, heart, and gut. This will help you open up and align your entire nervous system when you are mentoring.

The most important thing you can do as a mentor is to be fully present during your mentoring conversation. Focus on how you can achieve this and how you can stay present throughout.

Worksheet 10: W.R.A.P. exercise

If you are on a virtual call, share your screen with your mentee and show them the acronym W.R.A.P. You answer the questions one by one, and your mentee then does the same.

- WHAT CONCERNS have surfaced or remain?
- Is there anything that was RESOLVED after our session today?
- Has there been a new AWARENESS after our session today?
- What do you PLAN to do as a result of today?

Worksheet 11: L.E.A.R.N. exercise

The L.E.A.R.N. acronym may also be suitable.

L. What has been your biggest LEARNING today?
E. What are you most EXCITED about?
A. What are you most ANXIOUS about?
R. What RESONATED with you today?
N. Is there anything that you still NEED?

Worksheet 12: Key mentoring skills proficiency

Don't skip this! Do this exercise now on a piece of paper. Put a tick next to each statement that you feel reflects your skill.

Listening:
- I find it hard to just sit and listen – my mind keeps on wandering.
- I listen but I'm also listening to another conversation next to me.
- I listen but find that I wait for a pause so I can share my story with the other person too.
- I listen without interrupting at all and notice people's body language as well.
- I find it easy to listen and people often tell me I'm a good listener.

Reflecting:
- I never reflect back to people what I hear or see.
- I sometimes reflect back to the other person.
- I find myself often reflecting back what I hear or see.

Summarizing:
- I never summarize after I have heard what the other person has said.
- I sometimes summarize what I have heard.
- I always summarize what I have heard to make sure I understand what the other person is saying.

Questioning:
- I hardly ever ask questions.
- I sometimes ask questions when I feel the need to.
- I'm very curious and ask questions all the time.

Feedback:
- I never give feedback and find it very difficult to do so.
- I give feedback but feel uncomfortable doing so.
- I give feedback all the time.
- I don't like receiving feedback.
- I don't mind receiving feedback.
- I see feedback as a learning opportunity.

Advice:
- I always tell people what to do and love giving advice.
- I sometimes tell people what to do.
- I hold back on telling people what to do and rather ask questions.

Sharing experience:
- I don't like sharing my experience with others – I'm a private person.

- I don't mind sharing my experience with others.
- I love sharing my experience with others.
- I never ask permission to share my experience with others – I just do it.
- I always ask permission to share my experience with others.

Worksheet 13: Five steps to mindful listening

Exercise: Look at the five steps to mindful listening. Ask yourself the following questions and write them down:

Which step do you currently listen at? Where is your default listening?

_____

What listening step would you like to listen at?

_____

What can you do to listen at a higher listening level?

_____

Which person or people do you struggle to listen to?

_____

What can you do to listen to them at a higher level?

_____

THE FIVE STEPS OF LISTENING

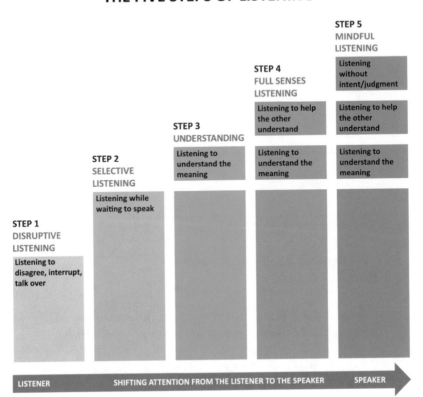

Worksheet 14: Skills to practise in your conversations

Go through the set of verbs below. Which skills do you need to improve in your conversations? Write each one down on a separate piece of paper or sticky note. For example, you may decide that being present, listening, asking, and empathizing are four key focus areas that you need to improve. Write each of these on a separate piece of paper or sticky note.

- Accept, don't judge
- Be present
- Listen
- Reflect
- Clarify
- Summarize
- Ask
- Empathize
- Share

In your next conversation, focus particularly on that one area that you wrote down. If you have genuinely achieved it, then put that sticky paper to one side and for your next conversation, focus on another area that you have written down. If you did not manage to achieve it, then focus on that skill again for your next conversation.

Commit to putting those sticky notes somewhere visible so they are a reminder for you to continue to focus on building these skills.

Worksheet 15: Powerful questions

Now is the chance to do some reflection by asking yourself some of these powerful questions. You can write the answers down or simply think about them. Most importantly, how did these questions feel to you? How do you think a mentee would feel if you asked them these questions?

- Who are you and who do you want others to think you are?
- Who is the person you aspire to become?
- What has fear (of failure) kept you from doing?
- What's the most courageous decision you've ever made?
- What's a conversation that you really need to have with someone, but haven't had so far?
- What dream have you yet to have the courage to act on?
- What self-limiting beliefs might be getting in the way of your own personal development?
- What mistakes do you find yourself regularly repeating?
- What have you learnt about yourself recently that has surprised you?
- With all that's changing in the world and in our customers' lives, what business are you really in?

Worksheet 16: Unlocking questions

Here are some examples of unlocking questions. Grab a pen and paper or your laptop and choose some that resonate with you. Take your time and answer them.

- If you were not to hold back in your life, what would you be doing?
- If you knew you were vital to your organization's success, how would you approach your work?
- If you were to become chief executive, what problem would you solve first, and how would you do it?

- If things could be exactly right for you in a situation you are facing, how would they have had to change?
- If you knew you had all the skills necessary, what would you do?
- If you were not afraid (if you were brave), what would you do?
- If you knew you were good enough, what would change for yourself?
- If you knew your children were taken care of in all aspects, what would you do with the rest of your life?
- If you knew you were worth it, what would you want?
- If you knew something wonderful was going to happen today, how would you feel?

You can now get the feeling of what that feels like. Truly liberating, isn't it?

Worksheet 17: Feedback

Take some time right now to answer the following questions about feedback:
- How do I feel about receiving feedback?
- What would make me more open to receiving feedback?
- How can I express this to my mentoring partner?
- How do I feel about giving feedback?
- How can I make my mentoring partner be more open to receiving feedback from me?
- Do I use feedforward?
- How can I use feedforward in my mentoring relationship?

Worksheet 18: Are you an advisor your mentee can trust?

- Credibility: Put down a number from 1 (not at all credible) to 10 (highly credible) rating how credible you are. How honest are you? If you say that you know something, how much do you know about it?
- Reliability: Put down a number from 1 (not at all reliable) to 10 (highly reliable) on how reliable you are. Do you follow through with your commitments all the time, or only some of the time? Can others rely on you all the time?
- Intimacy/vulnerability: Put down a number from 1 (not at all in tune with my feelings and emotions or unwilling to be vulnerable) to 10 (highly in tune with my feelings and emotions and willing to be vulnerable) on how vulnerable you are and ready to share your feelings with others.
- Self-orientation/ego: Put down a number from 1 (not at all self-oriented) to 10 (highly self-oriented) on how self-oriented you are. How important is it for you to be liked by others? How important is it for you to be right? Do you let your ego get in the way? Do you interrupt others, finish their sentences, or not listen to them?
- Now add up the first three numbers you put down for credibility, reliability, and intimacy. Divide that number by your self-orientation number and you will get your trusted advisor number. The higher the number, the more you are regarded as a trusted advisor. If you scored 9 + 10 + 8 = 27 / 3 = 9, then you are highly regarded as a trusted advisor. If you scored 6 + 5 + 3 = 14/7 = 2, then you have a bit of work to do to be regarded as a trusted advisor.

Worksheet 19: Can we score our relationship 100%?

Ask each other to write down on a scale of 1 to 100% how you would rate the relationship. Remember that not every relationship needs to be 100%. An 80% may be enough for some people.

Next, write down on a scale of 1 to 100% where you would like the relationship to be.

Now ask yourself:
- What can I do to get it there?
- What can my mentor/mentee do to get it there?

Share the information with each other. Now have the conversation and share what you have reflected on.

Worksheet 20: Feedback Survey

1. Are the mentoring sessions meeting your expectations?

1 Not what I expected	2	3	4	5 Exceeding my expectations
O	O	O	O	O

2. How is your relationship with your mentor/mentee?

1 Not good at all	2	3	4	5 Very good
O	O	O	O	O

3. Can you share two to three takeaways or learnings so far? What is going well? What are you struggling with?

MEETING AGENDAS

 MEETING AGENDA 1

The chemistry meeting agenda
(60 minutes)

1. BUILDING RAPPORT AND TRUST (20 MINUTES)
Get to know each other and build on this rapport and trust in further meetings. • Introduce yourself and give a little background – personal, family, career, interests. • What do we have in common? • Share something that the other person may not know about you.
2. AGREEMENT FOR ENGAGEMENT AND SETTING GROUND RULES (10 MINUTES)
What do you both agree on for you to engage with each other going forward? This agreement needs to be reviewed at each meeting. Draw up a list together. • Safe haven and confidentiality • Commitment to the journey • Honesty and openness • Being present • Actively listen • Desire for both to learn from each other • How to give feedback and how often • Challenging each other • Reviewing our relationship – how do we do it and how often? • What will we do if the other person does not commit to this agreement going forward? • How often should we meet and for how long? • Who drives the relationship and sets up meetings? • What boundaries need to be put in place? • How do we contact each other outside of this meeting? • What time commitment is expected for this mentoring journey? • Are we both prepared to commit to the time required?
3. ROLES AND EXPECTATIONS (10 MINUTES)
Discuss with each other the roles and expectations of a mentor and mentee. • What is my understanding of what a mentee should do?

Continued
• What are your expectations of a mentor? • What is my understanding of what a mentor should do? • What are your expectations of a mentee?

4. ASPIRATIONS AND GOALS (15 MINUTES)
Discuss your aspirations for your mentoring journey. Both to share. • What do you aspire to get from this mentoring journey? • Do you have any challenges, issues, or dilemmas that you are wanting to bring to the mentoring conversations? (Not to go into detail, but to share top level and then decide what to bring along for next meeting.) • Do you have any goals that you have been thinking about? • Do you want to list any primary goals that you would like to work on and any secondary goals? • How would you define those goals in one sentence or a few words?

5. WRAP UP AND APPRECIATION (5 MINUTES)
Closing the first meeting. • Set up a date, time, and place in the calendar for your next meeting. • Exchange any other contact details you may not already have shared. • Reminder for the mentee to send the agenda or list of discussion points a few days before the next meeting. • Appreciate each other.

 **MEETING AGENDA 2**

Regular Mentoring Meeting Agenda
(60 minutes)

Mentoring Meeting Agenda

1. UPDATE: (10 MINUTES)
<ul><li>Reminder of confidentiality</li><li>Check in and update of what has happened since last meeting</li><li>Action points from last meeting</li></ul>
2. ISSUES AND INSIGHTS: (20 MINUTES)
<ul><li>Current reality</li><li>Issues/challenges/topics to discuss</li><li>Desired outcomes</li><li>Review goals</li></ul>
3. EXPLORE POSSIBILITIES: (15 MINUTES)
<ul><li>Explore options to achieve outcomes</li><li>Strategies to achieve goal</li><li>Mentor sharing</li></ul>
4. BUILD CONFIDENCE AND ACTION: (10 MINUTES)
<ul><li>List actions</li></ul>
5. WRAP UP AND NEXT: (5 MINUTES)
<ul><li>Next meeting</li><li>Appreciation</li></ul>

 **MEETING AGENDA 3**

Regular Mentoring Meeting Agenda using The Conversation Flow
(60 minutes)

Mentoring Meeting Agenda

1. UPDATE: (10 MINUTES)

- Check in
- What has gone well for you since our last conversation?
- What successes have you had?
- What achievements have you had?
- What issues remain from the last meeting?

Admin
- When will we close this meeting today?
- Can we remind each other about our agreement for engagement and the confidentiality?

2. ISSUES AND INSIGHTS: (20 MINUTES)

CURRENT REALITY
- Where would you like to focus this session today?
- What would you like to work on today?
- What would you like to achieve from this conversation?
- What would you like to build on from the last session?
- What have you been avoiding thinking about lately?
- What thinking have you done so far?
- Can you put it into one sentence?
- How can I help you think this through?

DESIRED OUTCOME
- What is your vision for this area?
- How does it fit into your overall goals?
- At the end of this session, what would you have been pleased to have achieved?
- What is your desired outcome?
- What do you want to happen? Why?

THE MENTOR SUMMARIZES
- Summarize the key issue and the desired outcome.

---

3. EXPLORE POSSIBILITIES: (15 MINUTES)

- Would you like to explore some ways to move this new idea forward?
- How do you think we might move this insight forward?
- What are some possible paths we could take from here?
- What other options come to mind? (Summarize)
- What else could you do? (Summarize)
- What have you done before that could work well here?
- What could you do differently?

MENTOR SHARING:
- Mentor can now offer to share experiences, wisdom and offer suggestions if asked.
- Would you find value in listening to some possibilities that I've thought of?
- Would you like me to share some of my own experiences with you around this issue?
- Which questions would you like to ask me to assist you?

---

4. BUILD CONFIDENCE AND ACTION: (10 MINUTES)

- What steps and actions would you like to commit to, to make this goal happen?
- What other steps can you take?
- What other actions can you think of?
- By when will you do this?
- How committed are you to achieve this on a scale of 1 to 10?
- What could hold you back from achieving this action?
- How will you stay accountable to achieve this action?
- Is the action clearly worded? Realistic? Accurate? Focused? Does it have a timeline for completion?
- Summarize the actions written down.

---

5. WRAP UP AND NEXT: (5 MINUTES)

- Is the action aligned to the person's goals and values?
- Any further thinking?
- What issues have surfaced or still remain?
- What insights have you had?
- What ideas are you taking away?
- What intentions do you have as a result of today?
- When will we meet again? Date, time, place

---

6. APPRECIATION

Appreciate each other sincerely and graciously.

VALUES LIST

Develop a shortlist of your top values. Create a list of your top 20 values, without trying to order them at all. Do this by circling 20 of the values from the list below.

Once you have done that, what values can you let go of, so that you come up with 10 of your most important values.

Can these be narrowed down to five?

VALUES EXERCISE

Abundance	Emotional Intelligence	Integrity	Risk taking
Accountability	Empathy	Joy	Security
Accuracy	Enjoyment	Justice	Self-actualization
Achievement	Enthusiasm	Kindness	Self-control
Advancement	Equality	Leadership	Selflessness
Adventurousness	Excellence	Learning	Self-reliance
Altruism	Excitement	Leisure	Sensitivity
Ambition	Experimentation	Legacy	Serenity
Assertiveness	Expertise	Love	Service
Attention to detail	Exploration	Loyalty	Shrewdness
Authenticity	Expressiveness	Making a difference	Simplicity
Balance	Fairness	Mastery	Soundness
Being the best	Faith	Moral fulfillment	Speed
Belonging	Family-orientedness	Open communication	Spontaneity
Boldness	Fidelity	Openness	Stability
Calmness	Financial Security	Optimism	Strategic
Carefulness	Freedom	Order	Strength
Challenging myself	Focus	Originality	Structure
Collaboration	Friendship	Perfection	Success
Commitment	Fun	Patriotism	Support
Community	Generosity	Personal expression	Take responsibility
Compassion	Global awareness	Personal Growth	Teamwork
Competitiveness	Goodness	Positivity	Temperance
Consistency	Grace	Practicality	Thankfulness

Values list

Contentment	Growth	Preparedness	Thoroughness
Continually Improve	Happiness	Professionalism	Thoughtfulness
Contribution	Hard Work	Physical challenge	Timeliness
Control	Harmony	Play	Tolerance
Courage	Health	Power	Traditionalism
Creativity	Helping others	Pride	Tranquility
Curiosity	Honesty	Protect environment	Trustworthiness
Decisiveness	Honor	Quality-orientation	Truth-seeking
Democratic	Humility	Quality of life	Understanding
Dependability	Independence	Quiet times	Uniqueness
Determination	Ingenuity	Recognition	Unity
Diligence	Influence	Relationships	Usefulness
Discipline	Innovation	Reliability	Vision
Discretion	Inquisitiveness	Resourcefulness	Vitality
Diversity	Insightfulness	Respect	
Effectiveness	Intelligence	Restraint	
Efficiency	Intellectual Status	Results-oriented	

ACKNOWLEDGMENTS

The Mentoring Roadmap would not have been possible without the help of a very supportive group of people I'd like to acknowledge.

My husband, Nic, who has stood by my side and supported me on my mentoring learning journey since 2009. I could not have achieved what I have without him cheering me on, stepping in to look after our daughters and the business while I travelled, and encouraging me when he would have loved to have had me stop sometimes and just be. This book would not have been possible without you. Thank you for being my rock!

My beautiful daughters, Sarah-Jane and Emily, who have had to put up with having a busy mother who is often preoccupied with work and mentoring. I thank you both for your love, support and encouragement during this journey. Sarah-Jane designed and drew the line illustrations in this book and I want to thank her for this – you are so talented!

My loyal and committed graphic designer, Sophia Mortakis-Lasker, who has worked with me on this book, doing all the designs and illustrations as well as assisting me with designs and material for mentoring over the past 10 years. Sophia was instrumental in the design of the Catherine Wheel and all its iterations. She has also been my producer on my virtual mentoring workshops, quietly and diligently working behind the scenes so that they can be a success. Thank you for all you have done, I appreciate you so much!

My good friend, Sally Rutherford, who has worked with me on editing my mentoring materials over the past few years. She did an initial proofreading of the manuscript and gave me wise input on the cover and layout. You have such an incredible talent in making my words flow seamlessly and I appreciate your friendship and support over the years.

My friend and mentor, Rob Katz, who stood by my side and guided me for 18 months as a mentor during a time of transition in my life. Thank you for being the most amazing mentor to me. We became good friends and I always look forward to our catch-ups and conversations.

I would never have got involved with mentoring if it had not been for YPO (Young Presidents' Organization). During this time I was supported along my mentoring journey by so many incredible people. I will try my best to acknowledge those who helped me along the way, and if I leave anyone out, then I do apologize and want to say that I appreciate you!

Amy Hartlaub, the YPO mentoring manager at the time when I was on the international committees and with whom I worked for five years rolling out the mentoring program globally. Amy was the most amazing person to work with, always enthusiastic, willing, conscientious, supportive, and kind. We had quite a journey together and it was a privilege to work with you for so long.

Paul Lamontagne and Justin Taylor, both YPO members who were the committee chairs under whom I worked. Both of you were leaders I admired and it was a pleasure to work on your committees under your leadership. You both supported me, and I appreciate everything you did for me on my mentoring journey.

My colleagues who formed part of our global mentoring committee at YPO, Kavit Handa, Jayant Mammen Mathew, Brian Cohen, and Michael Bloch. Thank you for all you did to help grow mentoring within the organization and for your unwavering encouragement. We were able to laugh especially when times were tough!

The management of YPO, Sean Magennis, the ex-COO of YPO, who always held up the flag for mentoring and would be a sounding board for me when I needed it. Immanuel Commarmond, Karen Lindblom Morais, Joy Hayes, Sabrina Beleck, and Zoe Williams who worked so hard to roll mentoring out globally, as well as all the wonderful managers who were assisting at regional and chapter level.

There were so many fellow YPO members and spouses who encouraged me in YPO and helped to drive mentoring over the years. I thank all of you for your unwavering support.

I would like to acknowledge the mentoring facilitators who facilitated mentoring masterclasses around the globe, bringing mentoring to members, and making a difference in peoples' lives. A special mention to Roni Witkin, who together with my sister, Margie van Rensburg, helped me to start the juices flowing for the development of the Catherine Wheel.

My good friend, Anthea Boehmke, who assisted me when I first wanted to run mentoring workshops and facilitated the first workshops for YPO. It was fun having you by my side during those early days and I really appreciate you and your unwavering support and friendship.

A special thank you to our staff, especially our GM, Carol Osler, for keeping the business running smoothly and efficiently, affording me the time to spend writing this book. You are an amazing team!

David Clutterbuck, the pioneer of developmental mentoring, has been a huge inspiration and mentor to me since I first reached out to him in 2011. He has taught me so much about mentoring and I am forever thankful to him for taking the time, in the early days, to answer my endless questions and be such a great teacher. I admire the work he has done in the field of mentoring and coaching, and I'm in awe of the number of books he has written. Besides being such an incredible mentor, he is also great company and a raconteur at a dinner party.

I would like to acknowledge and thank Ravishankar Gundlapalli, the founder and CEO of MentorCloud, and author of *The Art of Mentoring*, with whom I have had the pleasure of working over the years. He has such a passion for mentoring, which I greatly admire.

The Mentoring Roadmap would not have been possible without the wise input from Sarah Bullen from The Writing Room, who gave me valuable counsel to get started, as well as feedback to improve my book along the way, including a very comprehensive manuscript appraisal.

A special thank you to Aimèe Armstrong, the publishing coordinator from Staging Post, part of Jacana Media, who was so professional at every turn and kept me on track. Thank you to Margot Bertelsmann, who was the copy editor for the book, and everyone at Staging Post who got involved in the various other aspects of production and contributed to the slick output.

Lastly, a heartfelt thank you to my supportive family and friends who have taken an interest in what I do and always asked me questions to find out how the book was coming along. This book would have been much harder to complete without you cheering me along the way. My only regret is that my father-in-law passed away before the book was published. He was so proud of me and could not wait to hold the book in his hands. I know he is watching me from somewhere, with a huge smile on his face as he sees this book come into fruition.

RESOURCES

Page 20

Mentoring is on the top list for L&D teams

Taylor, D.H. 8 February 2022. 'L&D Social Sentiment Survey'. https:// donaldhtaylor.co.uk/insight/gss2022-results-01-general/

Page 21

Mentoring produces employees that are more highly valued by the business

Knowledge at Wharton Staff. 16 May 2007. 'Workplace Loyalties Change, but the Value of Mentoring Doesn't'. https://knowledge. wharton.upenn.edu/podcast/knowledge-at-wharton-podcast/ workplace-loyalties-change-but-the-value-of-mentoring-doesnt/

Mentoring is an important career development tool

Balu, L. and James, L. 2016. 'Facilitating Employees Career through Mentoring Methods',European Journal of Business and Management, Vol 8, No. 7. www.core.ac.uk/download/pdf/234627135.pdf
Rapp, A. 2018. 'Be One, Get One: The Importance Of Mentorship'. www.forbes.com/sites/yec/2018/10/02/be-one-get-one-the-importance-of-mentorship/?sh=443e481e7434

Page 22

Mentoring programs boost diversity and retention in businesses

Hunt, D.V., Yee, L. and Prince, S. 2018. 'Delivering Growth through Diversity in the Workplace'. www.mckinsey.com/capabilities/ people-and-organizational-performance/our-insights/delivering-through-diversity

Mentoring supports women in executive positions which increases net profit

Noland, Marcus (PIIE) and Moran, Tyler (PIIE), February 8, 2016. Peterson Institute for International Economics (PIIE) https://www. piie.com/commentary/op-eds/study-firms-more-women-c-suite-are-more-profitable

Page 23

Mentoring in Fortune 500 companies

Knowledge at Wharton Staff. 16 May 2007. 'Workplace Loyalties Change, but the Value of Mentoring Doesn't'. https://knowledge. wharton.upenn.edu/podcast/knowledge-at-wharton-podcast/ workplace-loyalties-change-but-the-value-of-mentoring-doesnt/

Mentoring is a key criterion for graduates selecting an employer

James, L. 'Facilitating Protégé Career Development through Skills of Mentors'. www.core.ac.uk/download/pdf/234627135.pdf

Page 24

Benefits of onboarding mentoring programs

Reeves, M. 3 January 2019. 'Why your Onboarding Program Needs to Include Mentoring'. https://www.togetherplatform.com/blog/ onboarding-programs-mentoring

Page 25

Mentoring boosts careers of mentors and mentees

Quast, L. 31 October 2011. 'How Becoming a Mentor Can Boost Your Career'. https://www.forbes.com/sites/lisaquast/2011/10/31/how-becoming-a-mentor-can-boost-your-career/?sh=66cabccc5f57

Mentoring increases employee engagement

Martic, K. 14 January 2022. 'Who are Engaged Employees, How to Spot them and Keep them Engaged'. https://haiilo.com/blog/engaged-employees/.

Mentoring statistics from Fortune 500 companies

Cook, S. 2023. '40+ Definitive Mentorship Statistics and Research for 2023'. https://www.mentorcliq.com/blog/mentoring-stats

Page 26

Employee retention

The Deloitte Global 2022 Gen Z and Millennial Survey. 'Striving for Balance, Advocating for Change'. https://www2.deloitte.com/content/dam/Deloitte/at/Documents/human-capital/at-gen-z-millennial-survey-2022.pdf

Career development for Gen Z

Perna, M. 21 March 2021. 'Why Skill and Career Advancement are the Way to Gen-Z's Heart'. https://www.forbes.com/sites/markcperna/2021/03/02/why-skill-and-career-advancement-are-the-way-to-gen-zs-heart/?sh=70cb468222b5

Importance of learning and career development for employee retention

Hess, A.J. 27 February 2019, 'LinkedIn: 94% of employees say they would stay at a company longer for this reason—and it's not a raise'. https://www.cnbc.com/2019/02/27/94percent-of-employees-would-stay-at-a-company-for-this-one-reason.html

Mentoring's Return on Investment

Cook, S. no date. 'Mentoring ROI: How Mentoring ROI Works + Free ROI Calculator'. https://www.mentorcliq.com/blog/mentorcliq-roi

Statistics on the benefit of mentoring

LLC Editorial Staff. 16 January 2023. ' Mentoring Statistics 2023 – Everything You Need to Know'. https://www.llcbuddy.com/data/mentoring-statistics/?nowprocket=1

Page 32

Mentoring in tribes

McKay, B. & McKay, K. 19 June 2020. 'Lessons from the Sioux in How to Turn a Boy Into a Man'. https://www.artofmanliness.com/character/manly-lessons/lessons-from-the-sioux-in-how-to-turn-a-boy-into-a-man/

Mentoring used to connect indigenous tribes to their culture

Aschenbrener, C. and Pryce, J. 2019. 'Mentoring for American Indian and Alaska Native Youth'. *National Mentoring Resource Center Population Review*. www.nationalmentoringresourcecenter.org/resource/mentoring-for-american-for-american-indian-and-alaska-native-youth/

Page 38

Reverse Mentoring

Bates, Colin. No date. 'Reverse mentoring programs: examples and steps to success'. www.skillpacks.com/reverse-mentoring-programs/

Importance of training mentors and mentees

Clutterbuck, D. 2013. *Making the Most of Developmental Mentoring*. Liverpool: Wordscape.

Page 46

Mentor benefits

Allen, T.A., Lentz, E. and Day, R. 2006. 'Career Success Outcomes Associated with Mentoring Others: A Comparison of Mentors and Non-mentors'. *Journal of Career Development*, 32. www.researchgate.net/publication/234651061_Career_Success_Outcomes_Associated_with_Mentoring_Others_A_Comparison_of_Mentors_and_Nonmentors

Mentoring in prisons

Mosaic. 2013. 'Mosaic's Ex-Offender Mentoring Programme'. https://www.mosaicnetwork.co.uk/wp-content/uploads/Mosaic-Ex-Offender-Programme-Overview-011216.pdf
The Reasons Why Foundation. 16 March 2021. 'Why Mentor Ex-Offenders'. https://www.therwf.org/news/post/2021-03-16-why-mentor-ex-offenders

Page 50

Mentoring in youth programs

Youth Mentoring Initiative. 2021–2022 Review. 'Benefits and FAQ of Being Mentored'. 2021-2022 Infographic Review (ymionline.org)

Page 51

Mentoring in education

Partners for Possibilities. 2018. 'Partners for Possibilities 2018 Impact and Trends Report'. www.pfp4sa.org/wp-content/uploads/2021/03/2018_PfP_Impact_and_Trends_Report_1.pdf

Page 70

First impressions

Wargo, E. 2006. 'How Many Seconds to a First Impression?'. https://www.psychologicalscience.org/observer/how-many-seconds-to-a-first-impression

Page 71

Feedback

Rock, D. 2009. *Your Brain at Work: Strategies for Overcoming Distraction, Regaining Focus, and Working Smarter All Day Long.* London: Harper Business

Page 94

How to build a strong relationship

Maister, D., Green, C. and Galford, R. 2001. *The Trusted Advisor.* New York: Free Press.

Page 106

How to build trust

Glaser, J.E. 2021. *Conversational Intelligence: How great leaders build trust and get extraordinary results.* New York: Routledge

Page 107

Vulnerability

Brown, B. 'The Power of Vulnerability'. TED Talk, https://www.ted.com/talks/brene_brown_the_power_of_vulnerability/c

Brown, B. 2018. *Dare to Lead: Brave Work. Tough Conversations. Whole Hearts.* New York: Penguin Group

Brown, B. 2015. *Daring Greatly: How the Courage to Be Vulnerable Transforms the Way We Live, Love, Parent, and Lead.* New York: Penguin Life

Page 141

The three brains – head, heart and gut

Reynolds, M. 2014. *The Discomfort Zone: How Leaders Turn Difficult Conversations into Breakthroughs.* Oakland, C.A.: Berrett-Koehler Publishers.

Page 151

Insight

National Science Foundation. 2018. 'New Insights on Insight in the Brain'. https://new.nsf.gov/news/new-insights-insight-brain

Page 176

Listening with intent to understand rather than reply

Covey, S.R. 1989. *The 7 Habits of Highly Effective People: Powerful Lessons for Personal Change*. New York: Free Press

Page 177

The 10 components of a thinking environment

Kline, N. 2015. *Time to Think: Listening to Ignite the Human Mind*. London: Cassells

Page 189

Reflecting with questioning

Dewey, J. 1998 [1933]. *How We Think: A Restatement of the Relation of Reflective Thinking to the Educative Process*. Boston: Houghton Mifflin.

Reynolds, M. 2014. *The Discomfort Zone: How Leaders Turn Difficult Conversations into Breakthroughs*. Oakland, C.A.: Berrett-Koehler Publishers.

Page 194

Curiosity and questioning

Berger, W. 2014. *A More Beautiful Question*. London: Bloomsbury Publishing

Berger, W. 2018. *The Book of Beautiful Questions*. London: Bloomsbury Publishing

Page 201

Powerful Questions

Clutterbuck, D. 2013. *Powerful Questions for Coaches and Mentors*. Liverpool: Wordscape

Page 210

The neuroscience behind feedback

Rock, D., Jones, B. and Weller, C. 2018. 'Using neuroscience to make feedback work and feel better'. https://www.strategy-business. com/article/Using-Neuroscience-to-Make-Feedback-Work-and-Feel-Better

Triggering

Rock, D. 2009. *Your Brain at Work: Strategies for Overcoming Distraction, Regaining Focus, and Working Smarter All Day Long*. London: Harper Business

Page 225

A trusted advisor

Jones, C. No date. 'Are You a Trusted Advisor, or Just Giving Advice?'. www.catherinejohns.com/are-you-a-trusted-advisor-or-just-giving-advice/

Book References:

Berger, W. 2014. *A More Beautiful Question*. London: Bloomsbury Publishing

Berger, W. 2018. *The Book of Beautiful Questions*. London: Bloomsbury Publishing

Brown, B. 2018. *Dare to Lead: Brave Work. Tough Conversations. Whole Hearts*. New York: Penguin Group

Brown, B. 2015. *Daring Greatly: How the Courage to Be Vulnerable Transforms the Way We Live, Love, Parent, and Lead*. New York: Penguin Life

Clutterbuck, D. 2013. *Powerful Questions for Coaches and Mentors*. Liverpool: Wordscape

Covey, S.R. 1989. *The 7 Habits of Highly Effective People: Powerful Lessons for Personal Change*. New York: Free Press

Eurich, T. 2018. *Insight: How to Succeed by Seeing Yourself Clearly*. New York: PanMacmillan

Glaser, J. 2005. *Creating WE: Change I-Thinking to WE-Thinking; Build a Healthy, Thriving Organization*. New York: Adams Media Corporation

Glaser, J.E. 2021. *Conversational Intelligence: How great leaders build trust and get extraordinary results*. New York: Routledge

Kline, N. 2015. *Time to Think: Listening to Ignite the Human Mind*. London: Cassells

Maister, D., Green, C. and Galford, R. 2001. *The Trusted Advisor*. New York: Free Press.

Reynolds, M. 2014. *The Discomfort Zone: How Leaders Turn Difficult Conversations into Breakthroughs*. Oakland, C.A.: Berrett-Koehler Publishers.

Reynolds. M. 2017. *Outsmart your Brain: How to Master Your Mind When Emotions Take the Wheel*. Oakland, C.A.: Berrett-Koehler Publishers.

Reynolds, M. 2020. *Coach the Person, Not the Problem: A Guide to Reflective Enquiry*. Oakland, C.A.: Berrett-Koehler Publishers.

Rock, D. 2009. *Quiet Leadership: Six Steps to transforming Leadership at Work*. London: HarperCollins

Rock, D. 2009. *Your Brain at Work: Strategies for Overcoming Distraction, Regaining Focus, and Working Smarter All Day Long*. London: Harper Business

Zenger, J.H. and Stinnett, K. 2010. *The Extraordinary Coach*. New York: McGraw Hill

Made in the USA
Columbia, SC
11 March 2024

32933277R00178